Rockers

rock-er (rokr) n. 1. One that rocks, as: a vigilante cop. *Slang*. Out of one's mind; crazy

Stories

by

Thomas Fitzsimmons

Although Lost Love, Red Star of Death, and Dead Eye are true stores, names and locations have been changed.

Although inspired by real life characters and actual events, the remaining stories are works of fiction. Names, characters, places, and incidents are either the products of the author's imagination or are used fictitiously. Any resemblance to actual persons, living or dead, events, or locales are entirely coincidental.

Cover and text design: Tom Counihan, Jerry Cohen

ISBN 978-0-615-43416-2

Manufactured in the United States of America

For

Maureen, Robert, Patricia, Carol – thanks to our parents, Madeline and Tom, we all know how to spin a yarn

To the men and women of the New York City Police Department: "New York's Finest"
&
The New York City Fire Department: "New York's Bravest"

TABLE OF CONTENTS

Rockers   7

The Saint   37

The Ladies' Man   55

The Paranoid Elite   66

The Hoodlum Priest   98

Red Star of Death   111

The Defective Detective   141

Never Fire a Warning Shot   156

The Made Man   172

Bandit   179

Lost Love   189

Date with an Angel   215

Dead Eye   227

A Christmas Story   257

Bodyguard   284

The Faggot   292

Mad Dog Cole   299

The Demon Child   316

Rockers

rock-er (rokr) n. **1.** One that rocks, as: a vigilante cop. *Slang.* Out of one's mind; crazy

I

The morning rain soaked East Harlem an hour before dawn, purging the oil-slick streets and littered sidewalks, shrouding me in welcome shadows as I climbed the hurricane fence and dropped into the alley behind the tenement. I scanned the area for signs of guard dogs: chains, leashes, fresh excrement, gnawed bones.

There were none.

I pulled a black ski mask over my face, chambered a round in my semi-automatic, took a deep breath, then picked my way through piles of fetid kitchen trash that must have been thrown from the apartments above. I reached up, used my body weight to pull down a wobbly fire escape ladder, climbed five levels, and wondered for the hundredth time who or what awaited me---why had I been supplied with armor-piercing ammunition?

From my perch outside the fifth floor apartment, I looked past a flimsy, metal security gate, through threadbare pink curtains and guessed that the Hispanic man dozing on the plastic-covered couch was in his late thirties. He wore a New York Mets tank top, jeans, sneakers, and clutched a semi-automatic in his right hand.

I heard a knock on the apartment door. It was a soft knock---in code---and the dozing man startled awake. He checked his wristwatch, then relaxed his gun hand. He rose, stretched, shoved the automatic under his ample belly, into his waistband, moved to the door, and looked out the peephole.

"Keahy?"

The tin door came crashing in, its wood frame shattering, as four men brandishing wartime weapons and wearing black masks like mine rushed the apartment.

As I kicked in the security gate and stepped into the apartment, another man I hadn't seen bolted from a chair across the living room, shouting something in protest. To my horror, one of the intruders drew back his Uzi and slashed the barrel across the man's face; he collapsed on the floor.

"You crazy?" I screamed at the attacking intruder but my words were drowned by a third man speaking rapid-fire Spanish who ran in from the kitchen. Another intruder doubled him over with a kick to the stomach, then hammered him to the floor with the butt of an AK-47.

What had I gotten myself into?

Sounds came from another room---men yelling, a woman shrieking and children crying. Three more sleepy, dark-skinned men marched into the living room, their arms raised in soft surrender. They were ordered to lie on the floor.

One of the intruders held the captives at gunpoint while the others entered the bedroom and returned with a woman and four little girls, all howling, terrified.

"You shut those kids up or I will," the lead intruder, Mark Tesser said. The woman quickly gathered the children around her, hugged them, saying in broken English that everything would be all right.

Tesser grabbed one of the males by the hair and yanked him to his feet. "Where're the drugs?"

"No se." The man was defiant.

Tesser cracked the man on the head with his handgun. "That's from your landlord," he said as the man hit the floor.

The woman started screaming.

"Shut her up," Tesser ordered his men.

And she stopped---just like that.

Tesser chose another victim, dragged him to his feet and stuck the barrel of the gun under the man's chin, raising him on tip-toe.

"You comprende," Tesser said with a deadly gentleness. "Don't you?"

The victim spit in Tesser's face.

Tesser snapped. Bludgeoned the victim. Stuck the gun to the guy's head and cocked the hammer---my world stood still.

"Don't," I told Tesser.

"Let it go," another intruder said, backing me up.

Tesser glanced in our direction, kicked the victim aside and cued his men, who began ransacking the apartment. They tore apart closets, cupboards, tore open cereal and cookie boxes, used assassin's knives to gut the couch and all the bedroom mattresses.

"They're holding out," Tesser said.

I didn't like the sound of that. I hustled the woman and children into a safe corner, out of harm's way, just as the intruders launched a new assault against the men. They cracked skulls, broke jaws, and kicked prone bodies. I couldn't believe my eyes---the insane brutality. I saw myself being indicted as an accessory to murder.

"Mercy! Please! No mas!" one of the men cried, then dropped to his knees, clawed aside a frayed throw rug, pried up several splintered floor boards, reached into the opening, extracted and held up a black satchel. Tesser grabbed the satchel, looked inside, smiled. Signaled that it was time to herd everyone out of the apartment onto the street.

The woman, children, and other males exited without even the hint of resistance, begging for mercy every step of the way. When we finally reached the rain-slick sidewalk in front of the tenement, Tesser took one of the men aside, pulled out his gun and jammed the barrel into the man's stomach.

"Consider yourself evicted," Tesser said, the black mask unable to hide his smile. "If you ever go back in that building again, your woman and children die." Tesser gestured for him to go, and watched as he and his companions limped down the street through a maze of yawning puddles.

"Don't shoot. Don't shoot," the woman kept calling over her shoulder, begging the masked men not to shoot them in the back.

The masked men and I stepped to the curb where a nondescript, gray van waited. A black guy and a Puerto Rican, pulled off their hoods, laughing and exchanging high fives, thrilled that the operation had gone so well.

"I'd say we rocked their world," Tesser said, as he slipped off his own hood and smoothed an unruly, gray mustache.

"Won't see those dirty spics back again," a blond with blue eyes chuckled.

"Hispanics, to you," the Puerto Rican said, not joking.

"Touchy," the blond said, "aren't you?"

"Fuck you."

The black guy broke the tension by saying he wanted to go get a drink. Tesser and the blond were all for it.

"Can't." I pulled off my own hood, stunned by the brutality I'd just witnessed, and searched the eyes of the other ex-cops, some of whom I'd met only hours ago. "I've got things to do." I couldn't hide my contempt. "Appointments."

"'Fuck's your problem, Beckett?" Tesser said.

"You." I thumbed to his men. "And these psychos."

The blond spun to face me. "You got a problem?"

"You didn't have to beat those men," I said.

"So, you *do* have a problem," the blond said.

I looked to Tesser. He was holding the black satchel he'd taken from the apartment's inhabitants like a street-wise woman holds a purse on a crowded subway: under his arm, tight to his body.

"What's in that satchel?" I got in Tesser's face. "Money? Drugs?"

"You don't wanna know," Tesser said.

I grabbed Tesser by the shirt. "You set me up."

I felt a gun jammed into my back.

"Let him go," a voice behind me said.

I did as ordered.

The gun disappeared from my back.

Tesser reached into his pocket, counted out some cash. "Here's what I owe you."

"Shove it." I handed him back the weapon he'd lent me.

"Well, let us drop you off then. No problems. Really. You don't wanna be left up here, what with you being the only white face for miles. You know the rule: rockers take care of rockers."

"I'm not a rocker anymore," I told him. "I quit."

"What's *that* all about? Ain't you the guy crying poverty?"

I didn't answer. Just turned and walked away.

II

I had run into Mark Tesser two days before in an upper East Side Irish pub, Kinsale. I was sitting at the bar, sipping a pint of Guinness and moaning to my friend the bartender about the fact that, after three divorces and a dozen live-ins, I did not understand women.

Behind me some jerk with half-a-load-on was verbally abusing his wife.

"Whore," the jerk said, his voice just loud enough to be heard above the Irish music playing on the jukebox. "You're a goddamned whore."

11

I turned to watch.

"Please," the wife said, mortified. "Let's go."

"I'm not going anywhere," the jerk said.

A tough Irish waitress intervened. "I'll have to ask you to lower your voices." She placed their check on the table. "I'll collect that when you're ready."

"I'm sorry," the wife said. "We're leaving."

"Fuck we are," the jerk shot back and flung a scorching look at those sitting closest to him. "We're not going anywhere."

The wife snatched the vodka from her husband's hand.

And he slapped her, hard, across the face.

There was an audible gasp and the room fell silent.

I eased off my bar stool, slid into the booth beside the jerk, used my index finger and thumb to grab his ear and slam his face on the table, applying just enough pressure to immobilize him.

For the first time that night the jerk had no snappy comeback.

"You all right?" I asked the wife.

She nodded that she was. Tears were already beginning to well. "He didn't mean it," she addressed those around us. "He never hit me before." The remains of a bruise on her left cheek said otherwise.

"You go on," I told her. "Go home. I'll entertain your hubby till he cools down, sobers up."

"You won't hurt him?"

I assured her I wouldn't. She gathered her things and hurried out the door. A cell phone rang and the jerk started squirming. "I gotta get that," he managed to say.

"No, you don't." I tweaked his ear and he yelped in pain. I kept his face fixed on the table and told him I'd tear his ear off if he fought me.

"Michael Beckett," the jerk said. "You haven't changed a fucking bit."

I looked closely at the jerk; it took me a moment to recognize the former cop. "Mark Tesser?"

"That's me."

I released him. He sat up massaging his ear. "Fuck, Beckett."

Once a hard body, Tesser now looked like one of those cartoon characters who swallows an air hose and is blown up to four times his size. He wore a short-sleeved shirt that was two sizes too small and revealed a tattoo on the underside of his right forearm: an American eagle in flight. His stomach jutted out, hung over his pants. His hair was gray, thinning.

Tesser answered his cell phone. Told whoever it was, in hushed tones, that he'd call them back. "Move aside," Tesser told me.

I shook my head. "You heard what I told your wife."

"Gonna be my *ex*," he snarled. "She's a cheating slut."

"Slapping her around ain't gonna change things."

"No shit, Dick Tracy." Tesser eyeballed me. "You owe me a drink for nearly tearing my ear off."

I thought about that. "Not here."

We were ordering drinks at the next bar before Tesser spoke another word.

"Sorry you had to see that," he said, mulling over the ugly scene with his wife. An attractive female bartender set down Tesser's vodka, rocks, and a pint of Guinness for me.

"Wanna talk?" I said.

"Not about my problems." Tesser's awkward smile revealed alarmingly neglected teeth. He lifted his glass, toasted. "It's good to see you, Beckett." He threw back his drink. Ordered another. "So, tell me, you married?"

After some get-reacquainted-small-talk, during which Tesser fielded several more hush-hush cell phone calls (he would excuse himself, walk outside and complete each call), he bought me another drink. And it soon became apparent that, although we hadn't laid eyes on each other in years, as two ex-New York City cops we still had much in common. We both admitted having regrets about leaving the NYPD---Tesser retired on a disability pension. I resigned – a long story – and opened a failed restaurant. We both missed the camaraderie of "the job." And then there were the financial ups and downs former cops so often face.

"Hell's an ex-cop suppose to do?" Tesser said after the bartender had refilled our glasses. "I mean, all we're trained to do is catch the scumbags of the world and put 'em behind bars. Am I right?"

I had to agree. Tesser went on to say that, since retiring from the force, he earned a degree in political science from a local university, tried his hand at substitute teaching. Sold real estate, then insurance. Hated all of it.

I recounted the horrors of financing and operating a restaurant/bar in mid-town Manhattan---dealing with my limited partners and their blood-sucking lawyers, New York City health inspectors, building department inspectors, the bartender's union, various purveyors. And then there was the unfortunate low-level mobster who tried to convince me that I needed his protection from all types of street thugs---I stuck a gun in his mouth, he soiled himself, and I never heard from him again.

I left out the part about Enia, the man-eating waitress who had stilettoed my heart and helped wreck my business. When we broke up and the restaurant closed I lost almost everything.

"These days," I said, "I'm making my living with a gun as a private investigator/bodyguard." I sipped my Guinness. "Business sucks."

"Bummer," Tesser said. "How'd you like to make two hundred and fifty bucks for an hour's work?"

I laughed. "Who do I have to shoot?"

Tesser smiled, then glanced around to see that no one was close enough to overhear. "I'm a rocker."

14

As an Irish cop raised in a family of Irish cops, I'd known about rockers since I was a boy---ex-cops who protect businesses and individuals from organized crime shakedowns, bar owners from local gangs, even evict drug dealers from residential building---for a price. Although many active duty cops deride rockers as commons criminals, others feel that they perform a necessary service. "After all," my police lieutenant father once told me, "rockers only deal with scum the law can't touch, and," he winked, "they never hurt anyone who doesn't deserve to be hurt."

Tesser said he'd been working for a local landlord who had purchased distressed buildings from the city. The buildings were now infested with squatters. If the landlord could manage to quickly evict those illegal tenants---the civil courts took too long---then rehabilitate the buildings, he could sell them for a handsome profit. Tesser said that's where he came in. It was his job to put together teams to go into the apartments and "rock" the squatters out.

I had no problem with rocking thugs and criminals, and I told Tesser so. But I wasn't about to forcibly evict some down-and-out family from an end-of-the-road, roach-and-rodent-infested, cold-water dive that served as home.

"Thanks for the offer." I drained my pint of Guinness and left a fat tip on the bar. "I'll pass."

"No, you won't." Tesser said. "Not a boy scout like you."

I gave Tesser a sideways glance. I didn't know if it was the vodka talking, but I didn't like his tone. "You got something to say?"

"Gotta admit." Tesser threw back his drink. "I wasn't surprised when Internal Affairs found heroin in your car."

"Really." I eye-strafed the former cop. "Why's that?"

"Relax," Tesser said. "I know you were framed. There's no way you'd filch drugs---that was your problem. You weren't a team player. S'why you never made detective."

Tesser gestured to the bartender. "Two more." He turned back to me. "Explain it to me; you arrest one of the biggest drug dealers in the Bronx. He offers you $50,000 to let him go. And what do you do? You charge him with attempted bribery on top of everything else---what is that? You should have taken the money. I mean, who would've known?"

"I would."

"See? That's the difference between you and me, Beckett, you always took policing personal, like you were better than the rest of us. Like you were some sort of white fucking knight."

Frankly, I was taken aback. I didn't know that Tesser, or anyone else, felt that way about me.

Tesser rested his elbows on the bar. "Look, I know all about your baby sister, that she died from a drug overdose."

I bristled. "Leave her out of this."

"Fine. Point is, you hate all drug dealers, even the good ones."

"There are no good ones."

"That's exactly the attitude that got you fired."

"I resigned," I said.

"You were forced out," Tesser said, "for having a pound of heroin in your car." The bartender served our drinks. "The drug dealers won." Tesser toasted. "You and your integrity lost."

I placed my right hand on the bar, thinking I just might crack Tesser on the mouth.

"These squatters I'm gonna rock," Tesser said, "are the enforcement arm of a drug gang. They beat the living hell out of the owner. Threatened his kids if he went to the police. Question is, you gonna let them get away with it, or you gonna help me kick some ass?"

Drug dealers---Tesser was baiting me. "Kids?" I said.

"A two and a five-year-old."

I took a swallow of the fresh Guinness.

16

"C'mon, Beckett," Tesser said with sudden, warm, back-slapping familiarity. My eyes met his, then went to the tattooed American eagle on the underside of his forearm. And I noticed that the eagle had a sword run through it. Odd.

"Trust me," Tesser said. "These gangbangers are real punks. The eviction will be a piece of cake."

A piece of cake....

The words rang in my ears as I made a right on Park Avenue and stepped into a different world. A haughty, umbrella-carrying businesswoman high-heeled past me on her way south. An L.L. Bean-outfitted professional dog walker, pulled by several purebreds, made his rounds. A regal, whistle-blowing doorman hailed a cab. A lone, sleek limousine raced by, probably carrying someone to their seven-figure job in the financial district.

At a corner I stopped when I heard a siren, watched the flashing dome lights as a radio car raced up the avenue. A sudden sadness overcame me---my heart was with those guys.

As a police officer in a sector car in the notorious South Bronx's 41st Precinct, I'd worked chaotic days and nights, punctuated by acts of violence. What I saw changed me. From sensitive, naïve, gung-ho rookie to hardened, emotionally-spent veteran, all but numb to the sufferings of others---and then my sister died.

Since then my life had been filled with an overwhelming sadness, and not a little hatred. Yes, I wanted the drug dealers responsible for my sister's death brought to justice. But what I had helped Tesser's rockers do that morning was dispense *vigilante* justice. And I felt no satisfaction. Not with a sadistic head-case like Tesser.

Everything Tesser's rockers did was overkill. The military-issue weapons, the brutal assault on the occupants.

The pilfering of the satchel that must have contained money or drugs---was Tesser a user or a dealer?

And Tesser's men had approached the whole operation like a band of rag-tag amateurs. They had exited the van and sauntered into the tenement like a group of street thugs, no discipline, no plan.

By the time the sun came up I was in my apartment, cursing myself for not recognizing Tesser's set-up, gazing at a gold-framed photograph of my deceased sister: she was seventeen-years-old when the high school yearbook picture was taken. Thanks to a Bronx drug dealer, she never saw eighteen.

"Michael," a voice said.

I looked at the beauty stirring in my bed.

Marilyn, my live-out girlfriend, flung the blanket aside, revealing toned, sensual curves everywhere. I stepped out of my clothes and slid in beside her.

III

I was eating dinner at the bar in Kinsale that evening---Marilyn, a flight attendant, was out of town---when the bartender, O'Malley, asked me to speak to some landlord friends who were in trouble. They owned two buildings that had been overrun with vicious drug dealers.

"They go to the cops?" I said, knowing full well that there was nothing the police department could do, short of conducting a full scale undercover narcotics investigation---not likely.

"They did. And got no satisfaction."

"Tell them to go to landlord tenant court," I told O'Malley.

"They tried that too," O'Malley said.

I thought about recommending Tesser and his rockers. But the memory of busted heads and blood everywhere sent a shiver up my spine.

"At least talk to them, as a favor to me," O'Malley said. He gestured to a table. "That's them in the corner. Alex and Enia Brucia."

My stomach did something painful and unnatural when I looked and saw who was sitting there---it couldn't be. I thought about getting the hell out of there. But the Brucias approached. Alex stuck out his hand. He seemed like a nice-enough guy: scrawny, nervous, had a Russian accent of some kind. But his wife Enia---a savagely attractive woman with thick black hair, large green eyes, wide mouth and flawless skin, was another story.

"Hello, Enia."

"Hello, Michael."

"You two know each other?" Alex said.

"We've met," Enia said. "Let's see, the last time was -?"

"Over five years ago," I said. "Bruno's restaurant."

"How nice. You remember."

"We sat upstairs, corner table. Shared the Carpaccio Di Pesce appetizer, a rare porterhouse steak, bottle of red wine."

"No dessert?" Alex said half-jokingly.

I looked at him. "Warm Truffle Gateau." I turned to Enia. "You threw it in my face."

"Seemed like a good idea at the time."

Alex laughed. "She's done the same to me."

"Red wine," Enia said, "makes me crazy."

We sat. O'Malley bought us a round of drinks.

Alex, a former dental lab technician, told me he had invested his life's savings in order to secure New York State-backed financing that would allow him to purchase two run-down Bronx apartment buildings. It took him eight months to renovate the buildings, locate and rent to decent, hard-working tenants. But in the past year, drug dealers had moved in, terrorized and run off all the good tenants.

"I'm on the hook for a half-million dollars," Alex said. "We lose the buildings, Enia and I will be destitute."

I told the Brucias that I could recruit a couple of ex-cops to hang around the buildings as part time security guards, make dealing drugs impossible, eventually starve or scare the dealers off. But Alex insisted that would take too long. He wanted the bums out now.

"Go to the cops," I said.

"No," he said. "No more cops."

"I'll make a few calls," I said. "Put you in touch with the right cop. Yours is not a typical landlord tenant problem."

Alex lit a cigarette. "Enia?"

Enia pulled back her hair---there was a long, angry red scab on the side of her throat, several inches below her ear.

"They used a butcher knife," Alex said.

"Christ," I said.

"They promise to cut her throat, for real, if I go to the police again."

Enia let her hair fall back into place.

Alex lowered his voice to a whisper. "I've heard about groups of ex-policemen called rockers."

I took a moment, sipped my drink. "They do exist."

"The two buildings in the Bronx," Alex said. "I'd pay $5,000 a piece to clean them out."

"Thought you were broke," I said.

"You know any Rockers?" he said.

I looked at Enia. Remembered the evening we met, what had first attracted me to her besides her breath-flinching beauty---a shrewd intellect. After hiring her as a waitress in my restaurant, a pyrotechnic, six-month relationship followed. Bickering had escalated to a final, violent confrontation over her ethical lapses---Enia was a pathological liar, something I could not live with. I held Enia's gaze, and something passed between us; I didn't know whether I felt more like slapping her or screwing her.

"Well?" Alex said.

"Yeah," I heard myself say. "I'm a rocker."

I knew better than to trust anything Enia was involved in. Had to be certain that she and her hubby were not just another set of greedy New York City landlords, hell-bent on evicting law abiding, rent controlled tenants so they could raise rents. Had to be sure that Enia was not using me, again.

The once familiar stench of rotting garbage nearly gagged me as I climbed the subway stairs, stepped over a comatose homeless man, and onto that ghetto street. Even though it was nearly pitch dark---the drug dealers had, no doubt, shot out the street lights---and I was wearing raggedy clothes that blended seamlessly into my surroundings, the watchful eyes of fleet-footed drug sentries pinned me. I legged into a bodega and came out carrying a six-pack of ice cold beer. Crack vials, like so many of the drug-dead, crunched beneath my heavy-soled shoes as I walked halfway down the block, entered a rat-hole across from one of Enia and Alex's tenements, and climbed the stairs. I waited only long enough for my eyes to adjust to the darkness, then, gun extended, I stepped out onto the roof and did a series of crouching 360s. After establishing that I was alone, I took a position out of sight of the drug sentries that afforded me a good view of the tenement. I pulled out a beer, popped it open, took a sip, watched, waited.

There was a steady stream of drug buyers, some of them white, suburban teens driving late model cars---like my sister had---entering and leaving the tenement.

The violence erupted without warning.

Two females vaulted down the tenement stairs. A pack of thickly muscled pit bulls overcame them, took the screaming duo down hard, tore into them. A Hispanic man strolled casually down the same stairs a moment later, laughing and berating the two women for not going along with his sex-for-drugs offer. Then the man---he fit the description of the drug dealer who'd cut Enia---said something in Spanish and the pit bulls stopped. The women, crying, limping and bleeding, managed to get into their Porsche and drive away.

I'd seen enough.

IV

Early the next morning, I met the four men I trusted most in the world at a restored 100-year-old farmhouse in upstate New York. At the meeting, decked out in a designer suit, was my ex-cop partner Dave Robbins---black, charming, sophisticated in the Sidney Poitier mold. A former U.S. Marine Corp boxing champ, once renowned for demolishing heavyweight bad-asses with a single, sledge-hammer blow, Robbins had become a softy, totally incapable of defying his pint-sized, domineering wife or disciplining his daddy-worshipping, doe-eyed young daughters. Since retiring from the force he had been working as a salesman in Bergdorf Goodman's, Fifth Avenue men's store.

The diminutive, bitterly divorced father of a troubled 16-year-old son---a hopeless drug addict who had been in and out of rehabilitation programs---Ernie "Bullets" Serria was a quick-tempered, former NYPD sharp shooting champion who, in my opinion, had a death wish. Since retiring from the force, he'd taken to skydiving, bungee jumping, dirt bike racing, and extreme skiing.

Sean Manning, Serria's chain-smoking, former radio car partner and best friend, was a wheezing, couch-potato-fat candidate for a quadruple bypass. An unofficial and unsubstantiated charge of cowardice marred Manning's last few years on the NYPD. Although he had punched out the cop who made the career-obliterating accusation, he'd been trying to live down the adhesive coward's reputation ever since. A never-been-married, self-taught computer geek, he had been involved in a string of disastrous, flavor-of-the-moment dot-com company startups.

And last, but not least, the owner of the farmhouse, a fifty-five-year-old, 32-year veteran of the NYPD, Hans Kohlman. The tall, loose-jointed, German-born father of two grown sons had fallen into financial red following investments in a variety of ridiculous, no-money-down, once-in-a-lifetime, mega-monstrous, "le crème de la crème", mother-lode cash-opportunity scams.

The reunion of aging warriors began with Kohlman trying to sell us on his latest investment scheme while his Clydesdale-bodied wife served over-stuffed knockwurst and potato salad sandwiches.

"Look," Kohlman said, gushing with unbridled enthusiasm. "I wouldn't bullshit you guys, ever. It's a 100% legitimate banking transaction, approved by the American Banker's Association, Federal Trade Commission, and the U.S. Treasury Department, the Attorney General of the State of New York, as well as all international banking institutions."

I did a mental eye roll.

"Let me see if I understand you correctly," Robbins said. "You saying that this is a jealously-guarded secret of the world's 'money elite' and 'international banking moguls?'"

"That will make you rich beyond your wildest dreams!" Kohlman said. "But it's a limited time offer valid for only two weeks."

Robbins said, "My wife'd never go for it."

"I don't have a pot to piss in," Manning chimed in.

"Same here," Serria said. "Count me out."

"Beckett?" Kohlman said.

I shook my head, signaled that he should ask his wife to leave.

Kohlman spoke to his wife in German. She set down five cold German beers, waddled from the room, and closed the door behind her.

"I got a job," I said, and the men pulled their chairs closer to me. "Pays $1,000 apiece per operation. Two operations. Could be dangerous."

Serria graced us with a suicidal grin. "Count me in."

Manning looked at him. "Dumb spic. You don't even know what the job is yet."

Serria grabbed his crotch. "Bite this, you potato-eating faggot."

The banter elicited laughs---just like old times

Manning shrugged. "The spic's in, guess I'm in too."

"Beckett needs me, I'm in," my ex-partner Robbins said resolutely, then crossed his right leg over his left knee at the ankle. The glare from his handmade, calfskin wingtips was blinding.

Kohlman stood and towered over all of us. "You're not bullshitting me, any of you."

"Yeah. Yeah. 'Sieg heil', old man," Manning said. "Now sit down before you fall down."

"None of you give a shit what the job is. You just want to strap a gun on again. Get back in the action."

Eyes found the floor in the silence that followed.

Kohlman was right.

As decorated cops in the free-for-all, high-crime 41st Precinct, we had been altruistic, adrenaline junkies. And we all missed those days: the primal rush associated with midnight pursuits along perilous ghetto streets, the perennial possibility of a gunfight, the satisfaction of catching a felon in the act.

"That mean you're in or not?" I said.

"*Klar ich mach mit!*" Kohlman said and clicked his heels.

"Guess that's a 'yes'," I said.

"Not for nothing," Manning said, lighting a joint and passing it to Serria. "What is the job anyway?"

I looked around the room. "We're gonna be rockers."

As I detailed the evictions to the men and fielded their questions, I felt an elation I hadn't experienced in a long time. Sure I was going into a potentially deadly situation--- these drug dealers would be well armed---but I was going in with men I'd worked with for years, real pros, men who were combat veterans and followed orders, men adept at the arts of gun-point persuasion and violence---the best of the best.

"What about weapons?" Serria said.

I looked at Kohlman.

Kohlman led us out to his barn. Inside he pushed aside an old VW bug, opened a hidden trap door and we descended into bomb shelter that he had built with his own hands. Lining the two-foot-thick, cement walls stood shelf after shelf, rack after rack, of weapons sophisticated enough to make a terrorist proud. There were AK-47s, shotguns, Uzis, laser-sighted sniper rifles and handguns, bulletproof vests and night vision goggles.

Serria picked up a weapon, checked the action, smiled his approval. "Since when did you become a gun collector?"

"I'm not a collector." Kohlman pointed to a framed, official looking document that was nailed onto the wall. "I'm a licensed dealer. I tried to cut all of you in a few years ago. Remember?"

"I remember," Robbins said. "The government was planning to make it more difficult for someone to get a dealer's license. You wanted us to buy in before the new regulations went into effect."

Kohlman had told us that a gun dealer's license was like a city taxi medallion, that it would go up in value and could later be sold for a huge profit.

"But the government outlawed selling the old licenses," I said.

"The government screwed me," Kohlman said.

"Seems everyone's always screwing you," Serria said. "You dumb kraut."

V

In the pre-dawn hours the following day, a plain blue rented van roared up an avenue and came to a glass-crackling stop in front of Enia and Alex's tenement. Hans Kohlman, masked, night vision goggles hanging around his neck, radio in hand, slipped out the back door on his way to the rear of the building and to a fourth floor fire escape landing.

I sat in edgy silence inside the van, took several deep, calming breaths, watched in the reflected glow of street lights as the remaining rockers checked their weapons and racked rounds into chambers.

"Looking good," I said.

"Do it," Kohlman's voice crackled over the radio.

"10-4," I said.

On my signal, Manning, Robbins, Serria, and I pulled black ski masks over our faces, charged out the van's rear doors, and into the building in standard attack formation.

Several guard dogs barked on the lower floors as we made our way through the busted vestibule door, down a refuse strewn hallway, and up unstable stairs.

"Halt," Kohlman said. I paused the men on the fourth floor landing.

"Movement?" I said into my radio.

"Pitbulls," Kohlman said. "Front door."

"10-4."

We moved down the hall to the victim's apartment and Manning pulled a thin hose from a fanny pack, unrolled it, slipped it under the door, and allowed a flavored sedative to ooze out.

"Drinking," Kohlman said.

A few minutes later, we heard movement behind the door and flattened ourselves against the wall---all but Serria. The crazy bastard stepped in front of the door directly into the line of fire. Shit.

The locks clicked, the doorknob turned.

We all pointed our weapons.

The door swung open. "Greetings, *schweinehunde,*" Kohlman said.

I let out a deep breath.

We stepped over the pack of snoring dogs, entered the apartment. In the bedroom, we weapon-nudged five stoned Hispanic drug dealers awake and ordered them to lie on the floor. Manning handcuffed their hands behind their backs as the rest of us tossed the apartment. We flushed the coke and heroin we found, confiscated a half dozen handguns, and helped ourselves to more than $6,000 in cash. Kohlman called the ASPCA and arranged for them to pick up the sleeping pitbulls. Minutes later we marched the half-naked dealers out onto the street.

"You ever come back," I said as I un-cuffed the gang leader---the one who had sicked the pit bulls on the two women, probably the same one who cut Enia. "You die." I slashed the barrel of my gun across the leader's face, laying the flesh open to the bone.

The rockers drove to my apartment, where we split the loot and drank copious amounts of beer and wine, embellishing old war stories---the time Serria and Manning collared a gang of armed female robbers; Serria wound up marrying one, thus his bitter divorce. Dave Robbins repeated the yarn about the "major" drug bust he and I made---we'd screwed-up by arresting several undercover DEA agents and blew their three-year sting operation. The women in our pasts were all somehow more desirable, and we had, in boozy retrospect, morphed from what we actually were---over-the-hill lawmen to Hollywood-handsome and heroic. The rockers stumbled out of my apartment building, blinded by sunlight, around noon.

I wined and dined my girlfriend Marilyn that night.

Even with Serria playing a female drug buyer---he looked like a gorilla in a dress---the second eviction went smoothly. Three Russian drug dealers were in the apartment, six guns, and $2,000 in cash for our team. One of the Russians asked Serria out on a date, seriously.

Alex, ecstatic with the results, paid me and told me there were other violent drug gangs squatting in Harlem and Bronx tenements bankrupting the building owners. He offered to recommended me to those landlords. I told him I'd get back to him, that I had to talk it over with my rockers.

"I could sure use the money," Kohlman said later that night at Kinsale.

"Count me in." Serria tossed back a double shot of tequila, his fifth.

"I'm with the spic," Manning said.

"Whatever Beckett decides," Robbins said.

Everyone looked to me.

I let the silence build, knowing that, deep down, they were saying what I wanted to hear. I'd helped Alex because of Enia---yes, part of me despised her, yet I could not bear the thought of someone harming her. But what I hadn't counted on was how those two rocking experiences would affect me: I felt that I was doing something useful for the first time since leaving the NYPD, protecting the weak against drug dealers. And yes, I was avenging my sister's death.

"No bullshit jobs," I said and lifted my Guinness in a toast. "We check out every assignment before we accept it."

"Yeah," Robbins said. "Don't wanna screw up another DEA sting operation."

"Or get duped into being bouncers for greedy landlords," Manning said.

"We rock only violent predators," I said. "Agreed?"

Everyone lifted their glass.

"Death to predators," Serria said.

VI

After we checked out each proposed rocker assignment and personally witnessed the surreal terror and brutality that is the drug trade, my rockers executed seven more evictions. Manning took over Serria's duties as the female decoys---a thoroughly revolting site. We rocked Arab, Mexican, Dominican, and Colombian drug dealers, seized a dozen weapons, $18,000 in cash, and, even though no one asked Manning out on a date---a fact that Serria would not let him forget---we partied into the wee hours after each raid.

But on the eighth eviction something went wrong.

Kohlman, at his usual post on the fire escape, radioed that there were six men playing cards in the coke dealer's apartment. My rockers were in the stairwell, flattened against a graffiti-covered wall, weapons ready. I played a bespectacled, yuppie drug buyer. Knocked on the door, and a furious face appeared in the doorway.

"Fuck you want?"

"Blow."

He looked down the hallway, reached into his belt, and suddenly a gun was pointing at my face. "Let's see your money."

I showed him.

The dealer scowled. "Who sent you?"

"Hector." Everyone knew a Hector, I hoped.

"Hector hangs out on 127th Street?"

"No." I sniffled, coke-wiped my nose the with the back of my hand. "The one hangs out over by Sylvia's restaurant."

"Don't know him."

"Sure you do. He's got a glass eye, hare-lip, walks with a limp." I scrunched up my lips, made a comical face, circle-limped, and spoke through the side of my mouth. "Tauks wike dis."

The dealer laughed, lowered the gun. "Let's have the money, funny man."

"Thanks, pal." I held the cash out and, when he went to take it, I grabbed his hand, yanked, and slammed his face against the door frame. Manning, Serria, and Robbins barreled into the room as Kohlman crashed in from the fire escape. We found we were facing five Jamaican men with guns in their hands---standoff.

Kohlman racked a round into his shotgun, underscoring the fact that we had them in a no-win crossfire---he was ready to shoot. The men exchanged glances, gauging their chances. They were not good.

"If we wanted you dead," I said, "you'd be dead already."

"You cops?" the one who had been at the door said, using his shirt to deal with a free-flowing bloody nose.

I shook my head. "We're here to evict you, nothing more."

One-by-one the men dropped their weapons. Serria gathered the artillery and I ordered the men against a wall. And as the tension subsided and Kohlman frisked the dealers, one of them pulled a small handgun. Manning pulverized him, shattered his jaw.

Things could have been worse, I later realized. But it was a sobering experience. The fact that the drug dealer saw even the hint of an opportunity to pull a gun meant that we were getting careless. I wondered if we might be losing our edge.

No one suggested going out for drinks after that raid.

For our next eviction, our ninth, I borrowed a uniform from FedEx---the number one drug courier in the country---and concealed my gun in the phony package. But when the drug dealer opened his door, and we charged in, his gang disregarded orders to freeze, ignored the ominous weapons, and started throwing punches. Serria was knocked to the ground. We had to rock them---split heads, cracked ribs---to force compliance.

I began to lose sleep, had nightmarish dreams of raids gone wrong, of killing people.

And Marilyn felt the pressure. The nights she stayed at my apartment she would lie awake and watch my fitful sleep, hear me talk in my dreams. My body would glisten with sweat, thrash in spasms. Sometimes I'd yell, "No!" and bolt out of bed, my heart pounding and fists clenched.

"What are you into, Michael?" she asked me early one morning. We were seated on my living room couch, drinking coffee, reading the paper.

"Into?"

"Your job."

"I told you, I'm a private security consultant." I would never tell her about being a rocker.

She put down the paper, crossed her arms tightly across her chest. "You scare me, Michael."

"I scare me sometimes."

Marilyn looked out the window. I saw tears in her eyes.

"You haven't touched me in a month."

I felt my face flush with embarrassment, my male ego bruised; she was right, of course. The stress of being a rocker was getting to me. I was letting her down. And yet I bristled at the fact that she was adding to the pressure already upon me. I shot to my feet.

"What're you, keeping count? There a scoring system here?"

"If you're not making love to me -."

"Oh, now I'm cheating on you?"

"Are you?"

"No."

"Who's Enia?" Marilyn said.

"Enia?" I was caught off guard.

"You called out her name last night."

I told her I didn't know who Enia was.

"I don't believe you," she said.

I kicked the coffee table. Marble bookends fell.

Marilyn drew back as if I might strike her next. Disbelief registered on her face. She eased silently from her chair, backed out of the living room.

"I don't want to see you again," she told me as she walked out my front door carrying her flight attendant bags. "Not until you're ready to be honest with me."

I did not try to stop her.

The tenth raid was a disaster.

We tried the Manning female decoy ruse, my yuppie drug buyer ploy, and the FedEx routine. Nothing worked. And so we broke into an abandoned apartment above the target apartment, opened all the faucets, blocked all the drains, stuffed and flushed the toilet flooding the place, and waited for the ceiling to fall below.

Half hour later, when the drug dealers attempted to abandon their waterlogged lair, we attacked. Robbins took a bone-crushing punch in the mouth. A Syrian drug dealer used a rifle butt to break Serria's arm. We retaliated, left the dealers broken, bleeding masses of flesh, lying on their sodden apartment floor.

"That was my last raid," Robbins said to me afterward, sitting in the van, nursing a fractured jaw and split lip. "We gotta face it, Beckett, we ain't young bucks anymore."

"I don't need this shit," Kohlman agreed.

"I'm a lover," Serria held his arm, winced in pain, "not a fighter."

"I'm with the spic," Manning said, touching up his lipstick.

"All right." I was relieved that my men had called it quits; I couldn't---I'd be letting my sister down. "That's that."

Alex called later that day and thoughts of Enia at once flooded my mind---I had to get her out of my life. She was poison to me.

"Just bought another building in the South Bronx," Alex said. "Got an easy eviction this time. You -."

"Sorry." I stopped him cold. "I'm out of the business."

"What? I've committed two hundred thousand. You can't do this to me!"

"It's done."

"I'll double your pay. No. I'll triple it -."

"Goodbye, Alex." I hung up.

Over the next few days Alex called me incessantly and left me messages. Seems the drug dealers in his newly acquired building had gunned down his superintendent. They were more brutal then he ever imagined. I did not accept his calls.

I phoned Marilyn and told her my life was back to normal. I begged her to meet with me.

VII

The restaurant was Italian, romantic. The service, food, and wine were superb. I told Marilyn over appetizers that I missed her. By the time we finished dessert she admitted that she missed me too.

"I need to speak to you, Michael." It was Enia. She was standing at our table.

"Not now, Enia."

"When? You won't return Alex's calls."

"Enia?" Marilyn said. "You're Enia?"

Enia raised an eyebrow.

Marilyn got up, crushed her napkin, threw it down and walked out of the restaurant. I followed her to the street. She said I had lied about knowing Enia. That she hated liars. Her cab nearly ran me down as it raced off.

Enia was sitting on Marilyn's chair when I returned.

"She's an attractive creature," Enia said. "If you like that sort."

I sat across from her. "Go to hell."

"Help Alex."

"No."

She reached across and touched my hand. "I'll do anything."

"Great." I offered her the dinner check.

"Then recommend someone else."

And so I recommended Tesser's rockers, but with a warning. "He's bloodthirsty, out of control."

If that concerned Enia, she didn't say.

Alex himself called a few weeks later. "I owe you, Beckett. Your associate Tesser is the greatest," he said. "Fearless. Thanks again."

And a week later Tesser called.

"Whatever it is," I said. "I ain't interested."

"Just called to thank you for the recommendation," he said.

"All right. You thanked me."

"And I wanna pay you commissions on the referral."

"Don't call me, ever again." I hung up.

And phoned Marilyn.

"Part of me wishes you hadn't told me," Marilyn said to me that night in Kinsale. She was working on her second glass of white wine.

"You wanted honesty. I told you, Enia is a part of my past I'd rather forget. She means nothing to me."

"I don't care about Enia."

34

"What then?" I was confused by her attitude.

"You're---a vigilante."

"You're being overly dramatic," I said.

"Being a rocker is illegal, not to mention immoral."

"Really." I pushed aside my pint of Guinness and turned to face her. "Tell me. How many violent drug gangs live in your doorman building?"

"That's not the issue."

"Oh, no? You're passing judgment on crime victims, those the law can't help, and me for protecting them."

"You said you got paid." Her words were tinged with contempt. "Didn't you?"

"To roust sub-humans who sell death to innocent teenagers -."

"Like your sister?"

That stopped me. "Yes," I said. "Like my sister."

Marilyn took my hand, spoke sweetly. "Don't you see? That still doesn't justify your actions."

"Yes." I pulled away. "It does."

O'Malley, the bartender interrupted. "Beckett. Phone call."

I slid off my bar stool, happy for an excuse to walk away and cool off. I moved to the end of the bar and picked up the house phone. "Beckett speaking."

A man's voice said, "I got a building up in the South Bronx that's overrun with drug dealers."

"You've got the wrong guy, mister."

"Aren't you Michael Beckett, the rocker?"

"Rocker? No."

"Look," the landlord said. "They're dealing drugs to my daughter. She's only sixteen-years old. It's only a matter of time until -."

I stopped listening and forced myself to breathe. It was then that I realized that my sister's role in my life had changed. It was the anger over her death that had defined my life ever since. I hadn't been rocking for the love of my sister; I'd been driven by my need for revenge.

And guilt.

I'd been a lousy big brother to her, never wanting her around, never remembering her birthday or even buying her a Christmas gift. And, yes, I'd felt guilty about all that when she died. But I now knew that vengeance was no cure for my guilt. Rousting drug dealers wouldn't change a thing. I'd loved my sister in my own way. Could only pray that she had known it. With this realization, I felt my anger subside.

"Go to the police," I told the landlord.

"I did. They did squat. I need rockers."

"Look," I said. "Everyone knows rockers are a myth."

"What?" the landlord said.

"There's no such thing as rockers."

When I got back to our seats Marilyn was gone. Left in her place were a half-empty glass of wine, a crushed, lipstick-stained cigarette, and money for her drinks on the bar.

The Saint

Bambi O'Toole, veteran exotic dancer, bleach-blonde hair swirling around sun-scarred shoulders, blue eyes blazing, was naked save for the six-inch stiletto high-heels and thong that should have been worn by someone eighty pounds lighter, twenty years younger. She sashayed across a parquet floor into a sun-drenched bedroom and draped herself provocatively in the doorway.

"Oh, Alfonso."

Alfonso Levine, in bed reading the latest issue of *Rotund Ladies Exposed*, looked up, dropped the magazine and took his time drinking her in: five-foot three, short chunky legs, ass like a sack of potatoes. Alfonso made no excuses for the fact he was into obese women. And Bambi, his live-in, sex-tub of the month, fit that description nicely.

"This about me fixing the Venetian blinds? The hot tub pump?"

Bambi frowned, shifted her ample weight.

"No, don't tell me," Alfonso said. "This is about that putz Rory Egan."

"Smart boy." Bambi smiled a quick little smile, lumbered across the room, turned her back to him, bent slowly and touched her toes. She was looking at him from between two pillars of tantalizing cellulite.

"Please help Rory?"

"I loathe the man."

"But he's my mother's brother." Bambi straightened and jiggled around the four-poster bed to some imaginary music Alfonso wished to hell he could hear. "You have to do this for me."

"No, I don't."

"Yes, you do."

"Tell Rory to go to the cops."

"He hates cops."

"He hates everybody."

Bambi began rubbing herself. Dancing and rubbing, rubbing and dancing. "You won't let those thugs hurt my Uncle Rory," she said. "Promise me."

"What do you expect me to do about it?"

"You're the tough guy. Always bragging about being connected to the New York mob. Or was that another one of your lies?"

Alfonso bristled. "I wouldn't lie about a thing like that." Which was the first time that month that Alfonso had told the truth about anything.

Alfonso had grown up in New York City, a petty crook and Mafia wannabe. After opening a small Italian restaurant and allowing the local capo to use it to launder money, he actually became an associate of the Gambino crime family. He was the gofer---the loser whose job was to fetch the boss's limo each morning, just in case an enemy had placed an explosive device in it. The dupe who was forced---sometimes at gunpoint---to walk in, or out a door just in case an assassin was waiting on the other side. One day the inevitable happened and Alfonso took a bullet intended for his boss.

After spending a week in a hospital room overflowing with noxious-smelling flowers and phony expressions of sympathy from steely-eyed mob butchers, Alfonso decided there was no longer a future for him in the Gambino crime family. Which meant there was no future for him in the New York tri-state area.

Alfonso abandoned his restaurant and fled west. Headed to a place he'd fantasized about since seeing photos in a travel magazine. San Diego, California, was a place where he was not known, where there was no Mafia, and where he could go straight, find investors, open a legitimate restaurant, and leave his life of crime behind.

Alfonso found the people in San Diego friendly and trusting of strangers. But when he discovered that they didn't lock the doors to their homes, left keys in cars, and women routinely left their handbags in their shopping carts unattended, he took preemptive action. Set aside his dreams of opening a restaurant and returned to his felonious ways. Alfonso burglarized homes, stole cars, filched purses, and pilfered everything not nailed down in an altruistic attempt to teach the naïve San Diegans a lesson. Wise them up before a mob scout discovered that southern California was prime virgin territory.

"My Mafia days are over." Alfonso told Bambi, scrunched up his thin-lipped mouth in a ridiculous attempt at a tough-guy scowl. "I quit the mob. Besides, I ain't sticking my neck out for an asshole like Rory. Fucking guy gives me agita."

"You're afraid."

Alfonso sprung from bed, faced Bambi, his five-foot-five bony frame looked even less imposing in his Scooby-Doo pajamas. "I ain't afraid a nobody."

Bambi seized Alfonso by the shoulders, picked him up, and threw him across the room. He bounced off a wall and hit the floor.

"You'll do as I say."

"Fuhgeddaboutit." Alfonso struggled to his feet.

Bambi attacked. Grabbed Alfonso by the hair, flipped him back onto the bed, ripped down his pajama bottoms and buried her face in his crotch.

"This ain't gonna work, Bambi. I'm telling you, it ain't gonna work."

Alfonso Levine walked into Jimmy O's, a sports bar in Del Mar, later that day. He liked Jimmy O's---the location, the eighty-foot mahogany bar, the floor plan, the warm feel of the place. It had a large state-of-the-art kitchen, a respectable seating capacity, a moneyed crowd. And the fact that the owner, Rory, was always talking about selling the establishment and retiring back to Ireland was never far from Alfonso's mind. It was the type of restaurant/bar he hoped to own some day.

Alfonso found the saloon packed with all sorts of characters: would-be film producers, surfer dudes, sports geeks wearing baseball caps. There were members of a computer company's coed softball team at the end of the bar, whooping raucously, celebrating their latest win. A group of horse-racing nomads from the world-famous Del Mar racetrack took up the center of the bar, guzzling martinis and hitting on the more-than-willing Irish waitresses. Above the bar, large TVs were broadcasting football, baseball, hockey, tennis.

Fitzpatrick, a twenty-something bartender from County Kerry---Rory employed only Irish immigrants---set a glass of red wine in front of Alfonso before he had a chance to order.

"Greetings, New York." Fitzpatrick, quick with a smile and off-color jokes, stuck out his hand. "How's it hanging, Alfonso?"

"Low and to the left."

"How's Bambi?"

Alfonso rubbed his bruised ribs. "Still a lethal weapon." He drank some wine. Watched a bit of the Yankees vs. Padre game---the Yankees were behind 3-2.

"Where's Rory?" Alfonso asked.

"In the back."

Alfonso took his wine and threaded deeper into the pub, exchanging greetings with a few local businessmen. He looked around, searching the crowd. Didn't see Rory, and didn't see anyone who looked like an off-duty cop. Knew that was only *one* of Rory's many problems. Back in New York City, either cops or the mob frequented most thriving restaurants and bars. If you wanted to stay in business, you entertained one or the other, you had no choice.

40

And Rory Egan was cold, aloof, never fraternized with his patrons---unlike successful New York City restaurateurs who were gracious and treated customers like family. The only reason he had a prosperous business in the first place was that Jimmy O's was situated in a prime location in Del Mar Village, a tiny, charming, ocean front community.

Alfonso spotted Rory at the rear of the restaurant, seated at a corner table, tinkering with an ancient cash register.

He recalled Bambi telling him that Rory was a classic American success story. Immigrated to San Diego from County Mayo, Ireland, about thirty years ago, broke and uneducated. Worked his way through night school. Graduated college. Assumed ownership of the run-down tavern, then gutted and modernized the interior. Successful from the day he opened, it was obvious to everyone that Rory made a good living from Jimmy O's. Yet word was that he was the cheapest guy in town.

"Break down and buy a new register, Rory," Alfonso said.

"New costs money," Rory said before looking up to see who was speaking. "Oh, it's you." He used a rag to clean the register grease from his rough workman's hands. "What do you want?"

"How much you want for the place?"

"Why?" Rory stuffed the rag into his jeans pocket. "You can't afford it no matter the price."

"I might have a few interested investors."

"Now, who in their right mind would invest with you?"

"That's it, Rory, suck up to me." Alfonso sipped his wine. "Bambi asked me to stop by, said you were having a little problem."

Rory crossed his arms across his chest. "And what problem is that?"

"Some guy, Frankie Rayo, is trying to shake you down."

"My niece has a big mouth."

"She cares about you."

"Tell her to care a bit less."

"Have you spoken to the cops?"

"No." Rory fiddled with the register's cash draw. "No cops."

"Look, Rory, if these guys were a couple of tanked-up bikers you might be able to handle them. But if they're connected to organized crime, if they're the real deal -."

"And what would the likes of you be knowing about that?"

Alfonso bit his lip, held his temper. "I used to live in New York. Had a restaurant. Had to deal with the mob -."

"And now you don't have a restaurant, and you don't live in New York. What happened, the mob run you out of town?"

"No one ran me out of town."

"Yeah." Rory sneered. "Right."

"Look, Rory -."

"No. You look." Rory stuck a finger in Alfonso's face. "Mind your own business, you little snit."

At 2:00 a.m. the following morning, a black Lincoln Town Car glided to a stop in front of Jimmy O's. The driver, Big Lou, a tower of muscle dressed in a circus-tent-sized Hawaiian shirt, stepped out and carefully scanned the deserted area. He did not notice Alfonso, standing in the darkness across the street. Big Lou opened the rear door, said something to someone inside about the coast being clear, and a man, Frankie Rayo, Alfonso presumed, stepped out.

The sight of the mobster made Alfonso's mouth go dry.

Alfonso had never seen Frankie Rayo before, but he had the classic "dapper don" look of a big city gangster. Average height but wide, thick, moved with a bulldog swagger---a man accustomed to being in charge, of getting his way at any cost. Alfonso knew the type all too well.

Frankie Rayo figured the Federal Witness Protection Program would be a life saver. And so he testified for the prosecution at a racketeering trial in which six members of the Detroit Mafia were convicted of eighteen counts of murder and racketeering, and sentenced to life in prison.

In retrospect, Frankie regretted testifying.

But the mob had caught him skimming profits from the lucrative extortion ring they had entrusted to him and ordered him "hit." Since Frankie happened to be in jail at the time the contract was issued, awaiting trial for an unrelated case, Frankie saw an opportunity to save himself. He agreed to testify against his former associates, if the U.S. Attorney dropped the extortion charges against him, and enter him in the Federal Witness Protection Program. And it seemed like a good deal---at the time. But the freaking U.S. Marshal's Service, which ran the relocation program, had dumped him and his wife Ditsy---a former call-girl---in San Diego and gotten him a job as a Toyota salesman.

Living the life they'd assigned to him was fucking impossible. There was no one who spoke his language, no one he could talk to, no knock-around guys. And there wasn't a single decent Italian restaurant in a hundred miles. Hell, you couldn't even get a decent cannoli or a passable slice of pizza---they put pineapple on their fucking pizza!

So Frankie and Ditsy's days in San Diego passed like years on death row. And as the weeks dragged on things turned from bad to worse; Ditsy tried to fit into her new surroundings by eating like a native, California girl. She stopped ordering normal bar food like fried calamari and clams casino, switched instead to hummus and ahi. Frankie was fucking horrified. Within six months Ditsy bolted--- fuck her. Then he was fired from his job as a Toyota salesman---fuck the Japs.

Feelings of loneliness and despair enveloped Frankie. He began to drink. Was tossed out of several restaurants for making loud, insulting comments about the "lousy fucking food." He was arrested for public drunkenness. Locked up twice for DUI. The booze would have killed him, if it hadn't been for the watchful eye of the U.S. Marshal's Service. They broke into his home one night, put him in a straitjacket, forced him into a substance abuse program and basically saved his worthless life.

Frankie had a revelation in detox. He'd rather have his throat slit or die in a hail of bullets than go straight and be a nobody. There was no way in hell he was gonna live the remainder of his life as an honest, hard-working schnook.

Alfonso watched Frankie Rayo light a cigar, shrug under his white designer suit, no tie, and enter Jimmy O's. He knew that Rory was about to be assaulted or worse. Knew that, for Bambi's sake, he should try to help him. But how? He wasn't carrying his gun. And physically he was no match for Frankie and his gargantuan driver---hell, he wasn't even a match for Bambi.

Alfonso thought about using his cell phone to call 911, tell the cops that there was an assault in progress inside Jimmy O's. But then the cops would have his voice on tape, and if Frankie had an inside man in the San Diego police department.... Alfonso decided against making the phone call. He quick-stepped from his hiding place and ran for his very life.

There are no secrets in a small town.

Within 24-hours the fact that Rory had been assaulted, his restaurant/bar trashed, was the talk of Del Mar. Cops responded on their own to the rumors of the extortion attempt. Over café-lattés in Jimmy O's, Rory told two San Diego detectives that the rumors were false, there was no extortion attempt, that he'd gotten his injuries---contusions, cracked ribs, black eye---falling down a flight of stairs. Said that the mirrors over the bar had been broken during a bar fight over a stupid soccer game---Ireland vs. Germany. As the detectives paid for their coffee, one of them handed Rory a business card with instructions to "call us when you stop the bullshit."

A goofball, alcoholic glazier who, while replacing the mirrors at Jimmy O's, had observed Rory in the company of the detectives, spotted Frankie Rayo at the Del Mar racetrack later that day and saw a chance to make a quick buck.

"I saw Rory talking to the cops," he told Frankie in confidence.

Frankie slipped the glazier $100, and told his driver, Big Lou, to snatch Rory's niece Bambi. "Put her on ice."

That night Big Lou staked out a topless bar that Bambi had danced in 100-pounds ago and was known to still frequent. When he saw her exit he hit the gas, screeched the Lincoln to the curb, hurried out, grabbed Bambi by a fleshy arm and tried to force her inside the car. Bambi wrestled away from her would-be abductor, told him to fuck off and said, smiling coyly, that she already had a boyfriend. Big Lou shivered with disgust, slapped Bambi across the face, called her a fat pig, and said if she didn't get in the car, he'd crush her fucking skull. Bambi, thoroughly miffed, kicked Big Lou in the balls, knocked several of his teeth out with a devastating right cross, and pounded him to the pavement. It took three bouncers from the topless bar to pull her off of him.

"Who did this?" Alfonso was holding a cold compress to his tons-of-fun's swollen right eye.

"Some Romeo in a Hawaiian shirt," Bambi said. "I kicked his fat ass for him---the insulting prick. He won't be back."

"Yes," Alfonso said. "He will." He told her that the Romeo was most probably part of the gang that was shaking down her uncle. That they could very well be members of organized crime.

"Organized crime." Bambi didn't like the sound of that. "You sure?"

"I'm not sure of anything---yet."

"What're we gonna do about it?"

"*You* do nothing," Alfonso said. "I'll take care of it."

"You?" Bambi made a sound that passed for laughter; coyotes within a fifty-mile area scattered. "You'll take care of it---right. Like you were supposed to take care of these thugs in the first place. Or how about having my car tuned up? You were supposed to do that last month. And repair the blinds, fix the fucking toilet -."

It wasn't so much his affection for Bambi or outrage that Frankie Rayo would sink so low as to assault a woman that caused something to snap in Alfonso Levine. It was the fact that he'd been slapped, punched, and kicked around by mobsters all his life, and he was sick of it. He had run three thousand miles to escape the Mafia's till-death-do-us-part, heavy-handed control. And he was finished running.

Alfonso knew that if he didn't stand up to Frankie Rayo, protect his girlfriend and her scumbag uncle, maintain what was left of his dignity and self-respect, he might never find the courage again.

But first he had to find out why Rory wouldn't allow the police to protect him---Bambi didn't know. And then he had to find out just who in the hell this Frankie Rayo really was.

It was 1 a.m. when Fitzpatrick, the bartender, exited Jimmy O's, his car keys in his hand.

"You got a minute?" Alfonso stepped from the shadows.

"Christ, New York," the young bartender said. "You scared the living bejesus out of me."

"I need to ask you a few questions," Alfonso said pointedly.

Fitzpatrick's eyes narrowed. "What kind of questions?"

"Let's walk a bit," Alfonso said.

"I gotta meet friends," Fitzpatrick said weakly, looking at his wristwatch. "Don't have the time."

"I'll walk you to your car."

Fitzpatrick shuffled his feet, sulked like he was being imposed upon, but went along.

They began walking west on 15th Street, toward the ocean. The night was clear. Temperature a typical southern California 75 degrees. An ocean breeze swept gently through the trees, flower gardens, and freshly cut grass. The heady bouquet reminded Alfonso why he'd fallen in love with this place.

"What's Rory's problem with the cops?" Alfonso said.

Fitzpatrick shrugged. "Ask Rory."

"I figure you're there five days a week. You'd know."

"Rory doesn't confide in me, or anyone else for that matter."

"Are you an illegal alien?"

Fitzpatrick stopped, faced Alfonso. "What is this?"

"Rory's running Irish illegals through the bar, isn't he?"

"Christ." Fitzpatrick was visibly shaken. "Why're you even asking? You working for the fucking INS?"

Alfonso held his hands up. "This is between us. I swear."

Fitzpatrick looked out toward the Pacific: the moon was low, full, its blue-white light a garland on the black, choppy ocean. "All right. Rory's been running Irish illegals."

Figures, Alfonso mused. That explained why he didn't want cops snooping around. If they uncovered his operation, he'd go to jail.

They arrived at Fitzpatrick's car, a 1965 mint condition VW Bug.

"Out of curiosity," Alfonso said. "What's the going rate for smuggling illegals these days, twenty, thirty thousand?"

"Rory doesn't charge," he said.

Alfonso laughed.

"It's true. Believe what you will, but Rory's been running illegals since he opened the pub. He's helped hundreds of us, lent us cash, got us jobs, places to live. Every ten years or so the government grants us amnesty. With Rory's help, God bless him, we hold out till then." Fitzpatrick stood a bit straighter. "Become American citizens."

"You expect me to believe that that cheap fuck Rory doesn't make any money on the deal?"

Fitzpatrick unlocked his car, opened the door. "I swear on me mother's eyes." Fitzpatrick made the sign of the cross. "Rory's never made a dime on any of us. The man's a bloody saint."

Alfonso watched Fitzpatrick drive off, then gazed out at the ocean---how could he have been so wrong about Rory? But he knew the answer: he'd associated with scum for so long, that he thought everyone was scum.

He took a bitter moment to let the "saint" thing settle in.

Alfonso walked into the Del Mar public library the following day, found an available computer, typed the name Frankie Rayo into a search engine, and nothing came up; he hadn't really expected to be that lucky. And so he began the tedious task of accessing and perusing various big city newspaper articles that dealt with organized crime.

"MARTUCCI TURNS RAT!" was the headline over Frankie Rayo's photo in a Detroit newspaper. A capo in a crime family, Frank Martucci had turned government witness and then vanished into the Federal Witness Protection Program. The article stated that the public was outraged over the fact that Martucci, a suspect in a dozen homicides, was able to avoid a lengthy jail sentence in

48

exchange for his testimony. The paper also claimed that the Detroit mob had a one-million-dollar cash bounty on Frankie's head.

Frankie Martucci Rayo, an unlit cigar hanging from his lips, strolled into Jimmy O's a few nights later after closing. He told Big Lou---swollen jaw, black eye, compliments of Bambi---to guard the front door.

The place was empty save for Rory, who was seated at the usual table in the rear under the silent flat screen TV, counting the night's take.

"How's my partner today?" Frankie walked over to Rory.

Rory slammed the tin strong box shut. "Tell your goon," Rory pointed to Big Lou, "to stay away from my niece."

"Yeah. Yeah." Frankie lit his cigar, his manicured fingernails catching the dim light, and dropped the match on the freshly swept wood floor. "So, what's so important it couldn't wait till a decent hour?"

"Important?" Rory looked genuinely puzzled. "Come again?"

"What do you wanna talk to me about?"

"Talk to you---are you drunk?"

"Look, dickhead. I got a message you wanted to talk. Now talk or that beating you took the other day will seem like a love fest. Capisce?"

"I didn't call you," Rory said flatly.

"You didn't?"

Rory shook his head.

Frankie thought about that. All expression ceased. "You sure?"

"I'm not senile."

Frankie studied Rory's face. He was telling the truth.

But someone *had* called. The call could have been a prank. It could also have set a trap.

"Lou," Frankie said. "Check outside."

"You got it."

Big Lou walked out. Then walked back in. "Check for what?"

"Just check, you fucking imbecile."

Big Lou hurried out.

Frankie looked at Rory. "Can't get good help these days."

"Hire the Irish."

Frankie stuck a finger in Rory's face. "You better not be playing games with me, hump head." He took a pull on his cigar and something caught his eye, an old fashioned jukebox. He walked over, scanned the music selection. "Hey, you got no Dean Martin, Sinatra, Jimmy Roselli--- fuck is wrong with you?"

"Now why would an Irish pub play grease-ball music? Frankie squinted at Rory.

The front door opened and Alfonso Levine walked in.

"Place is closed," Rory said.

Alfonso walked up to the bar. "Get me a glass of wine."

Frankie looked at Alfonso. "You fuckin' deaf?" Frankie threw down his cigar, crushed it under his foot. "The man said the place is closed. Now get the fuck out."

"Red wine." Alfonso was facing the bar, watching Frankie in the newly replaced mirror. "Merlot. And be quick about it."

Frankie studied Alfonso as if reading his DNA.

"Hey, fuck-face," Frankie said. "You don't get out, I'm gonna bust your fuckin' head."

Alfonso stood his ground. "Try it."

Frankie charged.

Alfonso spun. A gun was in his hand.

Frankie froze, eyes on Alfonso's weapon---the punk's gun hand was shaking. "How'd you like me to take that gun away," Frankie said with an evil grin, "and stick it up your ass sideways."

Alfonso cocked the hammer.

Frankie bristled. "You have any idea who you're fucking with?"

"Hey," Rory said. "What is this?"

"Stay out of it, Rory," Alfonso said.

"I'm talking to you, punk," Frankie said. "Know who I am?"

"I know." Alfonso motioned with the gun. "Get out, Martucci."

Frankie stiffened. The punk had used his real name.

"Get out and don't come back."

Frankie stood his ground, took a moment to consider the situation. "Where's Lou?"

"Don't know any Lou," Alfonso said.

"Right." Frankie took out another cigar. "*They* sent you."

"No one sent me."

"They're waiting for me outside, aren't they?"

"I don't know what you're talking about."

Frankie lit the cigar, looked around for a back door; there was none. "Next time I see you, you're a fucking dead man. Got it?"

"Dead man. Got it." Again Alfonso motioned with the gun. "I'll count to three: one, two, three -."

Frankie held a hand up. "I'm going." He walked to the door, looked outside, opened up, felt for his gun on the way out.

The night was still. The tree-lined streets deserted--- which was something Frankie always hated about San Diego. The entire city closed down, became a cemetery after 11 p.m. Frankie looked left, then right: his car was gone. No Big Lou. No anybody. And that meant no danger. He took a deep breath, blew it out, started to relax. He looked back at Jimmy O's---he'd come back in a few days, teach Rory a lesson he'd never forget, then kill that punk Alfonso.

A car engine roared somewhere in the distance. Where the hell could Big Lou be? Maybe he went for gas---no, they filled up yesterday. A cop could have made him move the car---no, they hadn't been double-parked. And cops on patrol were rare in Del Mar.

Frankie walked up the short hill to Del Mar's main street, Camino Del Mar, eyes sweeping the area; the luxurious L'Auberge Inn, the posh Del Mar Plaza with its pricey restaurants and costly boutiques---not a person or car in sight. Frankie heard something, saw movement out of the corner of his eye in the shadows off to his right. A man stepped into the light, a man from Frankie's past in Detroit: Benny "The Butcher" Salerno. Frankie knew at that moment he was about to die. He felt the blood leave his head, his mouth went dry.

"Benny?"

"Hello, Frankie." Benny wore a black silk suit, had dark tan skin and short, slicked-back hair.

All at once Frankie was surrounded by several large men in dark, silk suits. One of them reached into Frankie's waistband, removed his gun.

Frankie looked to Salerno. "Benny." He tried to smile. "Couldn't we do something, work something out, we were friends once."

"Friends?" Salerno laughed. "You got no friends, Frankie. Never did. Never will." Salerno snapped his fingers.

A thug said something into a cell phone and a long, black limo pulled to the curb. Big Lou stepped out of the limo's passenger side, opened the back door, stood aside and motioned for Frankie to get in---Big Lou was one of them now.

"Let's not make a scene," Salerno said. "Get in the car."

Frankie licked his lips, took a deep breath, hesitated only momentarily, and stepped into the limo.

"What's this all about?" Rory asked.

"Get me a drink," Alfonso said.

Rory walked behind the bar. Poured a glass of Merlot and slid it across the bar. Alfonso picked up the glass, noted that his gun hand had stopped shaking, and took a grateful swallow. "I think I shit my pants."

Jimmy O's door opened. Benny Salerno walked in carrying a black briefcase. He had the all too familiar look of a cold-blooded mob assassin.

"I'm looking for John Smith," Salerno said.

"We're closed," Rory said.

"I'm John Smith," Alfonso said.

Salerno glanced at Alfonso, did a double take. A look of vague recognition spread across his face. "I know you."

Alfonso shook his head. "Not possible."

"Right." Salerno smiled; he had pointy teeth. "My mistake." He handed Alfonso the briefcase, turned and walked out the door.

"Christ," Rory said. "Who was that?"

"My investor." Alfonso set the briefcase on the bar, opened it, and, careful not to let Rory see, examined the contents: one million in cash. "How much you want for the place?"

"Don't start that again, for Christ's sake. You haven't a pot to piss in, or a window to throw it out."

"How much?!"

Rory started. "You don't have to yell."

Alfonso took a moment, spoke calmly. "Just tell me how much."

"Well -." Rory thought about it. "I'd say $700,000 would do."

"I'll give you $600,000. In cash." Alfonso took out several stacks of $100 bills and slid them across the bar. "But you'll stay on for a month, help me get the hang of things."

Rory eyeballed the money. "Sounds reasonable."

"And we can continue helping the Irish immigrants."

Rory looked up, gaped. "Come again?"

"I know all about it. You've been helping illegal Irish for years. I also know you don't make money on them."

"Who told you?"

"We have a deal?" Alfonso offered his hand. "Or not?"

"Deal," Rory said and shook hands.

Alfonso closed the briefcase, headed for the door. "I'm taking Bambi on a little vacation. We'll be back in about two weeks. I'll take possession then."

Rory was counting the loot. "Sounds grand."

"Oh, and Rory." He stopped, and looked back. "Tell the chef he's gonna have to learn to cook Italian. Stop putting pineapple on the fucking pizzas. And, for Christ sake, get some Sinatra and Dean Martin on the jukebox."

The Ladies' Man

I couldn't take my eyes off of the leggy, leather-clad vision of erotica sitting across the subway car, reading an alternative lifestyle fashion magazine, ignoring me.

I thought about abandoning my seat, stepping across the daunting, four-foot abyss and sitting next to her. I imagined smiling and saying hello. Telling her that she was the most beautiful woman I'd ever seen. That the sight of her took my breath away. That she was the girl I planned to marry. That her hair, skin and lips made me think of tropical sunsets, roses in May, Morticia from the *Addam's Family*.

The train pulled into a station.

I could tell by the way the object of my x-rated fantasies gathered her belongings that she was about to leave, walk out of my life forever---this was it. It was now or never. I mustered up the courage, stood and approached her. But Morticia brushed past me and strode out the door before I could utter a word. My eyes and heart trailed in her wake.

I flopped back onto my seat and sank into a deep funk. She had been perfect for me: age, height, body type, the fact she was into leather. I cursed myself for hesitating and not approaching her sooner. Knew beyond a doubt that I'd never see another woman as perfect as Morticia, ever again.

And then I noticed a busty redhead waiting on the platform; she was the most beautiful woman I'd ever seen. Her hair, lips, eyes made me think of leisurely walks along the beach, Caribbean cruises by moonlight, happy hour at an S&M club -.

Movement to the right caught my attention.

A muscle-head in a wife-beater tank top lurched into the subway car. I felt the color drain from my face.

As the victim of several recent unprovoked street assaults, I knew by Tank Top's swaggering body language that he could be trouble. I sucked in a deep breath which puffed up my diminutive frame, fixed my eyes on the tops of my shoes, and did my best to hide the stomach-twisting fear I was experiencing. I reached under my jacket to feel for the illegal handgun I carried. Then, making certain not to make eye contact, I gave that maximum security prison castaway a once-over.

He had the tragic air of a fallen movie star who'd done prison time---handsome in a psychopathic way. Long hair slicked back. Face lined with years, battle scars, and festering resentments---if he felt like slapping you around there was nothing you could do about it.

Tank Top grabbed the nearest pole and held on as the door chimes sounded, the doors closed behind him, and the train crawled out of the station.

Predators know the look of fear and the absence of it.

I should know. I had been picked on by bullies since grade school: on the street, in the lunch room, the school yard. They would make fun of my demure, nerdy good looks, push me around. Stuff me into lockers. Steal my money and pound me to the ground.

Things had not gotten much better as an adult. Although I did learn to avoid situations where I could be victimized: I steered clear of high crime areas, city streets late at night, sports bars where jocks hung out, and Catholic churches. These days I prefer the intellectual haunts of Greenwich Village.

Even though I take precautions, I was set upon last week by a blind date---don't ask. The end result was that she cracked a beer bottle over my head. And so I took to carrying a gun.

I stifled a yawn, checked the time. I was on my way to meet a lady for early morning coffee, another blind date.

When my alarm sounded that morning, I left the warmth of the woman sleeping in my bed---a rotund, snaggletoothed, tattooed poet who began as a one-night stand and morphed into a three-night stand---so I could meet my newest, internet blind date. She was a blonde-haired, blue-eyed, raging beauty, according to her web photo, who stated in her sexually explicit dating profile that she was a dominant female searching for submissive slaves, and that she had an oral fixation.

The conventional singles scene never worked for me. Trying to meet a woman at a bar, night club, coffee shop, or at my job---I bag groceries at a supermarket while searching for a literary agent to represent my erotic novel--- usually resulted in me being told to "drop dead," "fuck off," or running from the cops the woman summoned.

Last month I was I sifting through the spam in my internet mailbox and discovered a free trial offer to an internet dating service. I was intrigued; this was a new source for females. And being rejected electronically couldn't be as painful as being slapped down in person. Right? So I took advantage of the offer, filled out a long-winded dating profile which included short essays, and, after being issued a user name and password, scanned the online ads for dates.

I scanned over three-hundred members and found only five women I was attracted to in my 30-to 36-year-old age range. I wrote them. Although they all responded, they insisted I email them my photo.

Now, I'm no dreamboat, more Woody Allen. So I dug through my photo album, found a picture of an old friend who was a male model, scanned it into my computer, and e-mailed it. I figured that, when I met the women, I'd say I was sent by the male model who had had a change of heart and ran off with his ex-girlfriend, or something like that. Then I'd make my move.

The ruse worked, sort of. All five women turned out to be as dishonest as I was. Their photos were heavily retouched, or very old. Everyone had lied about their age.

And, as mentioned before, the last one broke a beer bottle over my head.

The muscle-head in the wife-beater tank top scanned the subway car, his frown deepening. Everyone in the train was his enemy. If only he had a weapon---a flame thrower--- he'd use it. The men in their business suits were looking at him but avoiding eye contact---like job interviewers did whenever he searched for work. The look said he wasn't good enough. The fact he had served 25- years for killing a man confirmed that. Yeah. The men in their suits, he'd kill them first.

Like he did when he was attached to the First Marine Division's Forced Recon Unit at Chulai near Da Nang, Vietnam. Shoot from ambush. Then finish them as they lay there dying. Slit their throats. Take a scalp or two, or an ear, or fingers. Hang them around his belt. They'd kill *him* if they got the chance. He could tell by the way they looked at him. Not making eye contact, sneaky like Viet Cong. But "Charlie" couldn't fool him, never could, never would. The slanty-eyed, yellow demons had agents and spies everywhere, working to overthrow the U.S. Government. Well, that ain't never gonna happen. Not while this Marine was still alive. Yeah. Kill the men first, then the women.

And he liked killing women. Especially the bad ones. The ones who painted their faces and wore tight, short clothes, and did bad things for money---like his mother used to do. A seven-dollar-a-trick Georgia hole. Hung out downtown on Peach Tree: two dollars for the room, five for mother. Buy a $5 bag of heroin, shoot it, and turn more tricks. Turn a dozen tricks on a good night. Tank Top, then a little boy, would watch her, man after man, night after night.

Yeah, just like Nam. Kill 'em all and let God sort 'em out.

The express train sped past the 28th and the 23rd Street stations then slowed to a crawl as it approached 14th Street. I glanced at my wristwatch, moaned. Knew we could sit in that tunnel for minutes, or hours. I would probably be late for my blind date. I looked to gauge Tank Top's reaction. Straightened when I saw he was on the move. I held my breath as he stepped past me and the other commuters who were scattered about, nodding off, or reading early editions of the morning papers. He walked past a small group of immigrant Irish construction workers, past some grunge musicians with battered instrument cases wedged securely between their lanky legs, past a group of Asian tourists who were doing their level best to decipher a New York City subway map, and took a seat across from a woman.

The woman was reading the *Times.* She wore a conservative business suit, eyeglasses, and her hair was tied up in a severe bun---she possessed an authoritative demeanor that I found most appealing. If I had to guess, I'd say that she was a financial type, employed on Wall Street. An overworked stock broker with a busy unfulfilling life. I couldn't picture her as a wife or mother, but I could see her as a leather-clad dominatrix---in other words, she was my type, big time.

Amanda Traweek looked up from her copy of the *Times*, leveled a withering glare at the frightening looking man in the tank top who was sitting across the aisle gawking at her, and wondered: Why are losers like that always attracted to me? She turned to the business section, checked the day's price on her fiancé's stock---it had risen a full point---and vowed "no slip-ups this time." Marry 83-year-old Al Kevens and she could afford to give up her grifter's life forever.

Not that she had much of a choice, mind you. As a three-time loser, with two convictions for bank fraud and one for shoplifting an emerald ring from Tiffany's, one more felony rap and she'd pull a mandatory prison sentence. Besides, she wasn't getting any younger. Hitting the stair master, aerobics, and the weights five times a week at the health club was helping, but not enough.

Amanda glanced up from her paper, checked her reflection in the train's window, flashed a smoldering look---the one she learned from her older sister, the toxic tramp---and reset her sagging boobs. Thank God for the genius who invented the Wonder Bra.

Amanda Traweek had worked hard to lure the octogenarian financier and garrulous curmudgeon, Al Kevens, into her life. Had stalked him for months in order to learn his daily routine, passions, and weaknesses. Then, she orchestrated an introduction to him at one of his daily haunts, New York's Four Seasons Restaurant.

And as she knew he would, Al fell for her, hard. Bragged how he had made a fortune in the black market during World War II. How he had founded the Commercial Bank of New York, which he had then sold to the Arabs some thirty years ago for millions. And how, for the last twenty years, he had made a second fortune by installing asbestos insulation in government buildings. Later he removed the very same asbestos insulation at 15 times the profit. The old geezer still had several hundred million, and he told Amanda that he wanted her to help him spend it.

"Fuck off, Al," Amanda told him several times, playing hard to get. "You're too old for me." And then Al gave her a flawless, five-carat diamond ring and asked her to marry him. After an appropriate amount of time, she reluctantly agreed, sobbing, "This is the happiest day of my life."

Amanda was on her way to meet him now---that is, after her weekly appointment with her parole officer. She'd give the fat, old biddy cop the same routine as last week about how tough it was to get a decent job where the men don't sexually harass a "lady." Shed some southern tears. Then she'd get another lecture about the rewards of honest work

60

and clean living, and Amanda would act like she sincerely gave a duck's dick.

Then she'd take the train back uptown to where Al's stretch limousine would be waiting outside her apartment. Marry him later today at a ceremony at a local church, then figure out the best scam to separate him from his cash---maybe screw him into a heart attack. And there'd be no more hundred-dollar tricks, or fifth floor walkup apartments, or noisy, stinking subways for her. It was gonna be first class all the way. Amanda turned to the newspaper's metro section, and someone grabbed her newspaper. She looked up. The scary guy in the tank top was standing over her.

I couldn't hear what Tank Top was saying to the businesswoman/dominatrix. He was keeping his voice low. But the woman was looking up at him and I could see the fear on her face.

I shifted uneasily on my seat and was struck by diverse emotions: a shameful relief that it was not me who was being victimized, mixed with a bizarre inclination to protect the damsel in distress and somehow stop Tank Top. I could actually picture myself doing it---pressing my gun to Tank Top's head, making him drop to his knees and beg for mercy. Or spin him around, punch him in the face, knock him to the ground with a single sledge hammer blow. And the lady would show her undying gratitude by launching herself into my arms, fawning all over me, taking me home to her bed---whip me, beat me, get me published---in my dreams.

I shifted my gaze from Tank Top and the woman and shook the childish rescue scenarios from my mind---the lady was on her own. In all the times I had been the victim, no one had ever bothered to help me. Besides, I wasn't about to pull my illegal handgun---good for a mandatory year in jail---or get my brains beat out by Tank Top for anyone, especially a woman I did not know. A woman who would probably testify against me in court if I fired my weapon, or step over my broken and battered body without a word of thanks.

The subway began to roll forward, then jolted to an abrupt stop and the lights in the subway car flickered. The conductor droned into the blaring, static drenched sound system about how sorry he was for the delay and how the train would be moving shortly. Yeah. Right.

I heard the woman scream.

Saw Tank Top slap her.

One of the Irish construction workers, a big guy, sprang to his feet and got in Tank Top's face. Told him to leave the lady alone, or else. And Tank Top pulverized him with a series of body blows. The big guy's knees buckled and he fell to the floor writhing in pain.

The other Irishmen jumped up and came to their comrade's aid.

Tank Top charged them. Fists flying. Feet lashing out.

Then, for reasons I'll never understand, I rushed to the lady, grabbed her hand, pulled her away from the brawl, opened a connecting door that led to the next subway car, and pushed her though.

"You are so brave," the woman said after we were safely into the next car and out of harm's reach.

I didn't respond, was dealing with the hard fact that I'd actually taken action, risked my life for, let's face it, a chance to get close to the lady. Was I that far gone? That obsessed with sex?

"I don't know how to thank you," she said.

I detected a slight southern accent. "How about your phone number?"

Just then I heard the door we just came through crash open behind us. I turned. Tank Top was standing there, a knife in his hand.

The lady let out a scream that almost broke my eardrum.

The other passengers reacted, scrambled to their feet and fell all over each other on their way to the safety of the next subway car.

You hear about adrenaline, how it gives people superhuman strength.

Not me.

My legs felt like lead and my limbs began to quake. I was back to my old self---a pitiful, sniveling victim and coward.

Tank Top took a step toward us.

I reached into my jacket, clutched the butt of my gun, but did not pull it out---I couldn't shoot anyone. And there was the very real probability that, if I did pull the weapon, Tank Top would take it away from me and use it on us.

I felt the lady grab my arms.

"C'mon," she said.

We took a few steps back.

Suddenly the train rolled a bit, then pitched forward with a loud clang, and the train began moving.

So did Tank Top.

With barely a flicker of effort he knocked me aside, onto an empty seat, rushed past me, and cornered the woman.

I pulled myself together. Knew I should bolt. Get up and walk away, now. I was out of danger. Getting further involved meant stepping over the line, sticking my neck out, risking my life for a woman---not in this lifetime.

Tank Top yelled something in a foreign language, slammed the woman against the wall, and placed his knife to her throat.

And then I did the stupidest thing I'd ever done in my life.

I pulled my weapon.

"Stop," I shouted.

Tank Top turned. His eyes were on my .38 Special.

The train eased into the station, stopped, and its doors pulled opened. A dozen or so commuters stepped in. A woman spotted me holding the gun. And screamed bloody murder.

"He's got a gun!"

People on the platform scattered. Ducked behind tiled support pillars, behind stairwells, dove to the ground.

"Freeze!" A uniformed policewoman was suddenly there, in a combat position, her gun was pointed at my face.

"Drop your weapon," she said. "Now!"

I did as ordered.

The policewoman picked up my gun, rushed me, slammed me back against a wall knocking me breathless.

"Got a license for the gun?" She had large, wild green eyes, full lips, dark hair tucked under her hat---she was the most beautiful woman I'd ever seen. I felt my heart soar.

I gulped air. "He attacked a woman," I said. "He was going to stab her. I was only trying to stop him."

"Who attacked a woman?" the policewoman demanded. A crowd was forming. Everyone was looking at me.

"Him." I gestured to my right. But when I looked, Tank Top was no longer there. "He was here, officer, I swear. A crazy looking guy in a tank top. He had a knife."

The policewoman's expression gave new meaning to the word "skeptical." "Where's the woman he attacked?"

I looked to my left.

The businesswoman/dominatrix in distress was long gone.

"You gotta believe me, officer, she was here. I saved her."

The policewoman flipped me around, forced me to spread eagle, frisked me, and took out a pair of handcuffs. "You're under arrest."

"The lad's telling the truth," the big Irish construction worker from the other subway car said, rubbing his bruised jaw. "We saw the whole thing." His mates, also nursing their wounds, chimed in. "He saved the woman's life."

The cop's expression softened. "Where'd you get the gun?"

I had to think fast; if I admitted it was mine, I'd go to jail. "The guy in the tank top, it was his, I managed to wrestle it from him."

"What about it?" the cop said to the Irish construction workers.

"Yeah," one of them said. "That's what happened."

His mates nodded. One winked conspiratorially at me.

I held my breath waiting to see if lady cop believed us.

She took a second to look me over, smiled. "You must be tougher than you look." She put her handcuffs away.

I puffed out my chest. For the first time in my life I was a hero.

"You'll have to come with me," she said. "Look at some mug shots."

"Under one condition," I said.

"Don't press your luck." Her green eyes flared.

"Afterward, you have coffee with me."

She grabbed me by the scruff of the neck and flung me out the door.

I knew at that instant, I'd met the woman I was going to marry.

The Paranoid Elite

I

Something startled Bill Lally awake. He bolted upright on the sofa, heart pounding. Looked around the dimly lit room. Forced himself to wake and concentrate. What had disturbed him?

Lally leaned on an elbow, cocked an ear and scanned the home office of Claudia Gelman, the wife of the richest man in New York. Silhouettes of vaguely familiar objects stood around him: an antique rosewood desk, a computer, a high-back chair, a coffee table dominoed with family pictures. Lally checked his watch. It was 3:02 a.m.

Noise. Lally heard movement outside at the rear of the fifteen-million-dollar townhouse---the sharp crack of splintering safety glass. He rolled to a sitting position, felt a blast of frigid air, knew that the beveled glass doors at the rear of the house had opened and closed.

Someone had broken into the house.

Lally groped for his clothes, then recalled that he'd hung his shirt, pants and gun on the back of a chair behind Claudia's desk on the other side of the room.

The shadow of an intruder flitted past the entrance to the formal dining room.

Lally executed a Dali-clock slide from the sofa, crawled under the coffee table, across the thick pile carpet to where he left his clothes, and retrieved his gun. He stood now, inched his way to the dining room entrance. Stopped. Held his breath. Listened for a sound that would pinpoint the location of the intruder.

Suddenly a form cloaked from head to toe in Ninja black glided past Lally and into the office. When Lally turned, his ankle joint cracked, giving his position away. The intruder responded with a vicious kick to Lally's solar plexus. Lally's breath roared out. He dropped his gun. Collapsed hard to his knees and could no longer feel sensation in his arms or hands. The next blow struck him somewhere on the side of the head or face. He wasn't sure. All he would remember was the room spinning away.

II

"Not interested," Lally told Erin Kellogg two weeks earlier.

Kellogg, a shimmering 32-year-old former naval intelligence officer who supervised New York billionaire Don Gelman's world wide security network, was sipping cocktails with Lally at the Oak Room Bar in the Plaza Hotel.

"You haven't heard my offer." Erin spoke with an amusing, lock-jawed prep-school accent. "At least afford me the courtesy."

"Look." Lally adjusted his Valentino tie. "Your boss is a parasite."

"A businessman."

"An amoral, corporate raider responsible for a hundred thousand people getting laid off. The creep has more enemies than Smith & Wesson has handguns." Lally noticed that the silk blouse under Erin's pinstriped business suit was opened to the third button---intriguing. "And I've heard rumors about his psycho wife, Claudia. Another *prize*. I'd rather gut fish for a living than work for them." Lally slugged back his glass of imported beer.

"But you'd be working for me." Erin made a production of crossing her skyscraper legs. Lally made a similar effort not to stare.

"You stay in the Gelman townhouse overnight," Erin said. "Six p.m. to six a.m. You report to me, and only me, who comes and goes. Who calls. Your thoughts on security, the men, alarm system. How's $1,000 a day sound?"

Lally feigned cool indifference. Signaled for another beer. Thought about the stack of unpaid bills neatly piled on his desk in his home office. Debt his ex-fiancée had left him. He heaved his best theatrical sigh and took a strategic moment to consider the offer he knew he couldn't refuse. Glanced around and allowed himself to absorb the "Lion in Winter" feel of warm wood paneling and timeless elegance that was the Oak Room Bar. Thought about the fact that he had not known Erin Kellogg for long.

He'd first seen her a few years ago at a party in the grand ballroom in the Waldorf Astoria Hotel on the arm of a U.S. Senator. Some time later she caught his eye on Madison Avenue, exiting a limo with a well-known real-estate tycoon. Another time Lally spotted Erin at the Box Tree restaurant with a film star. To Lally she had seemed the kind of vision you admire from afar, unapproachable, certainly unattainable. And then one morning, six months ago, his phone rang.

"Mr. Lally? My name is Erin Kellogg."

Lally did not know her by name. "Are you selling something?"

"I am *not*." There was a hint of resentment in her voice. "I've been told that you're the kind of man who would help a lady in distress. Is that correct?"

"How'd you get my number?"

"Charles Roberts."

She meant Chuck Roberts, *Doctor* Chuck Roberts, Lally's dentist. A good-intentioned friend who was forever sending him hard luck cases. Patients who arrived at his dental office with their teeth knocked out or jaws broken--- the abused ones. Most of them Lally simply referred to the police. The ones the police couldn't help, Lally, a former member of the NYPD's elite Stakeout Unit, became personally involved with.

"Please, Mr. Lally," Erin said, "I'm being stalked."

Lally considered that. "Are you free to meet me?"

"When?"

"Half hour?" Lally said.

"Where?

"The Regency Hotel."

When Erin Kellogg entered the Regency Hotel's stodgy, elegantly appointed dining room every head turned---men gaped, women scowled, waiters lost focus. The maître d' fawned unabashedly as he escorted her to Lally's table.

Lally, who recognized her immediately, was on his feet with his hand out. She was even more beautiful than he remembered.

"I'm Erin Kellogg." She smiled a toothpaste-commercial-perfect smile and sat opposite Lally.

Lally ordered two coffees.

With little preamble, Erin began her story, her entire life story---a long-winded, pretentious, name-dropping narrative.

Born and raised in the Back Bay section of Boston, she loved her Ph.D. father, disliked her High Society mother, lost her virginity to her first boyfriend (a distant Kennedy relative), was high school homecoming queen, experimented with drugs, was head of her sorority at Harvard, had a college boyfriend (another distant Kennedy relative), graduated top of her class, spent five years working with military intelligence, married and divorced (yet another distant Kennedy relative). And then she arrived at the reason she'd phoned Lally in the first place.

Erin said that she was being stalked by an ex-boyfriend, a garment center businessman who manufactured women's apparel and bragged about his ties to organized crime.

"He violent?" Lally said, eyes on her full lips.

"He hit me once. But we were both drinking. You know how it is when everyone's drinking. People say things, get angry. I used to date the ex-governor's nephew. Anyway, when he drank he lost his mind. And then there was the Italian diplomat. He had a jealous temperament -"

"Have you been to the police?"

"I have," Erin said. "They suggested I take out an order of protection, which I did. But there're no police around when he comes banging on my door at midnight. And when I call 911 he runs. It's always my word against his and, frankly I'm terrified."

"Understandable."

Erin placed her hand on Lally's and gave him a look he felt in his toes. "Will you help me, Mr. Lally?"

"Call me Bill."

Erin smiled.

Lally smiled. "I'll see what I can do."

Erin's ex-boyfriend, the stalker, was visibly shaken when Bill Lally barged into his firm's garment center showroom the following day.

"You go near Erin Kellogg again," Lally said, picked up a sample table and threw it through a display case widow. "You'll do six months in the hospital."

Erin never heard from her ex-boyfriend again.

Nor had Lally heard from Erin. Not even a thank-you.

For a time Lally felt hurt, used by a woman he was attracted to. But it wasn't the first time he'd been forgotten by those he helped, and he knew it wouldn't be the last. And so he chalked the episode up to experience and put Erin out of his mind. Until she phoned him that day and asked if he could meet her at the Oak Room Bar.

Maybe the Gelman job offer was her way of saying thanks. Whatever the case, $1,000 a day bought a hell of a lot of absolution.

The starched Plaza bartender set another beer down for Lally and a martini, straight up, for Erin. She speared an olive and popped it in her mouth. Lally watched her chew, mesmerized. He shook a laundry list of salacious thoughts from his mind and shifted on his bar stool.

"The Gelman job," Lally said. "What would I be looking for?"

"Who comes and goes. Who calls. The security set-up. The men, alarm system---the alarm system is most important."

"That's it?"

"That's it.

"There's gotta be more for $1,000 a day."

Erin regarded Lally as if deciding whether to trust him. She glanced around, checked for eavesdroppers, then spoke behind her hand. "Someone's been trying to recruit a mercenary to break into Gelman's house."

Lally looked at her intently. "A kidnapping?"

Erin sipped her drink. "I don't think so."

"What's worth stealing in the Gelman house?"

"Please! It's filled with millions in original art. And you must know Mrs. Gelman is a gossip columnist. She appears on TV talk shows and writes a nationally-syndicated newspaper column."

Lally smirked. "Like I said, a real prize."

"She stores sensitive information on her computer in her home office, the names of secret sources. Probably even some organized crime, law enforcement and confidential government informers."

"You mean rats, don't you?"

"Some people would pay anything for the names of those sources."

Lally thought it over. "Will Gelman know who I am, what I'm up to?"

Erin shook her head. "No one will know. Only me. And no one can know of our association."

"So how do I get hired?"

"Gelman's local Assistant Director of Security, a former NYPD Chief named Vogt, does all the hiring. It's done word of mouth. You have to be recommended."

"You can't recommend me?"

"Not a chance. Vogt would resent me telling him who to hire. If he thinks I'm meddling, that could cast suspicion on you. Your undercover status could be compromised."

"I see the problem," Lally said. "You have a plan?"

She reached into a purse, took out a piece of paper with a name and phone number written on it, and handed it to Lally.

"Brian Keating?" Lally said.

"Know him?"

"Not personally. He's a retired NYPD lieutenant."

"He just left the Gelman job on good terms. Think you can get to him? Convince him to recommend you for the position?"

Lally thought about it. "I'll see if we have a mutual friend."

"Remember not to mention me," Erin said. "To anyone."

Lally pocketed the piece of paper. "If I discover anything criminal, will I be burned?"

"I'm afraid I don't understand."

"Burned," Lally said. "Reveal my true assignment and testify in court."

Erin lit a smoke, took in a lungful, made a point of turning and exhaling away from Lally. "It's possible."

"I get $2,500 a day to testify in court as an expert witness."

"$2,500 a day?"

"Erin, there're guys out there who'll work for you for $250 a day. Hell, $100."

"I don't want them. I want you."

"Why?" Lally said.

She responded with a smile. "I owe you, Bill." She put her hand on his, squeezed.

Lally felt his stomach flutter. He glanced down at her legs, then up to the bulging blouse; a fourth button looked as if it were about to pop.

"The security men," Lally said. "They cops?"

"Some are, some are ex-cops."

"I won't testify against them, no matter what."

She sipped her martini. "But what if they're involved in the conspiracy?"

"I won't testify against cops. Period."

"Do you know any of Gelman's security staff?"

"Not that I'm aware of."

"But you're saying that, even though you work for me, your loyalty is to men you've never met, strangers?"

"We have a deal or not?"

"All right." She bent forward to shake his hand, the valley between her breasts deepening. "I will not ask you to testify against other police officers." Erin extended a steady hand. "You have my word."

Lally regarded her briefly, considered the high pay and the fact that she'd agreed to his unrealistic demands---this was all too easy. His instincts told him that there was something Erin was not telling him. But he took the soft, perfectly manicured hand offered to him, and shook it.

"Fuck you wanna work for Gelman for?" Retired Lieutenant Keating asked over the phone that evening.

Lally was sitting in a home office in his 25th-floor apartment, looking out at the George Washington Bridge and snow-covered New Jersey Palisades. "I need the work. Got bills. You know how it is."

"Look, do yourself a favor. Get a job digging graves. Mug old ladies. Hell, go door-to-door and sell Dr. Kevorkian gift certificates. I guarantee you'll be happier, you know?"

Lally stifled a laugh. "The hours are good for me."

"Don't think you're gonna make friends with Don Gelman. Guy's got billions, but he's one-way. Does shit for no one. Wouldn't spit to give a bird a drink of water, you know?"

"I need the work."

A silence on the other end of the phone.

"Who'd you say gave you my number?" Keating said.

"Emmett O'Brian. Used to work with you in the 43 up in the Bronx."

"You know The Duke?"

"He said to tell you you're a cheap, shanty Irishman who never bought a drink for anyone in his life."

Keating broke out laughing. "That's him all right. Got a pen?" Keating gave Lally a phone number. "That's Dom Vogt's line. Used to be a Chief Inspector. Brooklyn Borough Commander. He runs security at Gelman's house."

"What's he like?"

"A real stand-up guy," Keating said. "A cop's cop. When you speak to him be sure to say I sent you."

"Thanks. Tell me something, Keating. Why'd you quit Gelman?"

"His fuckin' wife Claudia. She's the reason everyone quits."

"What's her story?"

"I'll give you an example. They have a movie theater in the basement. I mean a first-class set-up would impress Spielberg. Twenty seats, 35mm projector, Dolby sound system. And just outside the theater they've got a professional concession stand---candy, popcorn machines, the works. Claudia keeps it locked up. Sometimes she sneaks down to the basement in the middle of the night, unlocks the concession stand, and counts every single candy bar to make sure the security men didn't steal anything. Can you imagine? They got billions and that

74

paranoid bitch is counting candy. And then there are her midnight alarm drills."

"Drills?"

Keating laughed a little. "You'll find out."

III

Retired Chief Dom Vogt was a pleasant-looking, round man, and Lally liked him on sight. They met in the Madison Avenue offices of the Princess Cosmetic Corporation, one of the many subsidiaries of Gelman's holding company, Gelman International. Vogt, in suspenders, shirt-sleeves and loosened tie, sat behind a tin desk in a tiny, dimly-lit cubicle office scanning Lally's employment application.

Lally sat across from him in a gray suit, starched white shirt, and sensible rep tie. He noted the chief's impressive array of police department memorabilia: Vogt's shields; police officer, sergeant, lieutenant, captain, deputy inspector, inspector, assistant chief inspector and chief inspector, were mounted on a single plaque, documenting his rise through the NYPD. Photos of the chief with politicians and celebrities were scattered piecemeal around the room. A Bachelor of Science and a Master's degree in Criminology from John Jay College hung on a wall behind his desk. On a window sill stood a photo of the chief, his wife, children, and grandchildren.

"You ever work for anyone like the Gelmans before? I mean with their kind of money?"

"No," Lally had to admit. Living in Manhattan he had, of course, socialized with the rich---not an unpleasant experience. But he found most of them to be shrouded by their wealth, self-absorbed to a fault and insensitive to the feelings of others.

"The rich are different," the chief said. "Don't have the same insecurities the average person does. Few years ago the biggest thing in the Gelman's lives was finding the 'right' guru. Then it was the 'best' psychic. Then the 'most popular' personal trainer. Now it's who in their social circle has the 'best' plastic surgeon. It's a competition. Seems everything to them is a competition."

"I understand."

"Do you?" The chief laid down Lally's employment application and picked up a folder with "Lally" written across it in neat, block letters. Lally knew he had been investigated.

"Only one thing bothers me about you, kid."

"What's that?"

"Why'd you leave the police department?"

"Financial reasons."

The chief looked at him with weary eyes that had seen it all. "And now you need an $11 an hour position?"

Lally was taken by surprise---$11 an hour? He'd had no idea the Gelmans paid so little. Erin hadn't mentioned it. He shrugged. "I was engaged. Ran up debt."

"Uh-huh." Unimpressed. "How long you and she together?"

"Too long. I'm attracted to wounded birds, Chief. 'Course, I never know they're neurotic at the time, until it's too late. This one fooled me completely. I never knew about the Prozac. She liked the high life. Cleaned me out, stuck me with all the bills, and left me. Right now $11 an hour is a lot of money to me."

The chief rose, walked to a Mr. Coffee, poured two cups.

"Been married to the same woman for 29 years myself."

"You must have found a good one."

A smile lit up the chief's face. "That's an understatement." He handed Lally a coffee, sat back down and used an index finger to tap the Lally report. "Says here you were one hell of a cop, kid."

"I did all right."

"Stakeout Unit. Four confirmed kills."

Lally shifted uneasily in his seat. He never spoke to anyone about the men he'd killed. "Leaving the job was difficult for me, chief. When I was sworn in as a rookie I thought the justice system was on the level. Took me 15 years to figure out I was wrong. Dead wrong.

The chief handed a document to Lally. "Sign it."

"What is it?"

"A standard non-disclosure agreement. It states you will not speak or write anything negative about Don Gelman and his family. If you violate the agreement, he'll sue your ass into the afterlife. I guarantee it."

Lally glanced at the agreement, signed it and handed it back to the chief. Vogt took it, checked the signature, and looked thoughtfully at Lally.

"I won't bullshit you, Lally. You have the look they want."

Lally wondered what that meant.

The chief continued. "They won't have Blacks or Hispanics in the house. I told you about Mrs. Gelman. She's not easy on the help. How do you feel about that?"

"Long as I get paid."

The chief smiled. "Good answer." He stood. "You're hired, kid." He held out his hand. "Welcome aboard." They shook.

"Report to Bill Santic. That's him over there." Vogt pointed to a man seated at an obscure desk at the far end of a field of desks. "He's a retired detective out of Brooklyn South. Good man. Handles the payroll and scheduling for the security teams."

"Thanks, chief."

"Don't make me regret hiring you, Lally," Vogt said as he patted him on the back.

Lally wondered why he said that.

IV

Bill Santic was an affable, gap-toothed, ex-jock gone to pot. He wore a suit that needed pressing and a shirt that needed laundering. After some department small talk, Lally filled out the necessary forms, W-2, emergency notification in case of injury, and showed his full-carry pistol permit. Then he and Santic left the Princess Cosmetic building, bundled up, and walked through driving snow up Madison Avenue to the Gelman residence on East 65th Street.

"Gelman's got over fifty-five full time security men. You'll be assigned to his elite personal team, his 'Praetorian Guard,' which numbers about 12 men." Santic managed to light one cigarette from the glowing butt of another in the high wind.

"There are two men in the residence at all times, that's 24 hours a day. You'll be one of them. Two more men are assigned to Gelman personally, a driver and a bodyguard, both armed. Mrs. Gelman has an armed driver at her disposal. There's an extra driver for incidentals, case there's an errand to be run, or one of Mr. Gelman's, uh, 'lady friends' needs something.

Lally nodded.

"Look," Santic said as they slipped and slid across an icy intersection and negotiated over a snow drift onto a curb. "You should know these are not what you'd call salt of the earth people. I'd say they're more trailer trash. But they've got money, $6 billion -"

"And we put up with them."

The Gelman residence was a stately, five-floor, 45-thousand-square-foot townhouse on East 65th street, between Park and Madison Avenues. They entered through the service entrance, made an immediate left, and were

78

standing in the security command center: a tiny, ratty, walk-through room. On a homemade plywood desk sat several ancient Sony surveillance monitors, cellular phone charge racks, and piles upon piles of dog-eared magazines. The room had the feel of a 10-year-old's backyard tree house.

Santic introduced Lally to five beefy dark-suited men. There were handshakes all around. Suspicious eyes scrutinized the new hire---his designer trench coat, suit and shoes appeared overpriced for this job. One guy repeated Lally's name twice. Spelled it. Lally knew the moment he was out of earshot, every man present would be on the phone to check him out, determine if he could be trusted.

Santic led Lally through the security office and into the main house. Their footfalls echoed as they stepped across the formal entranceway: a vast, cold-tiled foyer with large wretched paintings on the walls. Lally mentally ruled out an art theft ring.

Santic led the way to a man seated at a desk situated at the bottom of an enormous, sweeping staircase that Lally could picture Norma Desmond swishing down.

"Mario," Santic said. "Say hi to your new partner. Bill Lally."

Mario, a studious, stiff sort, looked up from a book and gave Lally the once-over. The weak handshake and thin smile were an effort.

"Report here to the security office tomorrow at 5:00 p.m., Lally," Santic said. "It'll give you an extra hour for Mario to show you around the house, show you how to work the phones."

"Phones?"

Santic pointed to a confusing looking desktop switchboard with a dozen phone numbers listed on its face. "Every call for the Gelmans comes through those phones. You'll know where they are at every moment, here or Palm Beach or the Hamptons, and you route the calls to them.

It's a difficult system to learn, and Mrs. Gelman breaks water every time a new man loses a call or cuts her off."

"What's security doing fielding phone calls?" Lally felt Mario studying him.

"Everyone in the company seems to resent the security staff," Santic said. "Say we got a cushy job, sit around and do nothing, so they're constantly finding jobs for us to do."

"Where'd you work, Lally?" Mario asked.

"Stakeout Unit."

"Know Tommy Gannon?"

Gannon was a Stakeout Unit cop that had been arrested and prosecuted for beating a gunman to death. The gunman shot at Gannon, missed, and when Gannon got his hands on the guy, he went crazy.

"Sure. 'Nutsy' Gannon. He worked with McShane."

"McShane? Thought he worked with Richie Grabowski?"

Lally grinned. Mario was trying to be cute. "He worked with McShane. Grabowski worked with Harrigan."

"Oh," Mario said dryly and didn't say anything more.

"Here's that pussy from the Stakeout Unit," a big, garrulous Irishman said with a wry grin when Lally reported, as ordered, to the security office at the Gelman residence at 5:00 p.m. the next day. The other four men Lally met yesterday stopped to look at him. Lally smiled; he'd been checked out. He slipped out of his trench coat, shook the snow off.

The Irishman approached and introduced himself. "Terrance O'Rourke, Gelman's driver, at your service." He stuck out a giant hand. "The boys from Bronx Task Force send their regards. Say you can handle a shotgun, and your beer." He shook Lally's hand with a well-intentioned, bone-crushing squeeze. "We'll have to see about the beer."

The service entrance door swung open and a blast of arctic air followed Lally's new partner, Mario, in. He sloshed into the security office, slipped off a ski parka, stomped wet snow off his boots. And that's when a telephone rang. The five men straightened and a mustached guy, seated at the surveillance monitors, picked up the phone on the second ring.

"Security," he said, listened for a second, hung up and announced, "They're on the move."

All at once cigarettes were crushed out, last gulps of coffee swallowed, coats and gloves hurriedly pulled on. Lally and Mario watched as all but the mustached guy at the monitors rushed out of the office. They hurried outside, took posts on the street by the Gelman limo. One of the men, a tree-trunk bodyguard, stood inside at the front door and waited.

"What's going on?"

"The Gelmans are on their way out," Mario said. "Keep an eye on the gargoyle playing doorman."

Lally watched as Don Gelman, his wife Claudia, and a nurse carrying the Gelman infant exited an elevator directly across from the desk at the bottom of the sweeping stairway. The Gelmans were casually dressed. He was a short man, bald, had a long, fat cigar stuck in a friendly-looking face. Claudia was not unattractive. Doe eyes, full lips, slim. She looked in person better then she did on TV. The Gelmans grabbed their coats---hers a full-length fur, his a fleece-lined Marlboro---scarves and hats from a closet in the foyer.

The gargoyle opened the front door.

"What the hell is wrong with you?" Claudia shrieked.

"Excuse me?" the gargoyle said.

"You're letting heat out." Claudia spoke as if to a retard. "You have any idea what it costs to heat a home this size?"

"Sorry, Mrs. Gelman," the gargoyle said, red-faced. He closed the door, waited as the Gelman's slipped their coats on and bundled up.

"Mrs. Charm," the mustached guy at the monitors snarled to Lally. "I hate her fucking guts."

Mario gestured for Lally to follow him. He led him out of the security office, back to the rear of the house, and down a set of stairs to the basement. They passed the plush home theater and concession stand retired Lieutenant Keating had described. They pushed open a door and entered an overheated, makeshift locker room that smelled of last year's air with a hint of coal gas. Mario showed Lally where to stow his gear, a rusty locker. There was a coffee machine, refrigerators---pad locked. He pointed out the toilet. Lally looked inside and grimaced. He'd seen cleaner toilets in South Bronx gas stations. He would soon learn it was the only toilet they were permitted to use.

"I guess it's a good time to show you the house with them out," Mario sighed. A burden.

He led Lally back up the rear stairs, through the security office and into the foyer. Mario introduced Lally to the man sitting at the desk at the bottom of the sweeping staircase. Lally and Mario would relieve the man at the desk and the mustached man who was sitting at the monitors in the security room at 6:00 p.m.

Mario gave Lally the tour.

The roof door was alarmed and the roof itself monitored by motion detectors. On each floor Lally discreetly checked window and door locks, looked to see if alarm contact points were intact and scanned for functioning motion detectors.

In addition to a well-equipped gym, a library and an elaborate playroom, the fifth, fourth and third floors contained guest rooms, twelve in all, but most went unused. Mario said that as far as he knew, the Gelmans had no friends.

The second floor was the Gelmans' main residence.

"All windows on the second floor are bulletproof," Mario said. "There are panic buttons everywhere. The floor is soundproof. You could set a bomb off down on the first floor and they wouldn't hear it."

Mario guided Lally through the Gelman's enormous master bedroom. Then into the attached bathroom.

"This bathroom also functions as a 'safe room,'" Mario explained. "In case of emergency, the Gelmans would hurry in here and seal it off. The doors are reinforced steel, as are the walls, ceiling and floor. It is equipped with a stand-alone generator, cellular communications, food and water enough for seven days. And weapons."

The Gelman infant's room, which was next door, also had access to the bathroom/safe room. The crib stood in the center of the room and had a video camera positioned on the ceiling directly above it. The baby was watched and tended to day and night by nurses. At the rear of the house was a full kitchen independent of the large professional restaurant kitchen Mario said was on the main floor.

The Gelmans, Mario said, spent most of their time in this second floor kitchen watching TV, yapping on the phones, and gorging themselves on junk food.

At 6:00 p.m. Lally and Mario relieved the man at the stairway desk and the man at the security monitors. Mario pointed to the stack of six video monitors and told Lally that each one displayed a separate video feed from cameras placed strategically around the outside perimeter of the house. Then Mario demonstrated how to set the wall mounted alarm system. Lally noted the system was old, ancient by today's standards.

"What do those red lights mean?" Lally pointed to the two lights, knowing perfectly well that the system was not set properly.

"Those are motion detector sensor indicators. Falling leaves set off the roof alarm so we keep that one turned off. Mrs. Gelman demands we check the rear of the house every fifteen minutes, so rather than turn off the sensors in her office and dining room four times an hour, we keep them off too." Mario led Lally back to the stairway desk and pointed to the elevator directly in front of it.

"Now this is important. Anywhere between 3:00 to 3:15 every morning, the baby's night nurse feeds the infant, then unlocks the elevator and sends it down, empty. The Gelmans won't hear it but you will. Makes a racket that time of morning. The newspapers are delivered to the service entrance at 5:30 a.m. and one of us has to stick them in the elevator and send it back up. Understand?"

"Got it."

Mario took his seat behind the desk, opened a drawer and pulled out a cellular phone. "Use this if you have to make any personal calls. It's a company phone so don't use it unless you have to and don't stay on long. They keep track."

Mario replaced the cellular phone. "O.K., here's the deal. The Gelmans bolt themselves in on the second floor around 11:00 p.m. and almost never come downstairs. It's like lockdown in a prison."

"The paranoid elite," Lally said.

"Yeah. Unless Mrs. Gelman is in one of her moods, hits a panic button. That happens, you run up the back stairs to the second floor, I go up the front."

"Why would she hit a panic button?"

"To break our balls. Make sure we're alert. See how fast it takes us to get upstairs and locate her."

"She do that often?"

"When she and her husband are fighting---often enough." Mario leaned back, crossed his legs. "I'll stay up tonight, man the phones, check the back of the house, put the papers in the elevator at 5:30. You can go downstairs to the movie theater, stretch out, and get some sleep. Tomorrow night, it's your turn to stay up and I'll get some sleep."

"What about the security monitors?"

Mario raised an eyebrow. "What about them?"

"Who's watching them if you're at the switchboard and I'm downstairs?"

Mario studied Lally. "You wanna stay up all night and watch monitors, be my guest. Me? For $11 an hour, the Gelmans are lucky I even sleep here."

"Sounds good to me," Lally said.

"But one of us *has* to stay by the phones at all times. Even though it almost never rings past 11:00 p.m. We miss a phone call we're both fired." Now he pointed to a room, across the foyer by the front door. "See that door? That's the foyer toilet. Don't use it, ever."

"Why?" Lally asked, noting it was only twenty paces from where they stood, and far more convenient than trudging through the foyer, security office, back hallway, down the stairs, past the home theater, and through the locker room to the basement lavatory.

"Mrs. Gelman doesn't want security using it. You get caught using it, you're fired." He thumbed to a room next to them at the rear of the house. "That's Mrs. Gelman's office." Lally looked, noted it was more of a living room with a large comfortable couch. Great for sleeping.

Mario continued. "Do not loiter in Mrs. Gelman's office for any reason. If you sit on her couch she'll know it---don't ask me how---and you're fired. Ditto for the room next to it, the dining room.

"The main kitchen is also off limits, as is the candy concession stand by the theater in the basement. Mrs. Gelman catches you behind the concession stand, or in the kitchen, she'll assume you're stealing food and —"

"I know, I'm fired."

"Right. And she'll have you arrested for larceny."

Lally looked at him.

For the first time Mario smiled. "I kid you not."

The Gelman's switchboard lit up at 10:35 p.m. the following evening. Mario, seated at the bottom of the sweeping staircase, answered on the second ring.

"Security." He listened intently, slap-closed a book he was reading, shot to his feet. "Got it," he said, hung up, and double-timed it to the security office.

"Just got a call from Gelman's driver," Mario said. "They're on the way home."

Lally was face down on the floor, doing pushups. "Forty-eight, forty-nine, fifty." He squat-thrust to his feet, red faced, breathing hard. "So?" He used a moist paper towel to clean the floor dust from his hands.

"Mr. Gelman shacks up every Friday night with one of his lady friends," Mario said. "Claudia isn't going for his line of bullshit tonight They're fighting,"."

"Great," Lally said. "This should be fun."

"Stand at the front door," Mario said. "When you see them coming, open up, let `em in, then close it fast and go back to the monitors. Do not attempt to make conversation with them."

Lally moved to the front door, ten feet of solid oak, and waited for the Gelman limo. Five minutes later the limo rolled to a stop. Lally watched O'Rourke, the driver, hurry out and around to open the rear limo door. But Don Gelman was already out and storming toward the townhouse. Lally swung the door open and Gelman marched in. Claudia rushed in behind him followed by the nurse carrying the wailing infant.

"Shut that kid up," Gelman said.

"If I could stop babies from crying," Claudia said, "*I'd* be the billionaire." The infant's screams were ear-piercing.

"I can't stand it." Gelman threw up his hands. "I'm going out."

"You're not going anywhere." Claudia planted herself in Gelman's path. "You think I don't know where you go? The whole fucking world knows where you go."

86

"Take a valium." Gelman pushed past Claudia and walked out.

"Fuck you!" Claudia said, looked at Lally, and broke down.

Lally averted his eyes, closed the front door, locked it, and went back to the security monitors.

Mario phoned Lally a moment later.

"No one's sleeping tonight," he said. "Stay at your post."

It was 2:32 a.m. when the first alarm sounded.

Lally looked at the alarm system display panel---second floor, Gelman kitchen. Lally ran to the corridor, looked for his partner, but Mario was already racing up the sweeping stairwell. Lally ran back through the security office, down a long corridor, up the rear staircase, down a second floor carpeted hallway to the kitchen where Mario was waiting. The kitchen was empty.

"She's hiding," Mario said.

"From what?" Lally said.

"Us. It's a game she plays."

Lally and Mario began searching rooms: the Gelman's master bedroom, safe room, baby's room---the infant was missing. Lally raced into the hall, opened a linen closet.

"Time!" Claudia checked the stopwatch in her hand. "Pathetic."

"Are you all right?" Lally said.

"Where's your gun?" Claudia demanded.

Lally patted his waistband.

"Your gun should be out, ready to shoot."

There were two more alarm drills that night.

V

Lally met Erin at the Oak Room Bar at noon one week later.

"Anything to report?" Erin said, sucking a martini olive in a manner Lally found most provocative.

He handed her a list of the Gelman's phone calls and visitors. "All the visitors are business associates, or plumbers, gardeners, massage therapists. The calls are business related. No signs of any attempted break-in, yet. The alarm system's a joke."

"Be specific."

"The roof sensors are set off by falling leaves. So security turns them off. Mrs. Gelman wants the rear of the house checked every fifteen minutes. But that means security has to shut down the system beforehand, or the interior rear motion detectors will go off. So they keep those sensors off too."

"Easy access for a thief." Erin took out a pad and scribbled some notes. "Solutions?"

"No quick fix." Lally sipped his beer---the first one was always the best. "They need a whole new security system."

Erin kept writing. "And the men?"

"He has good men. But they would be ineffective in an emergency situation."

"How is that possible? How could good men be ineffective in an emergency situation?

"They hate the Gelmans."

Erin laughed.

"It's no joke. They pay security $11 an hour and get what they pay for, zilch. Know what we do all night instead of watching security monitors and patrolling the house? Sleep---that is when the Gelmans aren't fighting and Claudia isn't purposely tripping the alarm, running our asses all over the house."

Erin looked amused. "She does that?"

Lally huffed. "The inmates are running the asylum."

"So," she said, "if anyone made an attempt on the Gelman's lives —"

"Let's just say I wouldn't risk my life to save theirs."

88

Erin shook her head, made more notes.

Lally continued. "From what I've seen and from what the men tell me, the Gelmans are lonely, paranoid people. They trust no one, have few, if any, friends. Fraternize only with business associates and the occasional lackey who turns up every now and then. It's like they're prisoners of their own wealth."

"You sound like you feel sorry for them."

Lally thought about that. "I wouldn't trade places with them, even with their billions." He scooped up a hand full of cashews from one of the small crystal bowls set along the bar. "So, now what? I tell Chief Vogt I quit?"

"Not yet."

Lally tossed the cashews into his mouth. "Why not? The job's finished. You have your report."

"Stay through the weekend. That's two more nights, $2,000."

"I can't take Claudia for two more nights."

"Please, Bill?" Erin leaned forward and squeezed his hand. "Do it for me." Her words were like long fingernails drawn leisurely down his back.

"All right," Lally said. "For you."

Erin speared another olive, placed it in her mouth and sucked the red-pepper center out. Lally's heart skipped six beats.

"How's dinner sound," Lally said, "you and me, Monday night, after this gig is over?"

Erin kissed him softly, briefly on the lips. "I'll have to get back to you on that."

VI

It was after 11:00 p.m., Lally's last night, when he opened the front door and the Gelmans came stomping into the house, bickering with each other and the driver Terrence O'Rourke.

Lally closed and locked the door behind them.

"And you," Gelman said, addressing O'Rourke. "You're the dumbest white man I know. Even Trump's nigger driver beat us to the front of the hotel."

"Mr. Gelman, the traffic was impossible."

"I don't wanna hear it. Next time my car is not in front of a place, *first*, you're out of here. Understand?"

O'Rourke hung his head. "There's no way I can control traffic."

"You've got a gun don't you?" Claudia shouted. "What the hell are we paying you for?"

"To guard your life." O'Rourke's jaw was tight. "Not pull a gun on some double-parked fool who inconveniences you."

Don Gelman threw his cellular phone. It struck O'Rourke on the head, shattered. The big ex-cop yelped, grabbed at the pain.

Mario, seated at the foyer desk, watched, eyes satellite-dish wide.

"Don't you *ever* argue with my wife," Gelman said.

There were tears of frustration in O'Rourke's eyes.

"You got that?" Gelman said.

Lally waited. Thought for a moment that O'Rourke was gonna lose it and pummel Gelman; he smiled inwardly at the prospect. But O'Rourke just stood there in humiliated silence. His eyes found the floor.

"Got it."

The Gelmans were mumbling something about maybe firing the impertinent son-of-a-bitch O'Rourke as they piled into the elevator, rode up to the second floor and bolted themselves in.

O'Rourke looked at Lally.

"I know what you must be thinking," O'Rourke said, face flushed with embarrassment. He used a handkerchief

90

to dab the blood trickling from a small cut where the cell phone had struck him. "I need the job. I got kids. A sick wife. Mr. Gelman knows it."

"Yeah," Lally said. "Sure."

O'Rourke looked beseechingly at Mario.

But Mario looked away.

A half hour later O'Rourke and the other drivers, bodyguards and security men signed out and left for the night. It was Lally's turn to stay up all night. Mario gathered up his gear, headed to the basement movie theater, and stretched out on a couch.

Lally was sitting at the foyer desk when the Gelman's phone rang at 11:55 p.m., a rare occurrence.

"O'Rourke still there?" It was Mr. Gelman himself speaking.

"He signed out for the night," Lally said.

"Make a note: notify Chief Vogt that O'Rourke is terminated."

Gelman hung up in Lally's ear.

Lally sat back, placed both feet up on the desk and decided he'd had enough of the Gelmans. He got up from his chair and disconnected the phones from the wall jack. Then he walked across the foyer, entered the forbidden, foyer lavatory and carelessly relieved himself. He made certain to leave the toilet lid up, then unroll an entire roll of toilet paper on the floor. He made a soapy, watery mess washing his hands, then used the clean cotton towels, all ten of them, and left them piled on the gleaming tile.

Lally sauntered into the Gelman's main floor kitchen, a vast stainless steel affair, and searched the three giant refrigerators until he had assembled an assortment of cold-cuts, cheese, tomato, spreads, pickles and bread. He stacked himself an immense sandwich and left the entire mess sitting out on the kitchen counter.

Lally realized he craved something sweet. He moseyed down to the basement movie theatre concession stand, pried open the candy display case, stuffed his pockets, then dumped several boxes of candy on the basement floor.

A half hour later, stuffed with candy, Lally entered Claudia's office, stripped down to his jockeys and tank top, hung his clothes and gun on the back of a chair behind her desk, lay on Claudia's couch and fell fast asleep.

VII

The side of Lally's head hurt where the intruder had struck him. Slowly he regained consciousness. Had the presence of mind not to move in case the assailant was near. He forced his mind to explore his body to determine the extent of his injuries; his head was throbbing but he felt sensation in his hands and feet. Good. The attacker had not broken his neck.

Lally heard a noise, the tapping of computer keys. He opened one eye and saw a dark, hooded figure sitting at Claudia's computer a few feet in front of him. He scanned for his gun as best he could. It was nowhere in sight.

Lally knew it would be impossible to move without the intruder seeing him. And he had no way of knowing if his body would respond or how much damage had been done by the assault.

Lally heard the elevator. The infant's nurse was sending the elevator down for the daily papers as she did each morning.

But the intruder did not know that. He switched off the computer screen, stood and pulled a pistol. He moved swiftly across the office and ducked behind a heavy floor-to-ceiling window curtain.

Lally rolled clumsily to his feet, limped to Claudia's desk, picked up a paperweight, lurched across the room and struck the bulge behind the widow curtain.

A phone rang in the darkness. Erin Kellogg turned on her bedside lamp, squinted at the clock, 3:45 a.m., and picked up the receiver.

"Yes?"

"It's Lally."

Erin's eyes opened. She sat up. "A break in?"

"Yeah. Got the guy cuffed. He broke the glass on the rear door. I'll call 911 and —"

"No. Don't call anyone. Don't tell anyone. I'll be right down."

An hour later, Lally heard rapping at Gelman's service entrance.

It was Erin. She was not alone.

Lally led Erin and two men---a thick, scary looking, bald brute dressed in black leather, and a blue-collar, reed-thin guy carrying a pane of glass and glazier's tools to Claudia's office.

The intruder lay, comatose, face down on the carpet, handcuffed.

Lally pointed the glazier to the door with the broken glass.

Erin rolled the intruder over, pulled off his ski mask: male, white, mid 30s, looked to be in excellent physical shape.

"Know him?" Lally handed Erin the intruder's gun.

"No," she said, taking the weapon and expertly examining it. ".22 Berretta. Seven in the clip. One in the chamber."

"He was carrying these." Lally handed her a sealed box of blank computer disks.

"So it was the computer information he was after." Erin motioned to the bald guy. "Take him out to the car." The bald guy picked up the intruder, shouldered him, and carried him out of the house.

Erin handed Lally back the box of computer disks. "I want you to backup Claudia's hard drive onto these floppies tonight, and bring them to me tomorrow."

Lally looked at her.

"I want to see what the thief was after."

"I can't copy someone's personal files," Lally said.

"Bill, I work for the Gelmans. There may be sensitive information in that computer I should be aware of —"

Lally shook his head. "Clear it with Claudia."

"Claudia's a pill. You know that."

The glazier interrupted. "Done."

Erin told him to wait outside.

The glazier picked up his gear and left.

"Do it for me, Bill." Erin moved close, put her arms around his neck and pressed her body against his. Lally felt heat come off of her.

"Please?"

Erin gently kissed his lips.

And Lally kissed her back, fiercely.

"All right," he said.

"Good boy." Erin patted his ass, took him by the hand, led him back to the service entrance, kissed him one last time, and told him to lock her out.

Lally returned to Claudia's office, sat at her desk---he could still taste Erin's lips. He flicked the computer power switch to "on." And as he waited for the system to boot, he wondered if Erin was planning to tell the Gelmans about the break in---knew she should. He walked to the foyer desk, pulled out the cellular phone, and made a single call.

VIII

"It's a blizzard out there," Erin said to a snow-covered Lally when he walked into the Oak Room Bar the following day. "They're expecting 18 inches."

"So I heard." Lally shook off the snow, slipped off his coat and draped it over an empty bar stool. He ordered a beer, then handed Erin the box of disks.

"This box hasn't been opened."

"No," Lally said. "It hasn't."

"But I told you to —"

"It's burglary, Erin. And you know it."

She shook her head. "You're just copying information. You're not stealing anything."

"Ask Claudia for the information." Lally's beer came, he sipped it. "Or get it okayed by Chief Vogt, in writing, and I'll copy the hard disk for you tonight."

Erin forced a tight smile. "I can't do that."

Lally nodded. "I didn't think so."

"This a shakedown?"

Lally smiled.

"I should have known. All right. How much?"

Lally laughed a little. "You don't get it do you?"

"No. *You* don't get it." She leaned close. "I've been offered a fortune by someone for the names of Claudia Gelman's confidential sources."

"I can't help you."

"Why not? I thought you hated the Gelmans."

"I'm not committing a crime for you."

"Stop with the honest Abe routine and name your price."

Lally shook his head.

"Oh, please. Don't try to tell me that in your years as a cop, you never took a bribe, skimmed some drug money now and then. Don't try to tell me that."

Lally looked at her and suddenly all the pieces fell into place. His suspicions had been correct. This was a set-up from the start. She had hired him for the sole purpose of supplying critical intelligence to the intruder so he'd know the safest route into the Gelman house---it was *she* who hired the intruder.

Lally had been duped, his life casually endangered by someone he'd thought was special. He cursed himself for being so blind, for allowing her to use him, again.

"That's exactly what I'm telling you, Erin. I never took anything."

Erin's zeal waned, but only for a moment. She made a show of crossing her legs, leaned forward, and placed her hand on his. "I'm not doing this just for me, Bill. I'm doing it for us."

"Really."

"With the money we'll make we can go away. Take a month in Fiji. Be together. You'd like that, wouldn't you?"

"Yes," he admitted. "I'd like that."

"Then copy the hard disk tonight." She pushed the box of floppies in front of him. "Meet me here tomorrow. Same time." She kissed him squarely on the lips, her entire demeanor now a promise of erotic delights to come. "I'll make it worth your while."

But Lally did not return the kiss. He pushed the floppy disks back in front of her. "Thanks for the beer, Erin." He stood and shrugged on his coat. "We won't be seeing each other again." He turned and walked out of the bar.

Lally buried his head in the collar of his coat as the snow pulled in around him. He walked to the corner, crossed the street, approached and knocked on the passenger side window of a parked, black, four-door sedan. Slowly, the window powered down.

"How'd it go?" Chief Vogt said.

Lally reached into his inside suit pocket, took out a tape recorder, and handed it over. Vogt rewound the tape briefly, then clicked "play". The voices were loud and clear.

"You don't get it do you?"

"No. You don't get it. I've been offered a fortune by someone for the names of Claudia Gelman's confidential sources."

"I can't help you."

The chief stopped the tape. "Good work."

But Lally didn't feel like he'd done good work. He looked back toward the hotel. Spotted Erin hurrying out of the 59th Street entrance, and climb into the back of a waiting limo. The limo headed south and disappeared behind a veil of snow.

The chief said, "Give you a lift home?"

Lally thought about it. The snow stung his face and clung to his coat. "No thanks, chief." Lally turned and trudged north, feeling very alone, through the winter no-man's land called Central Park.

The Hoodlum Priest

The summer night had barely settled on East 88th Street when Father Terrence McCabe bolted from a moving taxi in front of the building.

Police cars were already on the scene.

McCabe hurried into the ramshackle, 5-story brick tenement, took the rickety steps three at a time and was gulping air when he finally reached the fifth floor. First he saw two grim-faced, uniformed New York City police officers guarding apartment 5A. Then he spotted the splintered door frame and the shattered locks.

McCabe moved to enter the apartment.

One of the cops blocked his path. "Sorry, Father."

"Out of my way," the priest said. His white cleric's collar belied a scarred, pug face that had rarely, if ever, turned the other cheek.

"No unauthorized personnel," the cop said.

"What're you doing here, Father?" veteran homicide detective John Sullivan said from inside the apartment. "Let him through."

The uniforms allowed McCabe to enter.

That's when he saw her lying on the living room floor, face up, in a pool of blood, a carving knife protruding from the center of her chest.

"Holy Mary, mother of God," McCabe said making the sign of the cross.

Detective Sullivan, a hulking giant who hadn't missed a happy-hour in 20 years, knelt down beside the victim. He took out a pack of intense, peppermint-flavored gum, shoved a stick into his mouth---knew his 3 a.m. pizza and beer breath was as deadly as roach spray. "Who did it, Ms. Shaffer?"

Gail Shaffer did not answer.

"Gail?" Father McCabe said.

Sullivan glanced over his shoulder and gave McCabe a look that said the victim would soon be DOA.

The priest joined the detective at her side.

"Can you hear me, Gail?" McCabe's voice was just above a whisper. He took her hand in his, held tight. "Would you like me to hear your confession?"

Sullivan backed off, gave the priest privacy.

Gail managed a slow, lingering look at McCabe. Her pale blue eyes, set in a model perfect face, were wide with bewilderment. She forced a thin, flawless smile. "Bless me, Father, for I have sinned -."

McCabe blessed his friend.

"I committed a mortal sin, Father."

McCabe bowed his head, listened.

"But I didn't think he'd kill me for it." Gail struggled to enunciate each word, fought for every breath. "He said he loved me." Now her voice had a bite to it. "You won't let him get away with it, will you, Father?" She dug her nails into McCabe's hand. "Promise me?"

"I won't let him get away with it," McCabe said. "I swear."

Gail's eyes found the knife that was buried deep in her chest. "It's a beautiful knife, Father. Really it is."

"Don't look." McCabe gently turned her face to him. "Continue with your confession."

Gail whispered into the priest's ear for what seemed like a long time, and then her whole body shuddered. Her life was slipping away with each wavering heartbeat.

"The ambulance is on the way," Sullivan said. "Just hang on."

Gail sort of nodded. Tears streaked down the side of her face, running her makeup, mixing with the blood on the bare wood floor.

"Ask her who did it, Father," Sullivan said.

Gail looked past McCabe at the detective. Moved her mouth in an attempt to speak. Her lips were forming a word, a name, when suddenly her eyes rolled back and she convulsed.

"Gail!" McCabe used both his hands to grip hers. Squeezing with all his strength as if his grasp could prevent death from stealing her. He began to administer the Last Rites.

Gail gave the priest a last vacant look, drew a deep, wet breath, and her hands went dead in his.

"Gail is a close friend of mine," McCabe said to Sullivan as they lingered on the sidewalk in front of her building. "I mean *was*."

Although the medical examiner had left, the police lab technicians were still scouring Gail's apartment for evidence; fingerprints, hair and blood samples for DNA analyses.

McCabe sat on the building stoop and fought to control his emotions.

Sullivan patted the priest's shoulder. "I'm here for you, pally."

The priest and the cop had been friends since childhood. They'd run in the same tough, Bronx Irish street gang. Had their first beers together, experimented with drugs, fought bar fights, stole cars, shoplifted, swiped cash from their respective fathers' wallets to buy beer and pot. Even enlisted in the United States Marine Corps together.

And after three, life-altering combat tours in Viet Nam, the two, decorated, honorably-discharged veterans heard a calling to serve mankind. Sullivan chose the police department, became a homicide detective, and spent his time bringing killers to justice.

McCabe chose the priesthood, selected as his flock those most in need of God's guidance---hoodlums like he and Sullivan once were. McCabe frequented the high-crime

100

areas of the city in an attempt to bring lost souls back to God. And he became known throughout New York as The Hoodlum Priest.

"I'm sorry about your friend," Sullivan said.

The priest did not respond.

"Who do you think killed her?"

The morgue wagon arrived. They watched the attendants remove the empty, black body bag from the rear of the van and carry it past them into the building. A chill shook Father McCabe to the bone.

"I asked you," Sullivan said. "Who did it?"

"I can't tell you anything," McCabe said. "The Seal of the Confessional is sacred. You know that."

"You're obstructing a homicide investigation, pally."

McCabe looked at him. "Arrest me."

Sullivan heaved a sigh, took out a pad, pen and sat beside his friend. "Tell me about Gail Shaffer."

McCabe took a moment to gather his thoughts. He told Sullivan that Gail's long-suffering mother---she never knew her father---lived in a sludge tenement in Our Lady Of Immaculate Conception parish, in Yorkville. Gail had become a drug addict and prostitute by the time she was sixteen.

"Her mother contacted me, asked if I'd help with Gail." McCabe said he got a tip a few days later that Gail was hooking around 8th Avenue and 47th Street in Hell's Kitchen. Said he recruited members of his flock, ex-convicts, to assist him.

"We duked it out with her pimp and his gang, but we got her away from there. Her mother signed the commitment papers. Gail was forced into rehab." McCabe's voice cracked.

"You okay?"

"Yeah." McCabe said.

"I mean, we can do this later."

"I'm all right," McCabe sniffled. "I've got her mother's phone number if you want it."

"I was hoping you'd do me a favor and notify her for me?"

"Of course," McCabe said.

Sullivan, like all cops, despised the burden of having to notify the next of kin of a loved one's death. This time he had a patsy; he knew his old friend couldn't say no.

Sullivan flipped a page on his notebook. "How'd she take to rehab?"

"Not well. She went through the program about five times. Six was the magic number. But then she straightened out completely. Attended the 12:45 mass every Sunday. Volunteered her time to church fundraisers. Helped out in the soup kitchen.

"We socialized often: church-sponsored lunches, dinners, parties, bingo games. I fixed her up once with a lawyer, a Fordham graduate." McCabe looked off and smiled at the memory. "That was an utter disaster."

"What did she do for work?" Sullivan asked.

"She attended the Culinary Institute of America. Worked her way through and became a chef. Was doing pretty well too. Apprenticing at Le Cirque. The money wasn't great yet, but in a few years -."

"She have any enemies you know of?"

McCabe shook his head. "Gail was incapable of making enemies."

"She date much?"

"No. She was particular. Wanted a family. Most of the guys she met were bozos, or married."

"She have a boyfriend?"

McCabe leaned forward, rested his elbows on his knees, eyes on his shoes. "Gary Gersh."

"Gersh?" Sullivan jotted the name down. "How long did they date?"

"On and off for the last few years." McCabe added, "Beside being a drunk and a crack addict, he has personality problems."

"Imagine that."

"He's insecure, competitive, jealous."

"You know him?"

"Gail introduced us," McCabe said. "She wanted me to help her get him off booze and drugs. But Gersh didn't think he had a problem. Typical. Wanted no part of rehab. As a result Gail tried to keep him at arm's length."

"Tried?"

"He asked her to marry him last year. Gave her a ring, but she wouldn't accept it. He started stalking her."

"Gersh have a problem with you?"

The question took McCabe by surprise. "Why would he?"

"You were Gail's friend, a priest."

McCabe thought a moment. "He didn't understand our friendship."

"So, what attracted Gail to Gersh?"

"I could never figure that out," McCabe said. "Other than Gail must have felt sorry for him. She was a caregiver by nature. Attracted guys with problems. Gersh probably sensed that in her. Took advantage."

"Was he violent?"

McCabe looked off. "He hit her once."

"You punch him out?"

"Talked to him is all. Told him if he ever hit her again, I'd have him arrested. He told me to go 'f' myself."

"You think he killed her?" Sullivan said.

"Seal of the Confessional. Remember?"

"Well, do you think he had motive?"

McCabe smiled---Sullivan was asking the right questions. "Four months ago, Gail told me that Gersh raped her."

103

Sullivan took a long, slow look at his friend. "She report it?"

McCabe shook his head. "I couldn't convince her to. She blamed herself. Thought it was her fault."

"You speak to Gersh about it?"

"She begged me not to."

"Anything else I should know?" Sullivan said.

"She was pregnant with Gersh's child."

"What?" Sullivan said.

"She wanted to abort it. I advised her to have the baby. Told her I'd help her any way I could. Help her put the child up for adoption if she chose. But she said she didn't want to bring a crack baby into the world. She told Gersh she was planning to abort it."

"Gersh objected?" Sullivan said.

"He told her, if she aborted his child, he'd kill her."

"I take it she aborted the child?"

"I can't tell you that."

Sullivan spit the wad of gum into the street. "Where's Gersh live?"

"The high-rise on 92nd Street. Yorkville Towers."

Suddenly, news vans were squealing around the corner, pulling onto the block, double parking. Cameramen hurried from the vans pulling out their equipment. Soon the place would be swarming with reporters.

"Anything else?" McCabe was anxious to get out of there before the press recognized him---The Hoodlum Priest always made great news copy.

"Yeah." Sullivan closed his notebook. "About your deathbed promise to Gail, not letting the killer get away with it."

"You weren't supposed to be listening."

"Stay out of this investigation, pally. I'm warning you."

"Sure, fat man. Whatever you say."

"Look, I'm not fooling around," Sullivan said. "My boss has had it up to here with you. Priest or not, you take the law into your own hands and I won't be able to protect you this time. You see Gersh, you call 911. You don't do a thing. Understand?"

"I swear." McCabe raised his right hand, placed his left behind his back and crossed his fingers. "Boy Scout's honor."

Sullivan was grumbling about the fact that McCabe had never been a freakin' Boy Scout, when the morgue attendants came out of the building, carrying the black body bag containing Gail Shaffer's remains. McCabe watched as they wedged through the swarm of onlookers and news people and placed her into the rear of the morgue wagon.

Cameras flashed and video tape whirled.

McCabe arrived at Our Lady Of Immaculate Conception rectory two hours later. He avoided conversations with his boss the Monsignor, fellow priests, and other church employees. He climbed two flights to his tiny bedroom, switched on the air conditioner and checked his cell phone answering service for messages.

There were messages from several members of his ethically-challenged flock asking if he wanted them to "neutralize," "take-out," "whack," or otherwise exterminate Gary Gersh. He returned each call and asked each anxious assassin to stand down. He would handle it.

After attempting to locate Gail's mother---she was not home---McCabe had scoured the upper East Side. He stopped by Gersh's residence, visited several scumbag bars that were known Gersh hangouts. He gave his phone number to the rummy bartenders and toothless waitresses with instructions to call the second Gersh showed his face. McCabe knew Gersh would not hide. It was just a matter of time.

McCabe had toyed with the idea of settling into one of those dilapidated taverns, and getting hopelessly drunk like he and Sullivan used to do. Anything to dull the pain of Gail's death.

McCabe grabbed a cold beer from his mini-fridge, opened it, took a swig, and gazed around his tiny room. On his bookshelf among volumes dealing with Catholic studies was a photo of Gail and him at a church function. McCabe pulled a photo album from the book shelf. He flipped a few pages. There was a picture of Gail as she left the drug rehab clinic for the last time. And another shot of them dressed in green on St. Patrick's Day, fresh from the parade on Fifth Avenue, eating plates of corned beef and cabbage at a local Irish pub with a gang of felonious cut-throats. God, they were having fun. And there was Gail at the surprise dinner party he had thrown for her after she graduated from chef school. Gail wore white, balancing a floppy chef's hat on her head, proudly exhibiting the professional carving knife McCabe had given her for graduation.

The same carving knife that protruded from her chest.

McCabe closed the album.

He wondered if Gersh had used that particular knife to murder Gail in order to send *him* a message. To strike back at *him* for failing to convince her not to abort his child. It was, after all, a priest's job.

But McCabe had been more then a priest to Gail.

Much more.

He had been her lover.

McCabe put the album away.

Their intimate relationship began soon after Gail's successful completion of the drug rehab program. A sudden and unexpected romantic liaison followed. And then came the wretched complications, the insoluble moral issues. McCabe had taken advantage of a vulnerable parishioner who trusted him, violating his fiduciary responsibilities, as well as his sacred vows. Yes, he truly loved her, was in fact in love with her. But the physical consummation of that love was, for a priest, forbidden.

106

Yet part of him wanted to remain a Catholic priest, to continue his work in the service of Christ. Another part of him had wanted to leave the church, marry Gail, get a job, raise a family, lead a normal life.

"I feel that I've lost my faith," McCabe told Gail while discussing their future options. "That I'm spiritually adrift."

"I refuse to be responsible for that," was Gail's reply.

And so after much discussion, soul searching and conflict, Father McCabe chose to remain a priest, reaffirm his vows, devote his remaining years to the service of Christ. Had he not, Gail would be alive today.

"Gersh is outside!" McCabe recalled Gail screaming into the phone earlier that day---it was to be their very last conversation. "He's threatening to break the door down."

"Hang up and call 911." McCabe could hear Gersh yelling in the background, calling Gail a murderer. Then he heard the door crack and cave in and Gail's terrified scream.

McCabe would never forget that scream.

Or the vision of her lying there with *his* carving knife stuck in her chest. Picturing Gersh doing it. Gail fighting for her life, the fear in her eyes, the horror on her lovely face.

McCabe fell to his knees and began to pray. He prayed for Gail's soul and for her mother's. And he asked God to forgive him for his lapses in faith, his fall from grace, and for what he was about to do---hunt down Gary Gersh.

McCabe's cell phone rang.

Something told him it was Gail's mother. She would be hysterical, blame him for her daughter's death. She had trusted him. How could he let this happen? Why hadn't he protected her?

McCabe took a deep breath, answered his cell phone. "Hello?"

"Father McCabe?"

"Yes."

"This is Vito, the doorman at Yorkville Towers."

"Yes, Vito. What can I do for you?"

"You asked me to call the minute Mr. Gersh came in."

"I'll be right over." McCabe hung up. Located a key behind a gold-framed photo of the Blessed Virgin, used it to unlock a desk drawer. He reached in and pulled out the .45 semi-automatic that he'd confiscated from a member of his flock several years ago. He racked a round into the chamber.

"He still upstairs?" McCabe asked Vito.

The doorman nodded. "Haven't seen him come back down."

A few moments later McCabe stepped out of an elevator onto the 37th floor. He moved quietly down the hall and stopped at apartment 37-J. He placed his ear to the door, listened. No sound. He pulled a credit card from his wallet, jimmied the lock. The door clicked open. Gun in hand, McCabe slipped inside Gersh's apartment.

McCabe closed the door quietly behind him, scanned the place; it looked like a bag lady had exploded in there. McCabe stepped over piles of rotting garbage, stacks of daily newspapers and heaps of unopened mail. Photos of Gail were tacked to the walls in every room. McCabe looked under the beds, in the bathrooms, in each closet. Gersh was not in the apartment.

McCabe pulled out his cell phone, dialed the doorman. "Vito, it's Father McCabe. Mr. Gersh come down?"

"No, Father," the doorman said.

"He have any friends in the building?"

"None that I know of."

"He's not in his apartment. Any idea where he might be?"

"Some tenants like to hang out on the roof," the doorman said.

The door to the roof was slightly ajar. McCabe pushed the door open slowly, stepped out onto the gravel-covered rooftop, careful not to make too much noise. He looked around, his eyes adjusting to the immediate darkness. He checked behind the door and above the exit overhang. No one there.

"That you, Father McCabe?" someone said.

McCabe followed the voice to the other end of the roof, up to a small, two story brick enclosure which contained the building's water tower. Saw a tall, bean-pole thin figure perched atop the enclosure, silhouetted by the glow of city lights.

Gary Gersh.

McCabe moved closer. Pulled his gun.

"I told her not to kill the child," Gersh said. "She wouldn't listen. It's murder, you know."

All at once McCabe noticed that Gersh was wearing football pads on his bony shoulders, knees and elbows.

"She left me no choice," Gersh said. "I'd do it again under the same circumstances." Gersh reached into an equipment bag, pulled out a football helmet and tugged it on.

"What're you doing?" McCabe said.

"My parents will want an open casket," Gersh said with all sincerity. "I loved Gail. I can't live without her. What I'm about to do will prove it. Will you tell them?"

McCabe realized Gersh was planning to jump, do a Peter Pan right there in front of him. He stuck the .45 into his waistband.

"I'll tell them," McCabe said.

All at once the night was filled with approaching sirens. Lights from arriving police cars pulsated rhythmically off nearby buildings, sporadically brightening the night sky. Vito the doorman would tell the cops that Gersh was not in his apartment, that Father McCabe was searching for him up on the roof. A dozen uniforms would burst onto the scene in a few minutes and attempt to stop Gersh.

Which is what McCabe, a man of God, knew he should do---try to talk Gersh out of committing suicide, a sin that would condemn his soul to hell for all eternity. Exactly what McCabe wanted.

Gersh moved to the end of the water tower and gazed down to the street 40 floors below. Then he looked at McCabe and gave the thumbs up sign. Held it.

McCabe realized that Gersh was waiting for him to return the signal, give him the okay to jump; thumbs up for death.

A stairwell door slammed open down on the 37th floor.

Cops would be on the roof in seconds.

McCabe held out his hand, returned the thumbs-up sign.

And Gary Gersh jumped.

Red Star of Death

Danny Noonan
with
Thomas J. Fitzsimmons

The true story of the second deadliest, and costliest fire in the history of the New York City Fire Department.

I

The stench of burning PVC caught me by surprise and forced me to stop and gasp for breath---an all-too-familiar, noxious odor that, if allowed to thrive, could kill.

I continued down the IRT subway stairs, side-stepping harried commuters, and searched the sweltering station platform for the cause of the acrid smell---saw nothing apparent. As a former New York City firefighter I knew that PVC smoldered somewhere. I dialed 911 on my cell phone and reported the condition to the emergency operator.

Fire department units responded minutes later.

My train roared into the station.

I stepped into the stuffy subway car, scanned for psychos, bandits and other dangers---saw none---and realized that the lingering odor of burning PVC was irritating my lungs. I took a standing position at the end of the subway car, produced my inhaler, breathed in three grateful pumps and recalled what my old friend and mentor Patty Sullivan had always told me: *"Being a firefighter is the best job in the world."*

Despite the danger inherent in firefighting, I had to admit that Patty was right. But fighting the New York Telephone Company fire, breathing PVC fumes, had killed Patrick Sullivan.

And my lungs had not been the same since.

Fifteen minutes later I hauled myself up the stairs to the balmy summer streets and Fire Department Headquarters at 9 Metro Tech, Brooklyn, New York. I had made an appointment with the Photo and Forensic Unit to upgrade components of the fire technology class that, since retiring from the FDNY, I volunteered to teach to local departments.

The building's air-conditioning cooled my scorched lungs and made breathing easier. As always, I stopped at the department's Wall of Honor, Patty Sullivan never far from my mind.

The 40-foot-long bronze memorial, with eternal torches burning at each end, is where the New York City Fire Department honors firefighters who have made the supreme sacrifice.

Since 1865, 772 firefighters' names, companies, and dates of death have been inscribed on individual gold tags. But Patty Sullivan's name, as well as the names of the many other firefighters who lost their lives as a direct result of the New York Telephone fire---the "Phone Fire"---were not listed. For Sullivan and the others had not died at the scene of the blaze. They had expired only after days, weeks, even years, of suffering from varieties of cancer, heart, and respiratory disease and received no department recognition of any kind.

"Guess who died," a voice with a noticeable wheeze on my cell phone had asked that very morning. It was the sort of call that I dreaded and had received far too often.

I took a breath, let it out. "A smoke-eater from the Phone Fire," I said. "From the first alarm assignment."

112

Six-hundred and ninety-nine fire fighters from 35 engine and 19 ladder companies spent more than 30 hours battling that stupendous five-alarm blaze---one of the most complex, costly, and deadly fires in the history of the New York City Fire Department. They literally gave their lives protecting the citizens of the City of New York. They deserved official department recognition. They belonged on that memorial wall.

Yet for years FDNY officials and its medical division had declined to acknowledge the deaths and illnesses resulting from that unparalleled blaze. Over the years many of us had made phone calls and written letters, urging the department's high command to address our unique medical problems. We've explained again and again that all 699 men who fought the Phone Fire suffer some form of respiratory distress---and virtually every firefighter who responded to the Phone Fire's first two alarms has cancer. We even invited the department to *use* us, the Phone Fire "survivors," to study the effects of toxic smoke on the human body in the hopes of preventing present and future firefighters from meeting the same fate.

The department's response in every instance was complete silence. They ignored us and did not acknowledge our written or verbal pleas in any way.

In time we were forced to concede that the fire department had, for all intents and purposes, abandoned us, given us the "Pontius Pilate kiss-off." Later, when we discovered that the medical division had actually stamped red stars on the covers of all 699 Phone Fire medical folders---"Red Stars of Death," we called them---we became angry. I was still angry.

Recently the mayor had appointed a new fire commissioner. I actually knew the guy. We weren't close friends, but we had worked together in the Fort Apache section of the South Bronx. As I stood before the wall, an absurd thought struck me: What if I showed up at the commissioner's eighth floor office? Would he agree to meet with me? No. There was no way a man that powerful and busy would see a retired smoke-eater unannounced and unscreened---if he even remembered me.

I shook the fool's folly from my mind.

And moments later found myself on the eighth floor, introducing myself to the commissioner's receptionist.

"My name's Dan Noonan." I smoothed my mustache. "I'm a retired firefighter, and I'd like to see the commissioner."

The heavy-set, older woman nodded. "Do you have an appointment?"

"No," I said. "No appointment."

She eyeballed me warily. "What is the nature of your business."

"The nature of my business," I said, "is to see the commissioner."

A cocked eyebrow. "With regard to -?"

To my right, a secretary picked up the phone and said something that sounded like "code blue." The next thing I knew, a fire-hydrant-thick man in a loose fitting suit---a Fire Marshal---was coming across the reception area. On his hip I saw a 9mm Glock.

"The Red Star of Death," I said to the secretary, knowing this would be my one and only chance to make my case. "Tell the commissioner I'm here to speak to him about the Red Star of Death."

II

The New York Telephone Company Main Switching Center building is a virtual fortress. The structure, designed to be earthquake and riot-proof, has windows constructed of heavy wire glass in reinforced steel frames that were mounted with ¼" Lexan---a bullet-resistant plastic. At the time of the fire, all windows at street level and on the second floor were covered with heavy metal cages to protect them from vandals.

For nearly a half-century, the art deco, 11-story structure served as the main switching center for the lower East Side. It serves a 300-square-block area and is equipped to handle 10,000 calls an hour. Its customers included major business, six hospitals, nine housing projects, three universities, 11 secondary schools, several police precincts, almost all units in the FDNY's First Division, and 92,000 residential phones.

On February 26, 1975 at approximately 4 p.m. a fire alarm rang in the New York Telephone Company lobby at 204 2nd Avenue. A building foreman discovered that the glass on an alarm box in the first floor stair landing had been shattered. Since the accidental breaking of the glass by workmen carrying equipment through the first floor had occurred before, the foreman had manually reset the alarm and reset the fan system, which had automatically shut down. With no replacement glass readily available, the foreman inserted a rectangular piece of plywood.

Meanwhile, a manhole crew working outside was trying to locate troubles in a trunk line leading into the 2nd Avenue side of the building. A card game was in progress in the 10th floor locker room. A craftsman took a nap on the couch.

At approximately 10 p.m., the lights over three public telephone booths in the lobby went out. The same building-foreman reset the circuit breakers that controlled the lights. The lights went back on.

At midnight an employee on his way home observed that the lobby clock did not agree with his wristwatch. A building service woman, also on her way home, noted that the clocks had, in fact, stopped.

At 12:05 a.m. there were 23 employees in the building: ten on the 5th floor, two on the 4th floor, five on the 3rd, four on the 2nd. On the 1st floor a workman was finishing a lengthy telephone call. The guard stood at his post in the lobby.

At 12:11 a.m. a telephone company employee entered the building, walked through the lobby, stepped into another room and saw heavy smoke seeping from under a door. He looked down a 2'-by-2' hole in the floor---a cable conduit---and saw a mass of burning cables glowing bright orange. The employee tried to telephone a fire alarm.

The telephones were dead.

At the same time the 5th floor began to fill with heavy black-gray smoke. "Fire!" a workman shouted as fire alarms started to sound all around him. He grabbed a phone, dialed 911; the telephone was not working.

Workmen on the 3rd floor also tried to call for help. Their telephone lines were dead as well.

As panicky employees began congregating in the lobby, the lobby guard tried his telephone---dead.

"For the love of God", the guard screamed to a workman. "Get the fire department. We have a serious fire." The workman ran to the corner. Pulled the fire alarm box.

At 12:25 a.m. a pull box alarm was received at the Fire Dispatching Headquarters in Central Park, transmitting Manhattan Box 465.

We'd experienced a typical February night at Ladder Company 3, located on 3rd Avenue and 13th Street on Manhattan's lower East Side. We were worn ragged from the crushing work load and lack of sleep. There had been a smoldering mattress fire in an East Side apartment, a car crash with fatalities, a dumpster fire, heart attack, calls from residents claiming they had no heat or hot water, a lost child, a stuck elevator and the usual dose of false alarms. Business as usual for a truck company in the FDNY.

Thirteen minutes past midnight I left the warmth of the firehouse kitchen and relieved another firefighter at the cold drafty house watchman's desk in the front of the firehouse. I hated working through the night. As a single person living on Manhattan's upper East Side, I knew that the dating scene would be in full swing right about now--- and I longed to be out there in the middle of the action. I thought about calling my girlfriend of two years, who was waiting tables at Suspenders, a firefighter's hangout at 38th Street and 2nd Avenue. Find out what my crowd was up to, which fireman was hitting on which stewardess. Who'd had too much to drink. If the guy who owed me $100 from a football bet had shown his face yet. But instead I broke open a paperback that I'd been trying to finish for months, sipped a cup of black coffee, and settled in for a long and, hopefully, uneventful night.

At 12:26 a.m. a radio dispatcher's broken transmission blared through quarters. "Ladder 3, respond."

I laid down my paperback. "Ladder 3."

Although the dispatcher's subsequent words were unusually difficult to decipher, what I understood was: "Report of a working *structural* fire, Box 465, 2nd Avenue and 13th Street. The New York Telephone Building. Acknowledge Ladder 3."

Having had only two years experience as a New York City firefighter, during which I'd fought all the typical fires---apartment, dumpster, mattress, car---a working *structural* fire meant that an entire building might be ablaze. A chill raced up my back.

"Ladder 3, 10-4." I reached to my left, struck the fire alarm buzzer, its loud, harsh sound always startling. "*Everyone goes*!"

Men stopped whatever it was they were doing---cleaning up after a stale meal that had been interrupted by three separate fire alarms, checking tools, repairing equipment---

and ran downstairs, slid down poles, slipped into fire gear and jumped onto the trucks.

As I ripped the paper from the printer that contained the written, hardcopy alarm information, I kept yelling: "Everyone goes. Chief goes, too."

I donned my own fire gear, handed our Lieutenant Pullano---a former stockbroker---the printout. In moments we were racing down 13th Street, our bare faces stung by a frigid wind as our air horn and sirens shattered the wintry night.

"Smell that?" Patty Sullivan stood beside me as our rig approached the scene of the alarm. "I've never smelled anything like that before."

I took a breath; the odor was sharply acrid. I looked and saw Telephone Company employees, faces smudged by soot, running from the building and retching.

Engine Co. 5 had been returning to their house following a false alarm and were the first on the scene. They had begun pulling hose lengths to the entrance in the structure.

"Engine 5 to Manhattan, K, 10:75," I heard them broadcast over our truck radio. "Working fire, box 465, New York Telephone Building."

Engine 33, Ladder 3, and Tower Ladder 9, all under the direction of Battalion 6, were also at the location.

As we turned the corner on 2nd Avenue, Lt. Pullano got our attention by pounding his fist on the glass partition separating the cab from the crew's assigned positions. "Bring Scott masks."

The clumsy, yellow 30-pound breathing apparatus is carried on the back and looks exactly like scuba gear.

The rig came to a halt in front of the building and I saw black smoke billowing from the telephone company lobby and more employees stumbling from the building, coughing and choking. We grabbed our gear, axes, halligans and other forcible entry tools and rushed inside.

We assembled in the lobby and were told that the fire had grown to a second alarm and the Battalion Chief had put in a call for an additional engine and ladder company. That the telephone service in a 300 square block area on Manhattan's lower East Side was out of service and that the department was communicating on its emergency backup system---that must have been the reason the dispatcher's firehouse voice transmission had been broken.

A moment later we learned that the Telephone Company's fire alarm display board indicated a fire three floors below in the vault of the sub-cellar. The Chief determined that, although the flames were not yet visible, an assault on the underside of these vaults had to be made. As the first "due" ladder company our responsibility was to make that assault and locate the seat of the fire---an essential step in the foundation of all firefighting strategies. Some firefighters were assigned vertical smoke ventilation duties, others horizontal.

"Let's get to it," Pullano said.

Patty Sullivan turned to me. "Remember to stay low, Noonan." He helped me check my gear. "This could be a bad one."

And then Patty did something I'd never seen him do before. He blessed himself, made the sign of the cross--- three times. Watching the fearless, gray-haired firefighter, I flushed with apprehension. What the hell were we walking into?

I was a seventeen-year-old and shucking clams at Fitzgerald's Ocean Front Clam House in New York's Rockaway Beach the first time I'd met Patty Sullivan.

I'd been raised in that small, suburban community---a peninsula separating Jamaica Bay from the Atlantic Ocean. I was, by my parents' design, isolated from the rest of the five boroughs. My father---an NYPD Detective---and my mother wanted to protect us kids from the perils of the inner city.

Summers in Rockaway Beach were a mix of blue-collar and white-collar families all escaping the stifling crowds and heat of the city. Every Memorial Day the area would morph from a sleepy ocean-front village to a bustling seafront community.

During one of those early summer months, I began working at Fitzgerald's and got to know a group of regulars, men whose boisterous banter and fun-loving humor always livened up the place. I soon learned that they were New York City firefighters. Since many of them were skilled in more profitable professions---accounting, physical therapy, construction---I learned that firefighting was more like a religious vocation than a regular job; they didn't do it for the money. Which explained why they were held in such awe by the bartenders, waitress, customers, and, as the summer progressed, by me.

"What's it like to be a fireman?" I asked Patty Sullivan one August afternoon.

Patty, father of three and volunteer firefighter on his days off from the FDNY, dressed boat-shoe casual and shaved only when absolutely necessary.

"Thought you were gonna be a cop." He puffed his pipe, sipped his beer. "Like your dad."

"He wants me to go to college."

"Good idea," Patty said. "Go to college."

"You didn't answer my question."

Patty looked at me thoughtfully, rubbed the stubble on his cleft chin. "Best job in the world," he said. "But a dangerous one. No margin for error."

"No margin for error . . .."

Those words pinballed in my brain as Patty finished checking my gear. He patted me on the back, flashed me what he tried to pass off as a self-assured smile. I could see fear in my friend's eyes.

"Ready?" Pullano said.

We donned our Scott masks and descended into the basement of the building.

The halls were long and tiled, with several steel doors. The smoke had gathered at the top of the corridors creating a dim mist that caused the fluorescent lights to give off an eerie glow. The constant ringing of the fire klaxons---identical to a submarine dive alarm---added to the confusion.

We walked through a door which read "Extremely High Voltage" and negotiated a narrow ladder that descended at a sharp angle to the smoke-filled basement below. Officers experienced extreme difficulties in communicating. We could barely see or hear simple commands like, "Don't let go of the hose line," and, "Stay together."

We searched for fire in the pitch-black smoke. Found none. Then we hit pockets of glowing cable and doused them with streams of water. But the fire was burning the polyvinylchoride insulation of the wires in the vertical piping of the 11-story building. Our efforts were futile.

"Holy Mary mother of God," someone said behind me. And then I could clearly distinguish a voice, the Engine Officer transmitting over his radio to the Incident Commander that our position was untenable and perilous. I realized he must have removed his face piece and breathed poisonous air in order to make the communication.

"Two telephone employees are unaccounted for," I heard someone else say over the radio. I overheard them assign a rescue company the task of searching the building for the missing employees.

"Come on, lads," Patty said as he led us along the inside of the 13th Street wall, searching in vain for the fire.

Fifty or so steps later we found ourselves enveloped by ten million cubic feet of zero-visibility toxic smoke. After several minutes of blindly cracking into walls, iron railings, and each other, we were forced to retreat.

As we pulled back along the same route, someone said, "Hey, where's the lieutenant?"

"Pullano?" Patty said into his radio.

No answer.

Since I was beginning to feel a bit disoriented, I imagined that Pullano had too and had wandered off. We spread out, searched as best we could; Pullano was no longer anywhere near us. We retraced our steps along the interior wall and through the sub-cellar down a long, narrow corridor through nearly impenetrable, toxic black smoke. There were no windows, no doors and no other source of breathable air or outside ventilation.

"Bang on something, Pullano," Patty said into the hand-talkie, a last ditch effort to locate the missing fire lieutenant.

We heard three loud bangs. Pullano was somewhere ahead of us shrouded in deadly blackness.

We inched forward, felt along the walls and discovered a metal door. I used my fist to bang on it. Someone banged back.

"Get me the hell outta here," Pullano's muffled voice came from the other side.

I tried the door knob, twisted it. Pushed. Shoved. It didn't budge. Patty elbowed me aside, jammed the working-end of a forcible entry tool into the door jamb above the lock, pressed forward then yanked back with all his considerable strength.

No movement.

Sullivan quickly reset the forcible entry tool. This time drove it deep into the door jamb, below the lock. He and Joe Rosa---a family man and restaurant co-owner who wore his love for Italian food around his waist---heaved their full weight against it and the lock shattered and the door ripped open. Lieutenant Pullano stumbled out.

"Thank God," he said.

Flashover.

A blue-green lateral flame exploded from the room Pullano had been trapped in and raced though the sub-cellar. I dove to the ground, rolled to my knees, crawled as fast and as far as possible from the inferno. And when I looked back through the blowtorch flames and bellowing soot, Sullivan, Rosa and Pullano were gone.

"Lieutenant, Patty, Joe?" My words were muffled by my face mask and obscured by the roar of diesel turbines. I crawled back to the flashover site, using my hands as eyes, felt around for my comrades, found no one.

I was alone.

My Scott mask low-oxygen alarm sounded. I clicked on my six-volt searchlight to check the oxygen gauge but the powerful light didn't seem to work. I jiggled the switch, clicked it on, off, banged the goddamned thing against my leg. Pointed it directly into my eyes through my face mask---saw light. It *was* working but could not penetrate the lethal smoke.

My Scott mask alarm continued to sound, indicating my air was fast dwindling. I had two minutes to make it to the stairwell and climb four flights. Two minutes to reach fresh air. Two minutes of life. I breathed a prayer.

More Scott masks, low-oxygen alarms sounded somewhere in front of me---or were they behind me? I realized I was lost, turned around, with no idea which way I'd come, which passageway and stairwell I'd taken. I felt the first twinges of panic.

Following a fire hose, a life-line to the world above, I backtracked and cracked into a wall, a dead end---the hose ran straight up a wall. I shuffled to the left and realized that, due to the bubbling tar and melting polyethylene, my boots were adhering to the surface of the floor. God, it was hot.

Following the wall I finally came upon a firefighter. Somehow he had a sense of where he was and pulled me across a six-foot abyss, into a narrow staircase clogged with other firefighters coming in the opposite direction, sent to relieve us. I was forced to give way to the reinforcements and heard more Scott mask alarms sounding behind us. And then I heard a single ping---I only had seconds of air left. I pushed forward, clawing my way, hit the deck and crawled as fast as I could up the slippery waterfall of a stairwell.

As the smoke became less dense I could see other firefighters---some were disoriented, others felled by the noxious fumes---all coughing, choking, vomiting. I took a deep breath, held it, and ripped off my mask.

I dashed up the last few steps, through the lobby---my lungs burning---and out onto the street. I exhaled, fell on all fours, heart pounding, sweat stinging my eyes, blinding me. I drew a series of deep breaths and realized the air outside was, in some measure, also contaminated.

"Sweet Jesus," Rosa said as he collapsed beside me and slipped off his empty air tank. "I've never seen such blackness."

"Where's the Lieutenant and Sullivan?"

Rosa gestured to the Telephone Company Building.

Lieutenant Pullano came out of the lobby next, sat down beside me. "I owe my life to Patty Sullivan." He gasped for breath. "Patty shared his oxygen with me."

I wiped the sweat from my eyes as best I could, scanned the mass of fallen firefighters: Patty Sullivan was not among us. "Where is he?"

"He was behind me." Pullano looked to the Telephone Company building entrance, waiting for Sullivan to come out.

He did not.

Pullano pulled out his radio. "Ladder 3 Alpha, What is your location, K.?" (Ladder 3 Alpha was the radio code assigned to Sullivan.) "Ladder 3 Alpha, come in." We waited. No response. "Patty Sullivan, talk to me."

"Patty's in trouble," I said.

"Patty Sullivan owes me five dollars," Rosa said.

Rosa, Pullano and I struggled to our feet, raced back to the New York Telephone Company building and were nearly trampled by a surge of frenzied firefighters escaping the lobby.

"What's going on?" Pullano asked a fire captain as we changed our oxygen tanks.

"South wall's cracked," the captain said.

"But that's reinforced concrete," Pullano said.

"Temperature's 1400 degrees Fahrenheit on the first floor, 1300 on the second. Chief's predicting a possible catastrophic building collapse."

"One of our men is missing," Pullano said.

"He's low on oxygen," I said.

"Hell, he's *out* of oxygen," Pullano said.

"Right." The captain took out his radio. "I'll see if the Chief will authorize a rescue."

"There's no time," Pullano said as we pushed past the captain, sliced through the escaping firefighters and entered the lobby.

The first thing I noticed was that a plume of thick, black smoke was billowing from the main stairwell which had become a literal sub-cellar chimney; the stairwell was impassable.

"Shit," Rosa said.

"Exactly," Pullano said.

"He won't even know street level," Rosa said.

"Then he's finished," Pullano said.

I felt sick to my stomach. It would take a miracle for Patty to survive.

"Even if we could make it down," Rosa said. "We could pass him on that stairwell and never know it."

"We could try spreading out," Pullano said.

"Lock arms?" I said.

"Yeah," Pullano said. "That might work." Pullano pulled out his radio. "Ladder 3 Alpha. Patty Sullivan, what is your location, K.?"

Noise---a grating sound like twisting steel came from somewhere overhead. I looked at Pullano and Rosa; they stood dead still, Frisbee-wide eyes watching the ceiling above us.

"C'mon, Patty," Pullano said into the radio. "Answer me for Christ's sake. What is your location?"

Silence.

Then static, a faint transmission---"3 Alpha to 3."

"That's him!" Rosa said.

"Patty where the hell are you?" Pullano said.

"I'm somewhere on the main staircase heading up to the lobby. Do *not* attempt rescue." Patty Sullivan coughed uncontrollably---his Scott mask had to be off. "Repeat," he gasped, his voice growing weaker with each word. "Do *not* send anyone. I'm on my way up -."

A sudden rumbling sound followed by a minor ground tremor came from the direction of the stairwell. A surge of soot bellowed out---a smoke explosion had detonated somewhere below.

Patty Sullivan's radio went dead.

Pullano, Rosa and I charged into the stairwell.

The heaving plume of searing black smoke struck us like a gusting wind, forcing us to step back. We grabbed onto the stairwell handrails. Reset our footing. Leaned into the current of hot air. Locked arms. Fanned out. And took the first, tentative, blind step down into hell.

Thirteen steps below, Pullano tripped over a prone firefighter: Patty Sullivan. I pulled my glove off, felt for a pulse. Sullivan was alive. His face mask lay beside him. Pullano took a deep breath, held it, slipped off his own Scott mask and fixed it to Sullivan's face. Rosa and I took turns sharing our oxygen with Pullano.

And then the rising current of muddy air became markedly stronger.

"Hurry," Pullano said.

We lifted Sullivan, carried him, slipping and sliding, up the wet stairs, through the lobby and out to the street as a force-five rush of inky soot surged around us.

III

"Dan Noonan," the barrel-chested fire marshal with the Glock said as he neared me. "Long time no see. Everything all right?"

The passage of years had changed him---all of us---but I now saw that I knew the guy. He had been a kicker on the fire department football team.

"I need to see the commissioner."

"See His Holiness without an appointment?" The fire marshal had himself a hearty laugh. "That's a good one."

I didn't smile. All I could think about was how Patty Sullivan, his lungs seared by the polyethylene, polyvinyl chloride, benzene, chlorinated dioxins, chlorinated furans, and hydrocarbon fumes of the Phone Fire, had taken two agonizing years to die. "I ain't leaving."

The smile slipped from the fire marshal's face. "Meaning?"

"I'll camp out here if I have to"

He sized me up. "Level with me, Noonan. What's this about?"

"The Phone Fire."

That gave the marshal pause. "Tell you what, Noonan. I'm not without influence around here. Sit tight. I'll see what I can do."

I knew this was it, my best and last chance. If the commissioner wouldn't see me I'd have to give up. I was weary of the struggle; being ignored all these years had taken its toll. But if I were fortunate enough to win an audience, I'd make an undeniable case, convince the fire commissioner to take advantage of us, the Phone Fire survivors: recruit us for medical surveys and studies. Use the data to develop preventive measures that would protect active duty firefighters---and recognize those lost in the weeks and months following the Phone Fire.

The fire commissioner had himself been a smoke eater. If I could just look him in the eye he would not, *could* not turn me down.

I heard a commotion behind me. I turned. Three burly, armed fire marshals entered the reception area and took positions around the room. So much for my request to see the commissioner. Given the incidents of workplace violence involving disgruntled employees in recent years, FDNY security was not taking any chances with the likes of me.

One of the marshals gave me a steely look. The other two stood at soft attention, either waiting for orders or for me to make a hostile move.

I swallowed hard, recalling an old saying about discretion being the better part of valor.

Someone said, "The commissioner will see you now."

The marshal built like a fire hydrant was holding the door open for me. He waved his backup off.

"C'mon, Noonan," he smiled. "This way."

I followed him down a long, mahogany-paneled hallway, glanced in an open door and saw a conference room packed with fire department brass that had obviously just finished a meeting.

Farther down the hall I could see the commissioner himself in the doorway of his office, the flags of the United States and the City of New York behind him.

"Noonan, come on in," the commissioner said. He was holding several of my letters. "I'm glad you stopped by."

We shook hands and he had me take a seat across from his desk. "We have a lot of work to do."

IV

The ten minutes I spent with the fire commissioner convinced me that my decision to barge into his office and request an audience had been, in many ways, fortuitous.

Von Essen---now an engaging, polished politician and not the rough-around-the-edges smoke-eater I remembered---treated me like an old friend, a trusted confidante. By the time I left his office, he had assured me that he---and the FDNY's Chief Medical Officer, Dr. Kerry Kelly, whose father was a former firefighter---would see to it that the medical surveys and studies of the Phone Fire survivors begin.

As I left his office and made my way down to the street---sniffling from the headquarters' air-conditioning, which triggered the first signs of the sinus infections I suffer occasionally---I knew Von Essen would keep his word, follow through.

And he did.

Within a few months almost every Phone Fire firefighter received a medical questionnaire. I filled mine out. Sent it back. And wondered how long it would be before we knew the results of the survey.

A short time later, I was sitting in my doctor's office waiting area for the third time in two weeks, annoyed by the fact that I'd been summoned for a consultation. I was inundated with life's responsibilities: the voracious needs of my saintly wife and two young daughters, scheduling and supervising a renovation of our house, preparing for the fire technology course that I volunteered to teach, and dealing with the recent death of yet another Phone Fire alumnus, Dick Andrews, who died at 55 from cancer of the liver.

I had no time for this medical nonsense.

I had made an appointment with my doctor a few weeks earlier, complaining of another, more severe sinus infection that I couldn't shake. The doc had examined me, drawn blood, given me a prescription, then made the standard follow-up appointment. I arrived for the follow-up, gave more blood. The doc checked me out and declared the sinus infection cured---have a nice day.

Then came today's call asking me to come to his office.

I flipped absently though old magazines and wondered what the doctor could want to see me about. Aside from my Phone Fire-generated respiratory problems, I felt good. I checked my wristwatch; how I was going to make up for this lost time? My kids needed to be picked up from school. Then there was soccer practice, picking up tonight's meal, and phone calls to family members in New York that needed to be returned. Oh yeah, and the house painter who ruined our living room last week---the paint he used peeled off the walls within 24 hours---was due back today to start all over again. I thought about calling my wife on her cell phone and asking her to quit work early, pick up the kids.

"Mr. Noonan?"

I looked up. A nurse was standing there.

"The doctor will see you now."

I tossed down the magazine, was led into the doctor's office and directed to the usual chair.

"How're things, doc?"

The doctor looked up from an open folder and something in his face made me wish to God I hadn't asked. In place of his normal pleasant expression was a look of grave concern. He slipped off his eyeglasses.

I stood quickly. Whatever was coming I wanted to take it standing up. "What is it?"

"Well, Dan," he said solemnly. "The recent set of blood counts seem to confirm my suspicions. But I'm going to be sending you to Scripps Hospital in La Jolla to confirm."

"Confirm what?"

"Leukemia."

"Leukemia." I couldn't even absorb what the word meant at that moment. I only knew it was bad. "No way."

"Let's not jump ahead of ourselves." The doctor motioned me to sit back down. "Let's see what the hospital tests show."

I walked out of the doctor's office in a daze, completed the remainder of the day's chores by rote. I succeeded in putting the cancer threat out of my mind, for the most part by convincing myself that it was all supposition, a mistake, or a misdiagnosis. On the drive home from the grocery store, I decided that I would not share the unlikely possibilities with my wife---why worry her needlessly?

We ate dinner at the usual time, helped the kids with their homework---I enjoyed that chore more than usual that night---watched TV, and went to bed after the late news. I kissed my wife good night, rolled over, and couldn't help but think about the future. I found myself praying that I'd live long enough to raise my children, see them married, know my grandchildren, grow old with my wife. I lay there, staring into the darkness, the limits of my mortality on my mind.

I gave blood at the Scripps Hospital in La Jolla the following day. And for the next 24 hours I allowed myself to be consumed by work; I didn't want to give myself time to dwell on worst-case scenarios.

I arrived home late, put my kids to bed, kissed them good night. My wife retired and I grabbed a cold one from the refrigerator, clicked on the TV, watched a Honeymooner's rerun. Went to bed at 2 a.m. utterly exhausted. I laid there the remainder of the night, eyes open, recalling the lost dreams of my youth; if it hadn't been for the Phone Fire I'd be a well-paid fire chief by now. I thought about mistakes in life I'd made, people I'd judged harshly or unfairly---there were situations I wished I could live over again. I looked out the bedroom window to a starlit sky and listened to the hum of the air-conditioner.

According to my caller ID, the 9 a.m. phone call was from my physician's office. I looked away from the phone, thought about not answering it, just ignoring the call, let my machine take the message. I picked it up on the fourth ring.
"Hello."
"Yes, Dan," the doctor said. "I'm afraid it's confirmed."
I felt my legs turn to rubber. I fell back onto a chair.
"Oh," was all I could think to say.
"We have made an appointment at the oncology clinic." The doctor switched the call over to his receptionist who recited the appointment information. I thanked her and hung up.

The moment of truth, I thought, as the oncologist entered the examination room at the cancer clinic the following day. A quiet-looking man, he had kind eyes and a pleasant, reassuring demeanor.
I had arrived for the appointment early. Took a seat in the waiting room. Saw things that unnerved me: fellow cancer patients who reminded me of the photographs I'd seen of the survivors of Dachau, Auschwitz, Treblinka. I was a nervous wreck.
"Dan," the oncologist said and we shook hands. He suggested I sit, made some small talk. And then he asked me some lifestyle-related questions. I told him that I was a retired New York City firefighter, a fact he found most interesting. Told him about my experience and health problems due to the Phone Fire.
He listened closely and with great interest to everything

I said, made some notes in my blood work folder. And then he told me that my exposure to the Phone Fire toxic chemicals could very well have caused my cancer.

"But," he added. "We've caught this nice and early."

"What?" I said, not sure I heard right. "Come again?"

The oncologist smiled warmly. "If we monitor you closely, your cancer should be manageable."

"Thank God." I leaned forward, elbows on my knees, and let his words sink in.

"No guarantees." The oncologist sat back, clasped his hands behind his head, and explained the nature of my leukemia, the prognosis and everything. I related to it in fire department terms: My cancer was in the smoldering stage, not yet an out-of-control blaze.

"We'll keep you on a program where we can monitor you." He closed my folder. "Meanwhile, relax, Dan." He smiled reassuringly. "I'll see you in about two weeks."

On the way home I stopped at the beach in Del Mar, California, not far from our family home. I needed to be alone, to find a peaceful place to consider my situation. To acknowledge that my prayers had been answered.

Now was clearly the time to share my condition with my wife. But my daughters? No. Little girls see their fathers as towers of strength, all but invincible. If the cancer became terminal, I wouldn't let them see me deteriorate. I would spare them, if necessary do a John Wayne act, visit my fellow firefighters in New York, shake hands with lifelong friends, and make my way to a hospice in Arizona.

And then my name would be added to the list of Phone Fire dead.

As I prepared to leave the beach, a memory shot into my mind. It was the last act I had performed before moving my family to southern California, visiting Sloan Kettering Cancer Center in New York to give my platelets to Jack Schnock, another member of Ladder 3, who lay dying of leukemia at 48. I thought of "laughing" Pete Houston, the enormous black firefighter who had died of lung cancer at an early age. I conjured up the face of Patty Sullivan---he left four daughters behind. I could still hear him in the firehouse kitchen, "Hey, kid," Patty would say. "You're up. Stay strong for those around you."

At that moment I realized what I had to do.

I drove home and, after an emotional discussion with my wife, placed a call to the FDNY's Chief Medical Officer, Dr. Kerry Kelly.

It took ten phone calls and two weeks before Dr. Kelly responded. She said that she was sorry for not calling back sooner, but that she was busy. I believe the truth was that she knew I would never stop calling, never go away.

I told her about my leukemia. She said she was sorry and asked if there was anything she could do.

"Yes," I said. "I've got a suggestion." I told her that it would be most helpful if the medical division sent letters to the Phone Fire survivors, urging them to see their doctors and be tested for the most prevalent Phone Fire cancers.

"I can't do that," she said.

I was stunned. "Why can't you?"

"The men should know enough to see their doctors for annual checkups," she said. "Any problems should be evident."

"What if they're not evident?"

"Look-"

"The point is you'd be giving the men a heads-up."

"I can't do that."

"I gotta say, I don't understand why not. You'd be helping to save the lives of firefighters---wasn't your father a firefighter?"

"Yes."

"What if he was sitting home, enjoying his retirement. And he got an official letter from the medical bureau. Wouldn't that motivate him to see his doctor?"

Dr. Kelly sighed.

"At least tell me the results of the Phone Fire questionnaire. When will we see the results of the survey?"

"Sorry, Dan. I have to go."

"But . . .."

Dr. Kelly hung up the phone.

V

My phone rang at 5:55 a.m. on a promising September morning. I rolled over, fought through layers of sleep, silently cursed whoever it was calling at that ungodly hour, knowing it had to be family or friends from the east coast---it was 8:55 in New York.

"This better be good," I grouched into the phone.

"Put on the TV," my brother Mike said from Florida.

"Know what time it is?"

"A jet just hit the World Trade Center."

"What?" I slid from bed, padded to the living room, and switched on the TV. I watched the thick smoke billow from the north tower and calculated the number of firefighters that would be in that building. Considered the time of day, the city's traffic conditions, the weather, first-through fifth-alarm assignments. The incident commander would probably transmit additional alarms. There would be hundreds of firefighters climbing the structure's stairwells. I imagined that members of my former company would be there---I feared for them. Fighting a typical high-rise fire was dangerous enough, but by the look of it, this promised to be the mother of them all.

My wife joined me a few minutes later just as a second jet, United flight 175, hit the south tower.

And then the news commentators and paid military experts began to speculate that the plane crashes were no accident. The United States was being attacked. I used the remote to surf from news station to news station and paused when I heard a talking head say; ". . . the Pentagon was just struck by another plane. We are at war."

I thought of my girls, still asleep in their beds.

At 9:59 EST the south tower collapsed and I sprang to my feet, tried to scream. I couldn't. My throat was constricted.

"My God," I said to my wife. "There had to be people in that building." We watched in stunned silence as, at 10:28 a.m., the north tower collapsed. I reached for the phone, dialed my former firehouse. All phone lines were dead. I tried an 800 number.

"Who're you calling." My wife handed me a cup of coffee.

"The airlines." I pointed to the TV. "I've gotta get back home."

It took me four grueling days to reach Newark Airport.

Another hour before I walked into my former firehouse, Engine 33 & Ladder 9, located on Great Jones Street in Lower Manhattan. My heart sank when I discovered that ten of our men were among the hundreds of firefighters unaccounted for.

I spent the next three days at the World Trade Center site---"the pile"---dealing with the city's systemic sadness, my own grief, and digging alongside my fellow firefighters for survivors.

We found none.

Like everyone else, I was sickened by the things I saw. Shocked by the sheer volume of lost life. Eventually a desire to seek revenge on those responsible for the cowardly attacks replaced my sadness.

Having leukemia was the last thing on my mind.

The day before heading back to my family in San Diego, my mind and body exhausted, my throat raw from inhaling the burning debris as well as the DNA cells of the thousands who were pulverized, I ran into Fire Commissioner Von Essen at a mass of remembrance at St. Patrick's Cathedral.

"Danny." He greeted me with a warm handshake. "We'll talk about the phone fire soon as –"

"Make the Phone Fire number 344 on your agenda," I told him.

There were still 343 missing firefighters at the World Trade Center.

A month later I received my latest copy of the FDNY's official magazine, *WNYF (With New York Firefighters)*. To my surprise it contained the results of the medical bureau's Telephone Fire medical survey. I switched on a reading lamp, turned the pages, and read the report with great interest.

The medical bureau concluded that no correlation existed between increased incidences of cancer and the deadly chemical toxins the firefighters had breathed in the Phone Fire.

"Bullshit," I said out loud in the empty house.

I couldn't believe what I'd just read.

Having only recently watched a special on PBS titled *Trade Secrets*, in which investigative journalist Bill Moyers conducted an in-depth study of the manufacture of PVC, I knew that the medical survey had been an appalling sell-out, a whitewash.

Moyer's investigation revealed that the manufacturers of PVC knew as early as the 1960s that PVC caused cancer and other illnesses---their workers were dying from exposure. Thirty-one executives of an Italian company were actually indicted and tried for manslaughter; they chose to ignore the overwhelming life-and-death scientific data in favor of the bottom line.

Could the FDNY be doing the same?

137

It was clear that if the FDNY Medical Bureau officially confirmed the obvious, its pension fund would have to pay out millions in line-of-duty disability benefits. To most, retired firefighters are old news, yesterday's heroes, already a drain on the pension system.

I tossed *WNYF* into the trash, weary once again of the Phone Fire battle. If the department could get away with refusing to acknowledge the sacrifices made by the Phone Fire firefighters, the surviving World Trade Center firefighters would fare no better; respiratory problems from toxic smoke were already plaguing them.

My two daughters tornadoed into the house.

One sat at the kitchen table and began her homework. The older one picked up the portable phone and headed to the privacy of her bedroom, both, as always, demanding food. My wife walked in a moment later, thoroughly exhausted from what would turn out to be another sixty-hour work week.

As I watched her set a pile of paperwork on a table, flop onto a battered easy chair, kick off her shoes, and stretch out, I felt a surge of anger and guilt---guilt that she had been forced into the role of primary breadwinner. Anger that I could not live up to my full earning potential. Thanks to the Phone Fire, my career in the fire service had been stolen from me.

"Iced tea, Danny," my wife said. "Please?"

I opened the refrigerator, took out the jug of iced tea and the makings for a snack: cookies, chips, and fruit.

Later, as I helped my youngest finish her homework, I reflected on the Bill Moyer PBS special, and it dawned on me that it was the PVC manufacturers who were to blame for the Phone Fire dead. In a way, they were the true culprits.

"Daddy," my youngest said. "Can Joan and Laura come over?"

"If it's all right with your mother."

"Danny." My wife was seated at her desk, buried in paperwork. "Will you make dinner tonight?"

"My world famous Rockaway Beach meatloaf?"

Everyone groaned.

While we ate dinner---hot dogs and beans---it occurred to me that the WTC firefighters had been exposed to many of the same chemical toxins as the Phone Fire casualties. In truth, toxic fires like the Phone Fire and World Trade Center fires needed to occupy a category all their own, in terms of the lasting deadly afflictions visited upon their firefighters.

The Uniformed Firefighters Association had the same viewpoint. They were urging all WTC firefighters to have medical checkups forthwith.

"Look at what happened at the telephone fire," Kevin Gallagher, President of the UFA had written. "There was no testing done and we had members coming down with all different types of medical problems years later. I pray that the World Trade Center firefighters do not share the same fate."

I finished clearing the dinner table, swallowed some damned pills---my cancer had apparently been stabilized--- and decided then and there to investigate the PVC manufacturers' complicity. If warranted, I would gather evidence, recruit all living Phone Fire survivors, find the widows, and in some cases the surviving children, retain an attorney and bring forth a class-action lawsuit---lest the World Trade Center disaster turn out to be another Phone Fire fiasco.

My wife and girls finished washing the dishes, took their usual position in the living room, and turned on the TV. The loud, aggressive competition for the remote control brought a rare smile to my face. I opened the refrigerator, uncorked a bottle of white wine, poured a glass for my wife and myself, sat down beside her. And as I helped to settle the TV dispute---a September 11 retrospective turned out to be a unanimous choice---I swore that, no matter where the battle took me, I'd make time to be husband and father as well.

The Defective Detective

From half a city block away, through windswept snow, talent agent Robert Vick thought it was a dog that the tall thug in the studded, black leather jacket had kicked in a burst of anger. It was the yelp the creature made when the boot made contact and the way it whimpered when it cracked into a tenement brick wall and dropped into the snow.

Vick, an animal lover, saw red.

The thug rushed the broken canine, taking measured steps as if preparing to kick a football. Vick yelled for him to stop.

He did.

Vick ran the half block to the creature lying crumpled at the base of the brick wall in a pool of its own blood. The warm crimson liquid emitted steam as it mixed with the frigid air.

It was a small boy.

Vick, the father of two, lost control. Threw a punch, a right-cross that connected. The thug's head snapped back and he dropped heavily to the ground and did not move again.

Vick scooped up the child.

The yellow cab nearly crashed into a row of snow-bound parked cars as it careened across ice and came to a salt-scattering stop at East 77th Street, Lenox Hill Hospital's emergency entrance.

Vick, cradling the battered child, bolted from the cab, stumbled through a snow drift, shimmied between parked cars, and barged into the hospital's emergency room.

"I need a doctor," he yelled as he pushed past bleeding car accident victims awaiting treatment, past a woman who was screaming that the Republicans had seized control of her brain. He grabbed a passing doctor and told him the child in his arms was dying.

The doctor, a young African with sinister-looking tribal scars slashed into his cheeks, lifted the child from Vick's arms, placed him on a nearby gurney, and checked for vital signs.

"How did this happened?"

"He was kicked," Vick said.

The doctor gave Vick a sharp, probing look.

Vick shook his head. "Someone else did it."

The doctor fired a series of commands which were echoed by a crew of faceless others. In moments, a trauma team assembled and flew into action; a ballet choreographed to save the child's life.

Vick used his cell phone to call 911 and report the incident to the police. He gave a through description of the child's assailant as well as his last location.

A short while later the doctor, pulling off a set of bloody rubber gloves, approached Vick in the emergency room waiting area.

"He's in critical condition," the doctor said.

Vick's cell phone rang. It was the office. He was late for an appointment with a set of production company lawyers. Knew he couldn't negotiate the self-absorbed, A-list actor's twenty-million-dollar film contract by phone.

"I've got to get back to the office." Vick searched his suit pockets for a business card, couldn't find one. "I'll leave you my number in case the police need to contact me." He borrowed a pen and pad from the Admitting Nurse and tried to write---found he couldn't.

"In case you don't know it," the doctor said. "Your hand is broken."

Vick usually felt anxious in police stations. Just walking into one gave him the willies, would trigger childhood memories of his father---a career criminal---being dragged off, handcuffed, kicking and screaming out of their home, into the night.

A producer of "B" pictures who financed his films by means of extortion and blackmail, Vick's father was, at times, violent. And Vick possessed the physical and psychological scars to prove it. Scars which compelled him to vow never to strike his five-year-old daughter and ten-year-old son. And he never had.

But Vick felt strangely at home in the 19th Police Precinct located at East 67th Street in Manhattan. The place was moodily lit, neat, clean, a Hollywood director's idea of what a police station should look like. Vick climbed to the Detective Division Squad Room on the second floor.

The detectives in the squad room also fit a certain Hollywood mold: razor haircuts, Armani suits, gleaming manicures. A dozen or so were milling around a coffee machine, some bathed in nostril-stinging, roach-spray-strong colognes. Vick wondered if these real life detectives copied the styles of their Hollywood counterparts or vice versa, an unanswerable, chicken-or-the-egg question.

"I'm looking for a Detective Bo Blosco," Vick said to a slicked-back detective, a poster-boy for a male escort service.

A voice said, "I'm Detective Blosco."

Vick turned to face a well-groomed, heavy-set cop with a strong, large-featured face. The detective had phoned Vick at his office late yesterday and asked that he come to the stationhouse today for an interview.

"You must be Robert Vick."

Vick said he was, slipped off his coat.

Blosco eyeballed Vick's $3000 suit, Rolex watch, high-gloss Gucci shoes and the fresh cast on his broken hand.

"How'd you break that?"

Vick told him.

143

Blosco led Vick to an orderly desk, between a palm and a corn plant, by a window overlooking the street. They could see a film crew setting up for a shot out front, using the stationhouse facade as a backdrop. A local TV news crew was shooting an *Entertainment Tonight* crew, shooting the film crew.

"Seems everyone's in show business in this town but me." Blosco sighed, turned from the window and sat behind his desk. "Thanks for coming down, Mr. Vick." He pointed Vick to a chair. "You want coffee or something?"

"No thanks." Vick sat.

"Hope you don't mind." The detective took out a tape recorder. "I'll be recording your statement."

"No problem."

Blosco pressed the record button. "Tell me about the incident."

"Well, I was on my way to work -." Vick settled back in his chair and recounted the entire episode, taking his time so as not to leave out any facts.

When he was finished, Blosco said, "Your alleged perp's name is Dan Arony. Male, white, age thirty-six, six-foot-three, two-twenty-five. Says he's an unemployed truck driver. Lives in the projects on Second and Ninety Seventh. Says his wife is dead. It's just him and the boy. No other family. He's hurt pretty bad. His neck may be broke."

Vick looked at his fractured hand and felt sick to his stomach---he'd never struck anyone in anger before.

"Why'd you attack him?" Blosco said.

"I didn't attack him. I hit him. Once."

"Why did you hit him?"

"I just explained that. He was brutalizing the boy."

"That didn't give you the right to hit him."

"What was I supposed to do?" Vick said.

"Restrain him, or call 911."

"But he might have killed the boy."

144

"So you say." Blosco glanced at a report on his desk. "He told the uniform cops that he was playing with his son, James, age three, when they were both attacked---by you."

"That's a lie."

"It's your word against his," Blosco said.

"Did you say the attacker was the boy's father?"

"That's right."

Vick shook his head.

Blosco switched off the tape recorder.

"When I get the chance, I'll run the father's name through N.C.I.C. See if he's got any priors. Warrants." Blosco placed the recorder in a desk draw. "I were you, I'd think about consulting a lawyer."

Vic was stunned. "Why would I need a lawyer?"

Blosco shrugged. "In case the boy's father wants to press charges against you."

"Against me?"

"Hey, this is America." Blosco chuckled. "He'll probably just sue you---you look like you can afford it."

Vick bolted to his feet. "That supposed to be funny?"

"I'm not through," Blosco said. "Sit down. Please."

Vick took a minute before he sat on the edge of his chair.

Blosco leaned back, appraised Vick for a long moment. "I made some calls. Asked around about you, Mr. Vick. You're a successful talent agent."

"By some standards," Vick remarked.

"You work for William Morris."

"Yes." Vick noticed for the first time that Blosco was wearing pancake and eye makeup and his styled, black hair was sprayed concrete hard.

"I hate most agents. They're bloodsuckers."

"I'm crushed," Vick said.

"Represent any celebrities?"

"A few. Look, detective, I really have to be going -"

"How do you envision this case being handled?"

145

Vick didn't know how to respond to that. "Come again?"

"What do you want to happen?"

"Well, the father should be prosecuted, of course."

"How important is that to you?"

"I don't understand what you're asking."

"Look, Mr. Vick," Blosco said. "You're a talent agent, I'm talent. Therefore, you're in a position to help me."

"You're joking."

"Look at me." Blosco's eyes narrowed. "I look like I'm joking?"

Vick didn't like what he saw in the detective's eyes. "I'm not taking on any new clients at this time -."

"I wanna be on TV. You know, be one of those 'experts' all the news and tabloid shows put on the air every time there's a major crime or terrorist attack."

Vick gaped, too flabbergasted to speak.

"If you agree to represent me, you know, be my agent, I'll give this child abuse case my number one priority, make a big deal out of it. I mean really play it up. Child abuse cases are always hot. You get your reporter friends or directors or whoever to drop my name everywhere. Get them to interview me on the news. I'd make a good criminal justice consultant for a talk show or movie." Blosco reached into a desk drawer, pulled out an 8 by 10 glossy publicity headshot and shoved it at Vick. "Great picture. Right?"

Vick glanced at the photo of Blosco's smiling fat face. Then shoved it back across the desk. "I didn't come here to do you favors, detective."

"Oh? But you want one from me?"

"I want you to do your job."

"Look, Mr. Vick, I got over fifty open cases." He slapped a pile of manila folders piled neatly on his desk. "So I ain't got time to be a fuckin' social worker. You want priority? You got it."

146

Vick didn't know what to say. He stood, gathered his coat. "If that's all?"

"You understand," Blosco said.

Vick stopped.

"If the boy's father wants to press charges against his assailant, I'll have to lock you up. Now *that* would be newsworthy, wouldn't it?" Blosco laughed a little. "Think over my offer, Mr. Vick. Let me know if you change your mind."

Vick walked into Lenox Hill Hospital fifteen minutes later. An extraordinarily perky octogenarian volunteer receptionist informed him that three-year-old James Arony had just been downgraded to stable condition, but was still in the Intensive Care Unit. Vick headed for the elevators.

A nurse receptionist was giving an elderly couple a hard time as Vick neared the doors that led to ICU.

"But we've been neighbors for twenty years," the man said.

"I'm sorry," the receptionist said. "Only immediate family members are permitted to visit patients in ICU."

Vick stepped to a pay phone, pretended to use it, and when the nurse became distracted, he took the opportunity to slip into ICU.

ICU was a quiet, dimly-lit, antiseptic room. There were about twenty beds, most empty. Vick browsed until he located James Arony's bed---he was so tiny. His little head was bandaged. An IV tube was stuck in his bone-thin arm, an oxygen apparatus was affixed to his mouth and nose. And then Vick noted something curious. The boy had one dark dot on each earlobe. Birthmarks?

A heavy-set nurse with large, friendly eyes waddled over to check James' vital signs. She took the boy's temperature, adjusted the feed rate on the clear IV bag tube, which hung from an overhead hook.

"Can I ask you something?" Vick said.

The nurse smiled and nodded.

"Does the boy have any scars, evidence of past abuse?"

The nurse thought a moment. "You'll have to speak to his doctor." She walked heavily across the ICU to an office. The office was a small cubicle with a large cutout window allowing the staff to observe and monitor all activity in ICU. Vick could see her speaking to a black man in a white medical smock and when the man stood and turned, Vick saw he was the same young African doctor from the emergency room. The doctor looked through the large window and saw Vick, nodded in recognition, exited the office and approached.

The doctor gestured to Vick's cast. "How's the hand?"

"Fine." For the first time Vick noted a hint of a British accent. The tribal scars seemed less sinister in the dim light of ICU.

"How long will James be in the hospital?"

"Well, he sustained some fairly serious injuries." The doctor checked the boy's chart. "Strong lad, though. He should recover nicely. A week, ten days maybe."

Vick thumbed to the boy. "His own father did that to him."

"I thought they were attacked. A mugger?"

"Who told you that?"

"A Detective Blosco. He called only moments ago to check on the boy's condition. I asked him what had happened to the child and he told me that -"

"He's mistaken." Vick pulled the doctor away from the bed. "Did you find any evidence of past abuse?"

"I'm afraid only family members are -."

"Then I'm the boy's uncle," Vick said.

"I'm sorry. I could lose my medical license -."

"His father could kill him next time."

"It is a matter for the police."

"I don't trust the police," Vick said. "Do you?"

The doctor looked at the boy for a long moment.

"Please," Vick said. "Help me help the boy."

The doctor took a thoughtful moment. "Come with me." He led Vick into the ICU office. He pulled a set of X-ray film from a file and clipped them to a wall-mounted light box. Switched on the back light. Studied the film.

"There is some scar tissue." The doctor pointed to one of the X-rays. "His arm's been broken. There are other signs of past head trauma." He switched off the back light. "But they are the kind of injuries a boy might sustain falling off of a bike."

"Or from beatings."

"Yes," The doctor said. "I couldn't rule that out."

Vick left the hospital, walked east to 5th Avenue, and then south along the Central Park side of the street. Snow was falling and muting the sounds of the city which, through the translucent veil of tiny white flakes, looked clean, safe, oddly surreal.

He saw children frolicking in the park, playing in the snow. And remembered playing in the snow with his own children, teaching them how to form the perfect snowball, ride a sleigh, ice-skate, ski. That was before his wife had left him, said that she simply didn't love him anymore. And then she took their children to Vermont to be near her family. Now, he only saw his kids four times a year. God, how he missed them.

Vick saw an exuberant little tike dive into a snow drift, head first, and wondered if little James Arony liked to play in the snow. Thought about the irony of the predicament he'd gotten himself into. His earnest effort to save the boy's life resulted in both criminal and civil exposure---a sobering development. Maybe he *should* consult an attorney. Or maybe he should just give in to Detective Blosco's demands, take him on as a client. At least that way he'd be certain that little James would get help.

Vick entered his office at William Morris, a corner berth with a million dollar view, and saw that along with a pile of messages a manila envelope marked *urgent* had been left on his desk. He tore open the envelope, pulled out a publicity photo of Detective Bo Blosco.

His telephone rang. "Robert Vick speaking."

"You forgot to take my photo when you left," Blosco said.

"You seem to have a one-track mind, detective."

"You have no idea. Soon as a TV network contacts me and tells me they want me to join their team, or a news crew shows up at the stationhouse to interview me, I'll give the Arony case top priority."

"You'll arrest the boy's father?"

Blosco cleared his throat. "If he even *is* the boy's father."

Vick stiffened. "What are you saying?"

"This day and age, anything's possible."

Vick tossed Blosco's photo aside, paced in tight circles. "I can't believe they let you carry a badge."

"Hey, hump, you're the one's been dragging his feet." Blosco hung up. Vick stared at the dead phone in his hand. He couldn't believe that a police detective would so brazenly extort him. He slammed down the phone.

Vic thought about calling his attorney, have him contact the detective's superiors, the District Attorney, the Civilian Complaint Review Board and the mayor's office, lodge official complaints against Blosco---maybe later. At that moment the boy's welfare was his only concern. But how could he, a civilian with no investigative experience, perform a police detective's job? Vic sat as his desk and brainstormed.

It made sense to him that Dan Arony was not the boy's father. No parent he knew could or would brutalize a three-year-old child. But if he was not James' father, who was he---a relative, family friend or---God forbid---a child abductor?

Vic turned to his computer and logged onto the Web. Using a search engine, he located and accessed several missing children databases.

Vick was horrified by the sheer number of children reported missing every day in the United States, as many as 2,000. There were so many open cases and photographs that it would take him days to conduct even a cursory search. Frustrated, Vick dialed the North America Missing Children Association's 800 number and asked for assistance.

He described the Arony incident to the concerned and helpful volunteer who answered the phone. Told her that there was a chance the boy's assailant was not the father. She in turn walked him through the process of conducting a missing child search. Using the search engine criteria, the boy's age, sex, and the birthmarks on his earlobes, he found James Arony's photo.

Three-year-old James Arony's real name was Bryon Robertson. He had been abducted by a person-or-persons unknown, while shopping with his parents in Newark, New Jersey, eight months ago.

"When will you notify the boy's parents?" Vick said.

"Soon as his identity has been verified." The NAMCA volunteer asked Vick to hold and then transferred him to an FBI agent.

"The man you say assaulted the boy," the FBI agent said. "Describe him for me."

Vick did the best he could.

"You at your computer?"

Vick said he was.

The agent recited the web address for America's Most Wanted and asked Vick to access it. Told him to type in the name Alan Pardes in the search field then hit enter. And Dan Arony's mug-shot appeared.

"That's him!" Vick said.

"'The Demon,'" the agent said.

"Child abductors have nicknames?" Vick said.

"This one does." The agent asked Vick a series of who, what, where, why, when, and how questions. Confirmed that Bryon Robertson/James Arony and The Demon were both at Lenox Hill Hospital, thanked Vick for calling and hung up.

Vick turned back to his computer and read the Alan Pardes/Dan Arony/The Demon file. A prime suspect in the disappearance of three children, The Demon had been in police custody, under lock and key, several times, but always managed to beat the charges.

"Mr. Vick." His secretary stepped into his office. "Your one o'clock is here."

"Shit," Vick groaned. The self-absorbed, pain in the ass, A-list actor was there with yet another laundry list of ridiculous demands for the studio that had just cast him as the lead in a feature film.

"Cancel it." Vick got up, slipped on his coat. "Tell him I had an emergency. I'll call him later."

"He won't like it," the secretary said.

Vick smiled. "You think?"

Vick hurried into Lennox Hill Hospital and made his way to The Demon's 3rd floor room. It was empty. Vick searched the hallway, checked the patient lounge as well as adjoining rooms. He asked a nurse if Dan Arony was taken to X-ray, moved or transferred.

"He can't be moved," she said, "with a broken neck."

"He's not in his room."

"Impossible," the nurse said and went to check.

Vick couldn't believe it. The Demon was gone. But where?---ICU. He could he be crazy enough to go after the boy.

Vick nearly knocked over a man on crutches as he darted into a stairwell and scaled the steps, three at a time. He ignored a protesting ICU nurse/receptionist, entered ICU and positioned himself at the foot of little Bryon Robertson's bed. And when hospital security arrived, he steadfastly refused to budge until the police or FBI arrived.

When the TV camera and reporter entered the 19th Precinct Squad Room a few hours later, Detective Bo Blosco was ready. He checked his face in the mirror, smoothed his hair. The afternoon light reflecting off freshly fallen snow, poured in the window, illuminating his face, he thought, with a warm, star-quality glow.

Blosco's heart pounded when he heard the reporter ask another detective where to find Detective Blosco---that twerp Robert Vick had actually come through. The detective tidied his desk, and wondered what questions the reporter planned to ask him. Not that it mattered---be it a Mafia bloodbath, a terrorist bombing, a bank robbery, he knew he could wing it.

Blosco glanced at his reflection in the window and made a pact with himself not to allow success to change him. Well, not too much. He vowed to remain the same honest, generous, self-sacrificing, paragon of virtue he'd always been.

"Are you Detective Blosco?" a pretty, young TV reporter with a cold, red nose asked as she pulled off a fur coat and flung it across an empty chair.

"Call me Bo." Blosco affected a Ted Baxter baritone and stood to greet the perky journalist. Instead of shaking his hand, the reporter pulled a brush through her hair, checked her reflection in a hand-held mirror, and said to the cameraman "How do I look, Rick?"

"Fine."

"Bella," Blosco added. "That's 'beautiful' in Italian."

The reporter rolled her eyes. "Let's do it, Rick."

The cameraman switched on a floodlight. Pointed the camera at the reporter. "Tape is rolling."

Blosco took a deep breath, rechecked his reflection in the window, his suit, shirt, tie, hair. Perfect.

"Action," the cameraman said.

"Eight months ago," the reporter began, "at a shopping mall in Newark, New Jersey, a two-year-old boy was abducted while his parents shopped for his birthday gift -"

Blosco stomach did a flip-flop. Newark? Child abduction?

"But in a bizarre case of police blundering," the reporter said. "The perpetrator of the child abduction was in police custody, but never arrested, and eventually disappeared."

Blosco straightened. Disappeared?

The reporter turned to Blosco.

"Detective Blosco, you *are* the detective assigned to investigate the brutal assault on three-year-old Bryon Robertson, correct?" She stuck the microphone in Blosco's face.

Blosco's mind went blank---who the fuck was Bryon Robertson? He looked to the other detectives for support. They all turned away.

"Well, I -"

"Is it true that you had his assailant, one of America's Most Wanted child abductors, a man known as 'The Demon' in custody? That he was left unguarded while at Lenox Hill Hospital?"

Blosco suddenly felt sick. "I wasn't aware -."

"Detective, do you even know who Bryon Robertson is?"

Sweat beaded on Blosco's forehead. He glanced around the squad room, all eyes were now on him. It was then that he noticed Robert Vick standing at the back, by the door.

They made eye contact.

Vick smiled.

"Detective Blosco," the reporter said. "do you wish to make a statement?"

"No," Blosco said as he fell back into his chair. "No comment."

Never Fire a Warning Shot

Former Navy Seal, Finbar Devine, was seated at Chuck & Harold's runway-length, marble bar on a sweltering August afternoon, sipping an ice cold beer and griping to a tutti-frutti bartender that the whole damn town of Palm Beach, Florida, stank of suntan oil.

"And what's with all these blue-haired, liver-spotted old broads running around in bikinis and high heels?" Devine, his back to an art deco wall, shivered as he watched two age-ravaged, pseudo-sex-pots prance merrily by. "I mean, Christ, there should be a law."

Just then a lone, ancient, femme-fatale, with a face like a sun-dried raisin, winked and waved at Devine from a table across the room.

He did a double take, couldn't believe his eyes. "She waving at me?"

"That's Dirty Moe." The bartender leaned close, spoke as if divulging a government secret. "One of the oldest, richest tarts in Palm Beach. I can fix it up, if you're into that sort of thing."

Dirty Moe was wiggling a set of caterpillar eyebrows, gesturing for Devine to come to her table.

"Wanna meet her?" the bartender said.

Devine straightened. "How'd you like your nose broken?"

Color drained from the bartender's face and he swished away.

Devine spun on his bar stool so his back was to Dirty Moe. He trained his eyes safely on the front door and saw a wimpy-looking bald man in an expensive tan suit, wearing tortoise rimmed eyeglasses, enter the stylish restaurant and leg to the bar.

"Pardon me," the man said. "Are you Finbar Devine?"

Devine nodded, offered his hand but did not smile. He hadn't smiled since his first tour in Vietnam.

"I'm Abe Seubert." Seubert's handshake was brisk, his skin upper-crust soft. He glanced at a platinum Piaget wristwatch. "Sorry I'm late." He pulled up a bar stool, grabbed a handful of drink napkins, and wiped the perspiration from his face. "I despise this oppressive heat."

"Anything beats the Bronx in the summer," Devine said. "Drink?"

"Beer. Thank you."

Devine signaled the bartender to bring two bottles of beer. "So, what can I do for you, Mr. Seubert?"

"Call me Abe. Thank you for agreeing to meet with me."

"Barry Wish asks me to meet someone, pays for my flight, hotel and rental car, I'm there. How is the cantankerous bastard, anyway?"

Seubert used what looked like a solid gold lighter and a shaky hand to light the first in an endless chain of cigarettes. Devine knew he was making Seubert nervous. His physical stature and aggressive manner made most everyone nervous.

"He flew to Canada yesterday," Seubert said. "Some sort of revolutionary holistic cancer treatment."

The beers came.

"The man's an iron horse," Seubert said. "Never gives up."

Devine took a sip. "Navy Seals never do."

"Barry told me that you and he graduated Seal training together."

"Yep. Seal Team Two."

"You certainly look the part." Seubert took a swallow of beer. "I hope you don't mind, but I asked a friend of mine

157

in Washington to fax me your service record." He removed the fax from his suit jacket pocket, unfolded and read. "Three tours in Vietnam. Won two Silver Stars, five bronze stars with a combat V, three Navy Commendation Medals and the Vietnamese Cross of Gallantry with Silver Star." He re-folded the fax, put it away. "The newspapers reported that the Viet Cong posted a reward of 100,000 piasters for you, dead or alive."

"Good gosh." Like most Seals, Devine did not like discussing the details of his military service with civilians. "So, how long have you worked for Barry?"

Seubert said he'd been employed as a commodities broker at Barry Wish's stock brokerage firm, Wish, Lowery, and O'Rourke, for the past five years. "It has been a most lucrative association."

"Where'd you work before?" Devine said.

"Bear Stearns in LA." Seubert said. He fiddled with an ashtray. "That's where I met my wife, a flight attendant with American Airlines."

"Married a stew, uh? I dated dozens of `em over the years."

Seubert looked off, lost in thought. "I was crazy about her," he said. "Sounds silly coming from a man my age, but I thought she was my first real love. I knew her only three months when we got married. Big mistake."

Agreed, Devine thought.

"First, she hated LA. Said everyone was a phony---they were. So we moved here. Then she hated Florida. Said there are too many old people---there are. Then she said having a baby would make her happy. I didn't want to, I mean, at my age? But, she had a way. So, at age fifty, I became a dad. Can you believe it?"

And now Seubert smiled. "Best thing I ever did." He pulled out his wallet and showed Devine a picture of his 4-year-old son. He was at Disneyland posing with Mickey Mouse. "His name is Anthony," he said proudly.

"Handsome boy," Devine said, even though the kid was the spitting image of his father---banana nose, buttonhole eyes, pencil neck.

Seubert studied the photo as if for the first time. "I try to be a good father."

"We all try -."

"It took my wife about six months to lose interest in motherhood." Seubert put the picture away. "She started going to parties, staying out late, doing drugs. Wrecked a couple of cars. Came home stumbling drunk most nights---if she came home at all. I made certain Anthony never saw her that way. Then after two DWI arrests, thirty days in the county jail, and a stint at AA, she stopped drinking.

"Things got better for a while, till she got bored again and insisted we join the Palm Beach Country Club." He lowered his voice so as not to be overheard. "She started having affairs." Seubert sipped more beer. "I had no idea till she ran off with her tennis instructor. Took the new Rolls I'd given her for her birthday, cleaned out one of our bank accounts. Never even said good-bye to Anthony." He lit another cigarette. "Not that I minded her leaving. Long as I had my son.

"But I wasn't prepared for single parenting, not with my work schedule." Seubert told how he was eventually forced to place Anthony in a day care center five days a week. The center, Our Lady Of Mercy Day Care, was exclusive, expensive, and managed by a renowned child psychologist and Catholic priest, Father Billy Ray Howe.

"Howe?" Devine said, recognizing the name.

Seubert's gray, tranquil eyes turned hard. He told Devine how his son changed after enrolling in Catholic day care. In a matter of weeks, he became irritable, withdrawn. He stopped eating and, after a fainting spell, Seubert rushed him to a local hospital.

"I was frantic. Couldn't imagine what was wrong. I mean, a four-year-old can't really tell you." Seubert swallowed more beer. "Next thing I know the police are at the hospital and the doctor tells me my son's been molested."

Devine straightened.

"I went crazy, hysterical," Seubert said. "What were they telling me? Not *my* son. Impossible. Who would do such a thing?" Seubert paused. "I could tell by the way the doctors and police were acting, they suspected me."

"They're supposed to," Devine said. "Unfortunately, from what I read, parents are usually the culprits."

Seubert crushed out the half smoked cigarette and immediately lit another. He said the cops did an investigation. Checked out anyone with possible access to Anthony: relatives, neighbors, friends. Then they checked Father Howe.

"Seems his former church superiors, the Archdiocese of Santa Fe, had quietly paid millions of dollars to settle cases involving Father Howe, and other priests, accused of sexually molesting children."

"I remember seeing it on the news," Devine said. "The sexual assaults were rarely, if ever, reported to the police."

"Howe was routinely transferred to other churches, in other states," Seubert said. "And the church didn't even have the common decency to warn the new unsuspecting parishioners that they had a career pedophile in their midst." Seubert shook his head in disgust. "Only thing that I can figure is that the church's hierarchy is comprised of perverts. I mean, why else would a legitimate, religious organization sanction a pedophilic subculture?"

Listening to Seubert, Devine recalled his own days in Catholic schools. Although he'd never experienced anything more physically damaging then the occasional beating by a sadistic nun, there was a priest that insisted that Devine's class, all boys, swim nude in the church's indoor swimming pool. Devine remembered several other priests leering at him and his naked friends from the

160

sidelines. Even at 10 years old, Devine knew that there was *something* wrong. And he refused to swim in the church pool ever again.

"The cops discovered Father Howe had been accused of over 60 child molestations in several states over the last twenty years," Seubert said. "Apparently, church superiors ignored the advice of doctors and therapists who warned that Howe was a chronic pedophile, most likely to re-offend."

"Makes you wonder," Devine said. "How does a criminal like that walk into Florida, open a church-financed, state-licensed day care center, and---forget the church---no one in local government bothers to check his background, or references?"

"It's mind boggling," Seubert said.

"I remember reading Howe's in jail."

"For the moment." Seubert fiddled with his lighter. "He retained a first class criminal attorney. And my boy may be too young to testify against him. That means there's a real possibility he could walk. I can't let that happen."

"The newspapers said Howe's still wanted in Dallas and Santa Fe," Devine said. "Even if he beats your case, they'll extradite him. He ain't going anywhere."

"A statute of limitations may prevent many of those victims from bringing charges against him. What then?"

Seubert had a good point.

"I can't sleep nights thinking about it, what he did to my boy," Seubert said. "I can't eat, can't work."

"I understand your frustration," Devine said. "But what's all this have to do with me?"

Seubert took a moment. "Barry said you help people in trouble."

"I try not to make a habit of it."

"He said you helped him find a friend's kidnapped daughter. Said you did in a few hours what the cops couldn't do in three months."

161

"She wasn't kidnapped," Devine said. "She was a runaway, in my home town. All I did was find her. Bring her home. I got lucky."

"Barry said you kicked down doors. Beat the information out of the drug dealers and procurers. Made them talk. He said you saved her life."

"He's exaggerating," Devine said.

Seubert shook his head. "Not Barry Wish."

"Get to the point, Abe."

"I want to hire you."

"To do what?"

"To kill Father Howe."

Devine glanced around the room. "You wearing a wire, Abe?"

"A wire? No. Of course not."

"Take off your jacket."

Seubert did.

"Give it here."

Seubert handed Devine his silk, suit jacket. He searched it. Nothing. He threw the jacket on an empty stool.

"Stand up and turn around, Abe."

Seubert did as ordered. Devine patted him down, tossed him so quickly and expertly no one in the place noticed.

Except maybe Dirty Moe.

Devine told Seubert to sit back down.

"You're talking conspiracy, Abe. Contract murder."

"I'm aware of that," Seubert said. "Name your price."

Devine had to stop himself from cracking Seubert across the mouth---he hated guys like him. Wealthy pukes who were supremely confident that their money could buy everyone and anyone. He pushed Seubert's beer away.

"Take a hike. This meeting is over."

"What would you do if he molested your son?"

"You don't wanna know," Devine said.

"If you won't kill him, teach me how."

162

"Not my line of work."

"I've got plenty of money."

"Buy a martial arts school."

"I want a Seal to teach me," Seubert said.

"Ask Barry Wish. He knows what I know."

"He's too sick."

"Look," Devine said. "You'll never get a shot at Howe. If he beats your case, they'll extradite him, under heavy armed guard, from one state prison to another. You'd only be wasting your money."

"It's mine to waste. I'll give you 25K."

"Not for 50K."

"75K," Seubert said.

Devine stopped. "Seventy-five thousand dollars?"

Seubert reached into his suit jacket pocket, took out a Mont Blanc pen and a leather checkbook. "Seventy-five, large."

Devine rested his elbows on the bar, peeled the label off his beer bottle---he needed the money. Since his honorable discharge from the Seals, his life financially had been a series of high altitude bungee jumps. He had opened a New York based martial arts studio. Was sued into bankruptcy after one of his students was injured in a bungled fight exhibition. As a tactical training expert, he occasionally landed gigs as a paid lecturer to elite law enforcement units nationwide. But he had problems with non-military authority figures and was labeled a troublemaker. He dabbled in the high-risk bodyguard business and liked the action. But because of the large numbers of retired cops with career-stifling, civil-service mentalities that dictated they work for insultingly low wages, the good-paying bodyguard jobs were almost nonexistent. Lately he'd been toying with the idea of drawing on his Seal experience in intelligence, counter-terrorism and special operations to write a book; *A Seal's Every Day Guide To Personal Success*.

But right now, he had bills to pay. A mortgage on a costly condominium apartment in the Riverdale section of the Bronx. Credit card debt. A school teacher wife with a bad attitude, (tempered by a body that could stop the next ice age), who was threatening to take their four school-aged children---two boys, two girls---and divorce him if he didn't find a way to earn some decent money.

Hell, he was desperate. The only reason he was in Florida in the first place was because his former Seal partner, Barry Wish, had insisted on flying him down, first class, all expenses paid, to meet Abe Seubert.

"Meet Seubert as a favor to me," was what Barry had said over the phone from his hospital bed. "He's a bit of a hothead. Calm him down. See if you can talk some sense into him." But Devine didn't see how he could help Seubert without being sucked into a murder conspiracy.

"We have a deal?" Seubert said. "Or not?"

Devine took a huge swallow of beer, and the solution came to him---just like that. He'd do what Seubert asked, put him through Seal training, work him hard, break him, destroy his will to seek vengeance against the pedophile priest. Devine studied Seubert, his sunken-chest and short, scrawny frame and decided that the rich little prick wouldn't last a single week.

"Payment in full, up front," Devine said. "No refunds if you wash out of basic training."

"Basic training?" Seubert made out the check. "All I really need to know is how to shoot, maybe handle a knife."

"Negative." Devine shook his head. "Handling small arms is last. You have to get into shape first."

"I don't need to be in shape to kill a man."

"It's the Seal way or the highway," Devine said.

Just then the bartender placed a white envelope along with a silver champagne bucket containing a chilled bottle of Crystal on the bar in front of Devine.

"Sir," the bartender said cautiously, keeping his distance. "Compliments of Dirty Moe."

Devine glanced at the beaming, depraved old hag. She lapped her tongue suggestively, then made a show of crossing her bony legs. A wave of nausea swept over the combat veteran. He opened the envelope and Dirty Moe's card with her phone number and address slid out along with a $100 bill.

"All right," Seubert said. "We do it the Seal way."

Devine crumpled the $100 bill, dropped it in the champagne bucket, pushed it away, and told the bartender to send it back.

Then he snatched the cigarette from Seubert's mouth, dropped it on the floor and crushed it. "I catch you smoking again, you wash out."

"You're kidding -."

"No booze. Junk food. Sex."

Seubert sighed.

"Don't fuck with me, runt," Devine barked in Seubert's face.

Seubert flinched. "Sorry." He stood, took a step back and smiled a crazy little smile. "When do we start?"

Training began the following morning at dawn on a deserted Florida beach. Seubert arrived driving a new Jaguar, attired in expensive, designer workout gear, a fact that annoyed Devine to no end.

"Puke," Devine barked as he knocked his new student to the ground, kicked him into the underbrush and forced him to strip and dress in regulation military fatigues.

The calisthenics and swimming exercises began slowly, painfully and became more difficult as the hot and humid summer days progressed. Once a week, every week Seubert was forced to run four-miles in boots and full military gear on a timed obstacle course---he fainted the first and second

week. Swim ocean distances up to two miles in fins---
Devine had to rescue Seubert from drowning several times.

But Seubert would not give up.

And every time Devine thought that Seubert couldn't
take any more punishment, couldn't possible run another
step, swim another stroke, do another pushup, he managed
to summon a courage that, Devine knew first hand, had to
come from someplace deep in his soul. And so after five
weeks of training during which time Devine did his best to
break his student, Abe Seubert completed an abbreviated
version of Seal indoctrination training.

The first morning of the sixth week Devine and Seubert
drove deep inside the steaming Florida Everglades. In the
distance, they could see ominous, black thunderhead
clouds, trailing massive bands of torrential rain behind
them. Devine steered his rented Cadillac off the main road,
parked alongside high grass on the banks of a snake-and-
crocodile-infested stream, and couldn't help but feel guilty
about taking Abe Seubert's money.

For one thing, Father Howe was in police custody and,
according to the newspapers, would remain there
permanently. There was no way that Seubert would ever
get close to him. Secondly, he'd grown to like his student---
albeit begrudgingly---respecting his can-do attitude and do-
or-die resolve.

Devine opened the Caddie's trunk and pulled out two
Glock 9mm semi-automatics. He stuck one gun in his own
belt, the other in Seubert's. Next he dragged out a sack of
empty beer bottles, carried them through the marsh to a
fallen palm tree more than 100 feet away and set them up
as targets.

"Now the first thing to remember, Abe, is: this isn't
TV." Devine finished placing the last of the beer bottles on
the fallen palm tree. "Guns are not toys."

They walked the 100 feet back to the car.

"You never let anyone know you're carrying a gun. You never threaten anyone with a gun." Devine slapped a mosquito biting his neck.

"You never a fire warning shot."

"Why's that?" Seubert said.

"Never give the other guy a chance."

"Oh."

"But the most important thing to remember is, whenever you do pull a gun, you shoot and shoot to kill."

Without warning, Devine spun on his heels, drew and fired. Bam! Bam! Bam! The sound hurt Seubert's ears, the muzzle flash hurt his eyes. A zillion startled birds screamed as they flapped into the Florida sky, virtually blocking out the morning sun. And when Seubert looked the first three beer bottles had been shattered.

"Wow."

Devine shoved the gun back into his waistband. "Your turn." He flipped the safety off Seubert's gun. "Aim for the three bottles on the right. Keep shooting till you hit them."

Seubert nodded his readiness. Took a deep breath. Drew. Fired. He hit a swarm of gators that thrashed away in a mad frenzy. He hit an enormous snake that came crashing through the palms, striking the ground with a soggy thud. He hit birds, lizards, palm trees, and a lot of swamp. After unloading a 14-shot clip, about the only things he hadn't hit were the three beer bottles. They were left standing, smirking insolently.

Seubert shrugged. "Guess I've got a lot to learn."

Devine snatched the gun back, ejected, then slammed in a fresh clip. And was thinking that, when it came to making some fast money, maybe Dirty Moe wasn't looking all that bad.

After 14 days of small arms training, Abe Seubert knew how to shoot. He was not fast, but he was accurate. And, much to Devine's delight, had completely given up the idea of killing his son's molester.

"You know all you need to know, Abe," Devine said as they drove out of the Everglades for the last time. "Go to a range twice a week and you'll keep your eye. You can rent their guns, or buy your own."

"Yeah." Seubert's mind was elsewhere.

"Abe, bubbeleh, talk to me."

Seubert lit a smoke---his fist since training had begun---inhaled deeply. "I attended a criminal court, motion hearing yesterday afternoon. The DA decided not to prosecute Father Howe in Florida."

"He say why?"

"He assured me they had a much stronger case against him in Dallas. The children he molested there are older. You should have seen Howe's face. He was smiling."

"Howe was there?"

"Yeah." Seubert glanced out the window.

"He'll be extradited to Dallas and convicted," Devine assured him. "He ain't getting away with anything."

"I know that, now." Seubert flicked his cigarette out the window. "Looks like I spent 75K for nothing."

"Hey, I warned you, didn't I? Told you you'd never get near him."

"Yeah," Seubert said. "You told me."

The Right Reverend Billy Ray Howe, clad in orange prison garb, shackled hand and foot and flanked by shotgun-toting, Florida state troopers, shuffled through airport security just as an intercom voice announced the final boarding of flight #102 to Dallas/Fort Worth.

Howe's entourage continued their march down the concourse, wedging their way through swarming reporters and throngs of rubbernecking travelers, never noticing the bald man in the expensive tan suit and tortoise-rimmed eyeglasses, hunched over the payphone just beyond, watching as they approached.

"Father Howe," a reporter shouted.

Howe turned to face the journalist. "Yes?"

"Did you molest 5-year-old Anthony Seubert?"

A dozen microphones were thrust at the aging Catholic priest and a grin broke across his prison pale face, a grin that said he loved center stage.

"Those charges were dropped, sir." Howe, a bear-like man with a reputation for an academic mind, had affected a southern drawl.

"The boy was too young to identify you," the reporter said.

Howe smiled a homespun smile that made it chillingly evident why his young victims trusted him. "The charges were dropped."

"Did you molest the 8-year-old boy in Dallas?" another reporter asked.

"Of course not."

"Then why has the church defrocked and excommunicated you?" another reporter said.

Howe made certain to look directly into a network news camera before saying, "Like Christ, I am being persecuted."

"Do you compare yourself to Jesus Christ?" The first reporter asked.

Howe responded thoughtfully. "I am a martyr. I was created in *His* image and likeness. So are you all." Just then a teenage girl threaded her way close to Howe, held out a pen and pad, and, with a coy look and a syrupy smile that meant Howe had reached rock star status, drawled, "May I have your autograph, Father Howe?"

"Did you molest the 10-year-old boy in Santa Fe?" another reporter called out.

"No."

A burly state trooper slapped away the girl's pad and pen and pushed her back. "That's enough."

The entourage then elbowed past the frenzied press corps, steamrolling their way to the Dallas flight, as video cameras recorded every move.

But not for long.

For as they passed the pay phones, the bald man in the tan suit and tortoise-rimmed eyeglasses, spun on his heels, drew a gun, and fired three quick shots into the brain of Father Billy Ray Howe.

Devine was asleep when the phone rang in his Bronx apartment bedroom later that night. "Hello?"

"Put on CNN," a voice said.

"Who -?"

"It's me, Barry Wish. Turn on CNN."

Devine reached to a nightstand, groped around, found the TV remote, clicked on CNN.

"*... gunned down in a hail of bullets fired by the father of the small boy Howe was accused of molesting. Abe Seubert is in police custody and . . .. *"

"I got it, Barry." Devine hung up. Sat in stunned silence and watched the slow motion playback of Father Howe's brains being blown out. Then the cameras found Abe Seubert as he dropped his gun, and raised his hands in surrender. State Troopers enveloped him. Cameras clicked and flash bulbs popped.

Devine's wife stirred in her sleep. "Turn off that god-dammed TV."

"Yes, chief." Devine picked up the TV remote and quickly zapped off CNN News. He got out of bed, padded past his kids' rooms, to the kitchen. He opened the refrigerator, popped open a can of beer, walked over to his living room window and gazed out at a panoramic view of the Hudson River.

"To Abe Seubert," he toasted and felt a smile---the first in recent memory---crack his face. "May the Reverend Billy Ray Howe burn in hell."

Devine drank down the whole beer in one long pull, then crushed the can and let it drop to the bare wood floor.

The Made Man

The sky was overcast, air stifling that August night. I stopped at West 49th Street under an overhead street light, flicked a spent cancer-stick out onto 8th Avenue, and checked my surroundings. Not a soul was stirring, except maybe a few rats. I glanced at my watch. It was 4:05 a.m.

I stuffed my hands in my jacket pocket and crossed the street, mulling over the fact that I knew better than to walk those pre-dawn, Hell's Kitchen streets---that could be dangerous; for muggers, cops, and even for members of organized crime, like me.

A crusty homeless man lay in the doorway of a stationery store, wrapped in newspapers, watching me. Something about him was disturbingly familiar. Across the street a burly man sat in the driver's seat of a mold-green private sanitation truck, pinning me with a killer's stare.

All at once I felt dozens of eyes watching me from the shadows, alleys, and darkened doorways, but when I turned to look---nothing. No one. I reached under my jacket, felt for the gun that I had never fired, and continued north toward the ATM.

I'd always been a reluctant mobster. Never really felt comfortable in my role as underboss. I was, in many ways, ashamed of my profession. But like many young men, I had followed my father into the family business, more out of lack of direction then any desire to be a hood. When I dropped out of college, I had nowhere else to go, nothing else to do, and I needed a job.

In my heart I knew I could never be a tough guy. I abhorred violence---a fact better kept to one's self. But I managed to fit into the life fairly well. I enjoyed the underworld camaraderie, gambling, hookers, all the freebies and prestige that came with being a quasi-celebrity gangster. Although I never did adjust to the fact that I was feared.

Especially after the night I was supposed to make my bones, kill a man. I couldn't do it. The terminally overextended gambler begged for mercy and promised me he'd disappear. I let him go. To this day, thank God, no one knew. Except my wife of six months, Colleen.

"Be careful, goombah," Colleen, an ex-nun, had told me only minutes ago as I left our apartment to draw the funds that would facilitate our life-or-death flight from the city. Colleen was the love of my life---my own personal angel---the reason I was "quitting" organized crime. The reason, since we needed seed money to start our new life together, that I'd skimmed $5 million in drug-trade profits.

"Only the good die young," I told her with a smile and a wink. I zipped up my jacket, put on a baseball cap, sunglasses, and felt for the gun that I'd stuck in my waistband.

I watched Colleen sink to her knees and say her prayers. She prayed for my safety, prayed for my soul, prayed that I'd stop getting drunk on wine, prayed that He would allow us to escape the Mafia. Not since my parents' death had anyone but Colleen shown me love, or cared if I lived or died.

A big, black guy ambled south on 8th Avenue on my side of the street. I could tell he'd spotted me too. It was the way his posture changed when he turned in my direction: a vigilant predator pinpointing its prey.

I picked up my pace.

Half a block later I dipped my ATM card in-and-out of a bank's auto-reader. And when it buzzed, I pulled the door open, hurried inside, yanked the door closed and held it until I heard the auto-lock engage. The black guy was right behind me. He hit the door hard and started pulling on it.

He even had the nerve to turn affable, asking me, real friendly like, if I'd open it up and let him in.

I gave the guy the once-over; he was thick necked, broad shouldered with intense eyes. But the most dominant feature on his pitted face was the knife scar that ran from his left ear along his cheek to his chin. He was something out of a child's nightmare.

I glanced at the guy's hands---no weapons that I could see. But I shook my head, no. At only five-foot-eight and 175 pounds, I wasn't about to let him through that door. He threw up his hands and let his eyes soften and register genuine hurt. I had to smile, the guy's routine was pretty good, but not good enough.

I turned and looked around the bank's long, narrow air-conditioned space which contained about twenty ATM machines, ten on each side, and relaxed a bit.

I heard then saw a stunningly attractive, tuxedo and evening-dress-clad couple huddled over an ATM---*Page Six* socialite types arguing over who was supposed to remember their PIN. I stepped over piles of scattered deposit receipts and bank envelopes and thought about how out of place the couple was; only cops, drunks, fools, or desperados, like myself, would be daring enough to use an ATM at this time of night.

"ATM's are death traps," I remember my father, a capo in the Bonanno crime family, saying. "Only assholes, or someone with a death wish, would go to a ATM after midnight."

I walked down the bowling-alley length aisle to the cash machine at the far end. I pulled a dozen ATM cards from my coat pocket, withdrew the maximum amount of cash from each account. And as I stuffed the money into my pockets, I heard the bank door buzz. Turned and saw a businessman walk into the bank. The big black guy stepped in behind him.

The businessman stepped to the nearest ATM machine. The black guy hung back, took a position by the door and looked out the bank window, probably scanning the street for cops.

Raised voices. The woman in the evening dress called her gray-haired companion in the tux a fool. She shoved him. He shoved her back---these two had to be married.

"Yo, bitch." The black man walked over to the couple.

I thought about the bank's security cameras---police detectives might later examine those tapes---and pulled my hat lower over my eyes. I moved to the next ATM and eyed the exit.

The man in the tuxedo gave the black guy a look of disrespect and opened his mouth with a follow-up that never came---the black guy punched him. Dropped him on the floor, just like that.

The woman screamed.

"Gimme the money, muthafucka." The robber drew a knife. Something about the way he wielded it made me think he was ex-military. The guy in the tux, his perfectly coiffed gray hair now comically askew, didn't even try to get up off the floor. But pulled out his wallet, took off his watch, and handed them over. The woman slipped off her watch and ring.

I continued inching toward the exit, careful not to make any noise or draw attention. I wasn't about to interfere with this robber's petty crime or get involved in any way. This was not my problem, none of my business. I was no hero.

Besides, Colleen and I were booked on a 6:00 a.m. flight, the beginning of a long and complex journey to safety. I could not, would not, let her down.

"Leave them alone," I heard the lone businessman say.

I froze, groaned; this was about to get ugly.

The robber turned and glared. "Walk away, Renée."

The businessman held up a cell phone. "I'm calling the cops." He punched in 911. And the robber threw the knife.

It struck the businessman in the throat. He went down, blood squirting from the wound, covering his starched white shirt and tie. He thrashed about, tried to speak. I knew he would be dead in moments.

"Muthafucka," the robber said as he walked across the room and stomped on the businessman's cell phone. Then he bent down and pulled his knife from the guy's throat, careful to avoid the blood.

I saw my chance to bolt and I did. Sprinted down the aisle, passed the terrified couple, passed the dying businessman and the robber. I crashed the door open with my shoulder and ran out onto 8th Avenue.

I made it to the corner. Cut left a quarter block, ran across the avenue, dodged a cruising cab, and stopped to catch my breath. I was checking that the robber wasn't on my tail when a thought occurred to me---that upscale couple had just witnessed a murder. The robber would have to kill them.

I spotted a pay phone and hurried to it, but it was out of order. I tried to remember which wise guys lived close by. Vito the Moron lived over on 1st Avenue and Tony No Nose had a girlfriend over on Park. But I had no way to contact either of them.

Reluctantly, I walked back to the bank and peered inside.

The robber had the terrified couple cornered in an ATM booth. He was yelling at them, brandishing the knife, no doubt telling them that if they didn't remember their PIN number he'd kill them. The dopes probably didn't realize that they were about to die anyway.

I took a deep, calming breath. If I didn't interfere the robber would kill the couple, of that I was certain.

Saving them was up to me.

But if I was forced to shoot the robber, Colleen and I could be in mortal danger. My picture would be on the bank's tapes and could be on television by morning. We'd be forced to delay our flight and go into hiding here in the city. Avoid airports, train, and bus stations, lay low to avoid cops and the army of mob assassins who would soon be hunting me for the heavy price on my head.

"Mind your own business," I told myself.

There was a time, not long ago, when I would have done just that. But that was my life B.C; before Colleen.

I heard a scream. The robber knocked the man aside, and put his knife to the woman's throat.

I slipped out my tarnished revolver, checked that it was loaded---it was. But with 20-year-old ammunition. I had no idea if the gun would even fire.

Again the woman screamed.

I dipped my bank card into the ATM auto reader.

The robber heard the door buzz and let the woman go. I heard him say something in hushed tones to the couple about keeping the fuck quiet. He glanced quickly over his shoulder and saw it was me---the third and last witness to the murder he'd just committed.

"Cops are on the way," I lied and stepped away from the door to where the dead businessman lay in a pool of blood, allowing the robber plenty of room to exit. "You leave now," I cocked the hammer of the gun that I concealed behind my back, "you got a head start."

The robber tried a smile, then lifted his right arm to throw the knife. I raised my gun and pulled the trigger; nothing happened. I felt my stomach do a 360 and braced for the impact of the knife.

But the guy in the tux hit the robber from behind with a kidney-crushing elbow. The women raked her long fingernails across his eyes and the robber went down cursing. In an instant the man in the tux was on him. He locked him in a death-grip headlock and twisted, quick and hard. The robber's neck snapped with a sickening crack--- very professional.

At that moment I knew the socialite couple were not what they appeared to be.

"You really call the cops?" the man said.

"No."

"Why the hell not?" the woman said.

"Because he's Joey 'Mad-Dog' Carbone," the man said.

The woman looked directly at me. "You're right. That's him."

I sighed, stuck my gun back in my waistband. "Huh-uh," I said. "Never heard of this Carbone. You must be mistaken. Capisce?"

The couple exchanged a look.

"Understood," the man said and put his arm around the woman. "Thanks, Joey."

"For what?" I turned, pushed open the bank door. "I was never even here." I walked out onto 8th Avenue, took out a pack of butts, lit up, turned south, and disappeared, once and forever into the Hell's Kitchen night.

Bandit

"He had no reason to shoot me," Becky Hoff told uniformed New York City Police Sergeant John Taylor at 3:05 on a stifling August morning. She was lying in a pool of her own blood, on a chipped tile floor, behind a deli checkout counter.

"I gave him the money. Didn't resist. He had no reason."

"Can you describe the bandit?" Sergeant Taylor wished he were any place but there, watching this poor old Jewish woman die.

Becky Hoff thought a moment, staring off at the tin ceiling she and her husband had painted only one month ago in a halfhearted effort to spruce up the shabby deli that they'd owned for thirty-two years. Her husband had taken care to cover the bullet holes in the ceilings, remnants of the last robbery.

"Like a movie star he looked." The old woman's breath rattled. "Did you call my husband?"

Taylor nodded as an ambulance screeched to a stop outside. Two EMTs burst into the deli, medical equipment and stretcher in hand. Sergeant Taylor moved out of their way as Becky Hoff, slipping deeper into shock, kept talking as if that mundane activity would tether her to life.

"I have a son," she said. "A good boy. A lawyer."

Taylor grunted involuntarily. Like most cops, he thought lawyers were lower then whale shit. "Want me to call him?"

"No." Hoff's eyes glazed the way they do when someone drifts off, lost in a memory. "He is ashamed of his parents, our accent. Changed his name from Hoff to Hall." Her eyes welled. "No time for his father and mother."

"Tell me more about the bandit."

179

The EMTs worked frantically to control the old lady's bleeding. They couldn't.

"A black man," she said. "Lighter skin than you. Six foot, maybe. Short hair. Twenty-one or so."

"What was he wearing?"

"Black T-shirt. Black jeans. Black shoes or sneakers, I think. Can't be sure. Sorry."

"You're doing fine, Mrs. Hoff. Anything else you can think of? Hat? Scar? Tattoo? Any accent?"

"No."

Taylor's partner, McBain, made a whispering comment. This bandit's physical description matched that of one who had mugged and viciously beaten another old lady several blocks south only hours before.

She was not expected to live either.

Taylor ripped off the page of notes and handed them to McBain, who hurried outside to the RMP to broadcast the bandit's description city-wide.

"For pleasure he kills, that one," Becky Hoff said.

"What?" Sergeant Taylor said.

"Killing. He likes it." She raised an arm that had a six-inch tattoo running down the underside of the forearm, showed it to Taylor---faded blue numbers, unreadable.

"Auschwitz," she said. "There were men like him there." She dropped her arm, convulsed, and drew her last breath.

Sergeant Taylor blessed himself, said a silent prayer for the soul of Becky Hoff, and asked the Lord to stop the bandit before he killed again.

Outside, McBain had finished broadcasting the bandit's description from the RMP when movement caught his eye. A man was standing in the shadows across the street watching him.

The man stepped to the curb and stopped under a street light. He was unkempt, probably homeless, a grizzled black man, at least fifty and dressed for the oppressive heat in a tank-top and shorts. Jailhouse tattoos adorned his arms.

The man took out a cigarette, lit it with a match. He had strong but haggard facial features, a cruel mouth---the type of face a cop would not easily forget.

I watched the uniform cop walk back into the deli. I dumped my smoke and decided to keep moving before the cops gave me a second look. Cops always hassled me. Besides, there was nothing I could do. A woman who had been kind to me lay dying on a delicatessen floor. At least I had her killer's description, courtesy of the loud police radio in the open car.

I stuffed my hands in my pockets, walked north on 3rd Avenue, thought about how short our time on this earth truly is. Wondered how I would finally meet my end. Would I always feel this alone in a city of eight million people?

I bent to pet a passing stray dog who growled at me---a kindred spirit---and thought about the fact that I was, once again, spending my nights wandering the streets with nowhere to go. But that was better than lying on a cot in a homeless shelter, staring at the ceiling, too frightened to drop off for fear of being murdered in my sleep.

No, better to wander the streets alone, at night. Because people made me angry. And when I got angry, someone got hurt.

It wasn't always that way.

I was once a productive member of society, married with a small condominium in the north Bronx. I'd served my country as a Marine in Vietnam, won a Silver Star. A Post Traumatic Stress Disorder diagnosis got me honorably discharged. And it was no lie: I experienced battlefield flashbacks. The VA docs told me that my volatile temperament could pose a danger to myself and others.

But with the help of the GI Bill, I attended City College and earned a degree in Physical Education. I became a high school PT instructor and coach of an all-boys baseball and tennis team. One day the father of a student cornered me in the school locker room. Demanded I allow his son, a below-average southpaw pitcher with a bad attitude, more playing time. He wouldn't accept no for an answer. A heated argument ensued and the boy's father punched me in the face.

A red haze settled over my eyes.

Manslaughter got me five years in prison. My wife left me. What few friends I had deserted me.

I was alone.

Danzel Warren thought being a famous criminal was gonna be easy. You commit a few heinous crimes, get a good agent, and if you look "good" like he did, hell, it was cake. Right?

Well, not so far.

And Danzel had a hell of a promising juvenile record going for him. At 12 he'd sexually molested a half-dozen of his female classmates. When disciplined by the school principal for those assaults, he'd set fire to the school.

As a 14-year-old he robbed another child of his lunch money at knifepoint. At 15 he was arrested for carrying a loaded gun to school.

The time he spent in a state youthful offender facility he used wisely. Lifting weights. Watching movies. His favorite---*Natural Born Killers*---he'd seen more than fifty times.

But after speaking with a couple of talent agents---both convicted felons so he knew he could trust them---he was told his juvenile criminal record would be useful only for background purposes. The legitimate news organizations went for that kind of bullshit---you know, "how the po' boy went wrong" story. But if he wanted to be on "Sixty

Minutes" and "Entertainment Tonight," if he were serious about becoming a media icon, he had to do something "in the now", something unique.

"High-end art and jewel thieves are always 'in,' Danzel, my boy," one agent told him. "Imagine a professional *black* burglar---a Cary Grant, '*To Catch a Thief*' type. Good for a book, a movie-of-the-week deal, minimum."

Danzel, embarrassed to tell the agent that he had no idea who in the fuck Cary Grant was, rented *To Catch A Thief* and was thoroughly inspired. Within a week he came up with his own master plan. Starting in January, he would embark on a killing spree. Women mostly, not that he was sexist---he wasn't. But killing women would get better press coverage. He'd kill a man on occasion just to show the public he wasn't weird or anything.

But the killings had to correlate to the number of a given month. For instance, since January was the first month of next year, he needed one victim, two in February, three March. Four victims in April. Five in May, and so on. December would be his crowning achievement, guaranteed to catapult him into the spotlight, the serial killer's hall of fame. And he was supremely confident that then, and only then, would Don King be willing to represent him.

Danzel could envision card and board games with his picture on them. Guest spots on "The Tonight Show"---from his death row prison cell, of course. A "Biography" episode. Move over Jeffrey Dahmer, you muthafuckin' has-been.

Danzel headed south on 3rd Avenue, checking out the ramshackle tenements, searching, as always, for unlocked doors or open windows, and saw something up ahead. A car had just turned off its headlights. A man was exiting on the driver's side, another person from the passenger side---a woman.

Danzel quick stepped into a darkened doorway.

The couple walked to the rear of their car, popped the trunk, and got busy removing various bags. Danzel took a closer look at the pair; they were old, fat, and dressed like po' folk. Their car was at least 15-years-old, a rusting piece of junk. They probably lived in one of the run-down tenements. It wouldn't be worth robbing them.

Killing them might be fun.

Danzel stepped from the doorway.

He strolled toward the unsuspecting duo, eyes moving, always moving, careful to stay in the shadows. Was about to pull his gun and blast away when he thought he saw the glow of a cigarette. Yes, there was someone across the street, in a pitch-black tenement doorway, smoking, watching him. Danzel relaxed his gun hand and walked past the couple. No use taking chances. Whoever was in that doorway was a potential witness against him; could even be a cop.

I knew instantly the boy was the one who had killed Becky Hoff.

I dropped my cigarette, crushed it under my size fifteen, walked casually down the broken tenement steps and followed him. I planned to stop the boy and ask why he killed that kindly old woman.

I had to know the reason.

But the boy kept walking, looking over his shoulder at me.

"Come here, boy," I said and picked up my pace.

The boy broke into a run and disappeared around a corner.

I made it to the end of the street, looked north, and carefully scanned the area. If he had run toward Harlem and the 96th Street projects, he'd still be in sight---he wasn't. That meant he'd run west.

At my age I could not hope to catch him. But I knew that neighborhood well and had a pretty good idea where

184

the young killer was heading. I knew where I'd go. I dug into my pockets, found my last crumpled $5 bill. Tried to hail several yellow cabs but they sped past, did not acknowledge me, wouldn't even slow down, not for a homeless black man.

I stuck out my hand one last time and a gypsy cab stopped. The driver, a friendly Arab with a quick smile, agreed to drive me over to Central Park.

I said goodbye to the Arab driver, got out at 90th and 5th Avenue across from Central Park. And the first thing I noticed was the air smelled fresh and clean.

The boy would come from the south. I searched for a place to hide, somewhere the army of street-wise doormen who guarded the entrances to 5th Avenue's multi-million-dollar co-op apartments would not notice me.

I walked half a block and found the perfect spot---a private entrance to a doctor's office whose overhead security light had apparently burned out. I stepped into the darkness, leaned against a highly-polished bronze door, lit a smoke, breathed the same air and enjoyed the same park view as the city's filthy rich. Watched and waited.

Five minutes later I spotted the boy come off 88th Street. He took his time walking up the block, glancing into parked cars, no doubt looking for an easy score. If he kept coming my way, I'd be on him before he knew it.

"Hey, what're you doin?" A doorman with a tough Irish face was standing there, a baseball bat in his right hand.

I startled. "Nothing." I noticed for the first time that I stood within range of a surveillance camera. "Just resting."

"Get the hell out of here before I call a cop."

"Yes, sir." I had no choice. I flicked my cigarette into the street, left my hiding place, and dashed to the curb with the intent of using a parked car for cover.

But the boy saw me and bolted across 5th Avenue. Scaled a four-foot limestone wall and disappeared into the gloom of Central Park.

I was only moments behind him. My bones creaked as I climbed the wall and my feet cramped when I hit the ground. I limped to the nearest tree, waited for the cramps to subside as my eyes adjusted to the blackness. I felt like I was back in the jungles of Vietnam.

I held my breath, listened, but there were no sounds.

I felt the ground until I found a rock. Tossed it, and listened as it cracked through bushes and hit the ground with a soggy thud.

Gunfire. Flashes of blinding light and ear-rupturing noise.

I heard the boy crash though the brush, heard him yelp in pain, stumble and fall.

I crept forward.

Found him lying on the ground rubbing his ankle.

He looked at me, a little dazed. "You a cop?" He was wincing in pain.

"I ain't no cop."

"What're you following me for, nigger?" The boy rolled to his knees and began crawling around, feeling the ground, searching for his gun.

"Why'd you shoot that old lady in the deli?" I said.

"I felt like it."

"That's no reason."

"Fuck it ain't."

I could feel my face flush with anger and my breathing quicken. "She was my friend."

"No shit?" The boy located his gun. Picked it up, dusted it off, and pointed it at me. "Fuck you and your friend."

He pulled the trigger.

The gun jammed.

The red haze settled over my eyes.

Sergeant Taylor responded to the call of "shots fired," which was called in by a 5th Avenue doorman. Within ten minutes he found the bandit's battered body in Central Park

186

and knew instantly he was Becky Hoff's killer. And there was something else.

Taylor had read several recent police reports about similar homicide scenes, the manner in which the bandit's body had been arranged postmortem, as if he were lying in a coffin. Head pointing to the north, feet south, hands clasped at the chest. And all the other victims in those police reports had been males with criminal records and a history of violence. Taylor took a closer look at the deceased. The bandit's face was beaten to a bloody pulp, his neck broken.

"You thinking what I'm thinking, Sarge?" McBain said.

"What're you thinking?"

McBain pointed to the bandit. "That's the work of the serial killer the papers call 'The Avenger.'"

"That's what I'm thinking." Taylor radioed for a team of homicide detectives, then ordered the other cops arriving on the scene to search the area for the killer. But he didn't think they'd find him. Taylor looked east to the rising sun and knew that, by some divine intervention, his prayer had been answered.

The bandit had been stopped.

I found myself in front of Hoff's Deli a few nights later. The place had been boarded up, a chain lock secured the front door. A handwritten, cardboard sign said that, due to a death in the family, Hoff's Deli was permanently closed.

I crossed the street and walked into the darkness of the playground, lit a smoke, and thought about the kindly old woman and her slayer, the boy I'd killed. I didn't remember what happened after his gun jammed. I blanked out. But I knew I'd killed him. He deserved to die, that one. I felt no remorse. No regrets.

A gunshot off to my left.

It came from a gypsy cab that had stopped at the corner.

I shrank back further into the shadows, watched as a man with a gun hurried out of the back of the cab and ran past me north on 3rd Avenue---I recognized him from the neighborhood.

I walked over to the taxi cab. Peered in.

The friendly Arab who had driven me to Central Park the night of Becky Hoff's murder, was slumped against the steering wheel. There was a bullet hole in the back of his head. An empty cash box lay on the seat beside him. It appeared that the Arab had handed over his money. The killer had no reason to shoot him.

I located the nearest pay phone and called 911.

And as sirens filled the air, I left the murder scene, walked north up 3rd Avenue in search of the cab driver's killer.

I was going to find him no matter how long it took.

Ask him why he killed the friendly Arab cab driver.

I had to know the reason.

Lost Love

"Who's this?" a man's voice demanded on my home telephone.

"Who's this?" I shot back.

"Who *is* this?" the guy growled.

"Hey," I said. "You called me, pal."

The guy paused. "My name's Farrelly." His tone softened. "Michael J. Farrelly."

Farrelly's voice was grating, irritating me. "Who you looking for?"

"Johnny Stallone."

"Why?"

"I need a private detective," Farrelly said. "Someone who can keep his mouth shut."

I took off my eyeglasses, pushed back from my computer, stood and stepped away from the email I'd been reading. My ex-girlfriend out in San Diego had written asking me for financial assistance---Wendy always did have more than her share of nerve.

I gazed out my fourteenth-floor window at an underwhelming view of the new fifty-story glass office building across Second Avenue. For ten years, until six months ago, I had enjoyed a sunny and nearly unobstructed western view clear across Manhattan to the New Jersey Palisades. Now my apartment was shrouded in twilight. "I'm Stallone."

"So, you available?" Farrelly said.

"Depends. How'd you get my name?"

"An accountant in New York," Farrelly said. "Charlie Orr."

I knew that name. Last year I'd performed a white-collar criminal investigation for Orr , a corporate bigwig. While surveilling a suspect, the case turned hinky; a gun was drawn, a shot fired. The altercation nearly cost me my private detective's license, not to mention my life. But in the end the Assistant District Attorney---an old pal from my NYPD days---exonerated me of any wrongdoing. And I was well paid, very well paid.

"Tell me more," I said.

"I'm an attorney with a practice in Los Angeles. I have a client who needs to find someone in the New York area. A woman. It won't be easy. I've been looking for her myself for months."

"Go on."

"Where shall I begin?"

I reached for a pad and pen. "Your firm's name and address."

"Concord Development Corporation." Farrelly gave an address in Beverly Hills.

"Subject's name."

"Her name's Pamela Watt. Originally from somewhere in Pennsylvania. She married, then divorced a golden boy Canadian hockey player around ten years back. They were together for five years, had two kids, lived in New Jersey."

"Where's the hockey player now?"

"Beats me, but I know he's not playing hockey anymore."

"What about Pamela? Age? Description?"

"Now she's around forty-two, five-nine, brown eyes and hair. She was a Ford model in the old days---a real beauty. Got older, left the big time about sixteen years ago and wound up with an obscure New York City modeling agency called Cy Perkins Models. That's the last time my client saw her."

"Got a date of birth? Social Security number? Last known address?"

"No. I told you it wouldn't be easy." Farrelly paused. "What about your fee?"

"Two-fifty an hour plus expenses."

190

"Two hundred and fifty dollars an hour. Can you do better?"

"You want a cheap detective, Counselor, try the Yellow Pages."

I heard the flick of a cigarette lighter, then Farrelly puffing away. "I suppose you want a retainer."

"A certified check for five thousand along with a letter of agreement which authorizes me to act on behalf of your client. Once the five is used up, I'll notify you and you'll inform me whether your client wishes to go further. Any questions?"

"What type of expenses should I anticipate?"

"Depends. Where did she divorce the hockey player?"

"We don't know."

"If she got a quickie divorce outside of New York State, say in Vegas, then remarried and changed her name, that would complicate things. I might have to travel, or hire investigators in other states---with your approval, of course."

"What about the model agent as a lead?"

"Cy Perkins died years ago."

"How could you possibly know that?"

"I used to date models, thirty-five pounds ago. Before I began parting my hair at the armpit."

Farrelly croaked. I think it was supposed to be a laugh.

"I'll get back to you," he said.

I hung up the phone, not expecting to hear from attorney Michael Farrelly again.

My ergonomic chair squeaked as I sat down at my computer. I forced thoughts of the Pamela Watt investigation from my mind---lawyer Farrelly was obviously price shopping---and located Wendy's email. Although, since our tumultuous breakup, we had exchanged occasional emails, I hadn't actually "spoken" to Wendy in over two years---our phone calls always degenerated into blame-game bickering. As a result Wendy forbade me to call her. And she never called me.

I reread the email, considered Wendy's bizarre request for financial assistance, and thought about the fact that I actually enjoyed communicating with the love of my life electronically. Although these days no matter how amiable and positive my emails were, Wendy, against all reason, found fault.

I finished reading the email.

Decided not to respond.

Deleted it.

Maybe now she'd call.

Federal Express was at my door by ten o'clock the following morning. Inside the overnight envelope was the signed agreement from Farrelly and a certified check in the amount of $5,000. I picked up my phone and dialed.

"How," White Dove Lenahan said groggily. She was my half-American Indian, half-Irish detective agency partner.

"How yourself," I said.

"What the hell time is it?" White Dove's yawn sounded like a Sioux war cry. "My sun dial seems to be broken."

"A little after noon."

"That's the middle of the night."

"You alone?"

"Hold on."

I could hear the rustling of bed sheets.

"No strange men, or women anywhere."

"Must be losing your touch."

"Bite me, white eyes."

When we were first introduced over ten years ago, I'd found White Dove, a fellow New York City police officer, broken-hearted and nearly destitute. She'd met, fallen in love, and cohabitated with a charming Brooklyn slime-ball who turned out to have connections to organized crime. That tabloid-ready relationship precipitated her hasty

192

departure from the NYPD, which left her alone, unemployed, and homeless. As a total sucker for beautiful women with hard-luck stories, I took her in, literally. Allowed her to sleep in my spare bedroom, albeit temporarily. Gave her a job.

Like every other man, and some women, I found the bisexual, green-eyed White Dove knee-knockingly attractive, though I never made a move on her, nor she on me. A state of affairs I never regretted. Being intimate with the in-your-face alpha female White Dove, I always knew, would have been an exercise in masochism. It would have ruined our relationship.

I picked up the Farrelly check and examined it. "Looks like we've got a paying client."

"Eye-talian speak with forked tongue."

"A lawyer from L.A."

"A lawyer? Get the money up front."

"I'm way ahead of you."

"What kinda case?"

"Missing person. A woman."

"My specialty."

"Before you put your ear to the ground," I said. "Do me a favor and check out the Concord Development Corporation in L.A. I want to know who's behind it. And check out a California lawyer Michael Farrelly. The usual stuff."

"I'll get right on it."

I hung up. Sat at my computer. Thought about how to locate Pamela Watt. Since she had children with her former hockey player husband, locating him and asking where his ex-wife resided was one alternative. There was another, ridiculously obvious option. I toggled to an Internet phone book, entered the name Pamela Watt. Searched the tri-state area.

A dozen Watts appeared on the screen. There was only one Pamela. The phone listing was for a residence in

Oyster Bay, Long Island. I recalled Farrelly saying that he'd been searching for Pamela for months---not surprising. Amateur sleuths often overlook the obvious. Of course, I'd never tell the lawyer that.

"Got her," I told Farrelly two days later, a respectable amount of time---sixteen hours at $250 per---to have located a missing person. It was 9:01 a.m., L.A. time.

"Where is she?" Farrelly said.

"Long Island," I said, and gave him the address. "The last U.S. census indicated that six people are living there. Four adults and two children. There're two phones listed. One to Pamela, another to a Robert Winston. I checked the local marriage records. She's married to Winston."

"I'll call the client and get back to you." Farrelly hung up.

I dialed White Dove. "Get anything?"

"Concord Development Corporation is a Delaware-based real estate holding corporation. All company documents have the lawyer Michael Farrelly's name on them. He graduated Harvard Law, class of `83. Passed the California bar back in `84. No sanctions or other disciplinary problems I could find."

"And the money man?"

"Does Donald Browdy ring a bell?"

The name was indeed familiar. "Not Browdy World Syndicate? Talk shows? Game shows. Movies?"

"The same. He *is* Concord Development Corporation."

"Then he's our client."

"And one big asshole. Locked up for DUI half a dozen times. Likes to fight cops. Been convicted of felonious assault. Beats his wife. A real skell. I did a quick financial on him. The guy's conservatively worth seventy million."

My call waiting beeped. "Hold." I flashed to the next line. "Stallone."

"The client wants more," the lawyer Farrelly said.

"Like?"

194

"He wants to know everything about her. Is she happy? Are she and her husband financially set? Any debts or trouble of any kind? Is the husband a good guy or a bad guy? And remember, this has to be kept strictly confidential."

"Can do," I said. "I'll probably need more cash."

"You'll have it by tomorrow," Farrelly said.

"Anything else?"

"The client wants pictures."

"Pictures?" I thought about that. "Look, I don't peek in bedroom windows."

"No. Nothing like that. He wants to know what she looks like these days, that's all."

"Why? What's this all about?"

"My client was involved with Pamela once. Now he's having some marital problems. All he can think about is her, his 'great lost love.'"

Lost love. The words triggered memories of my own lost love.

The days when Wendy and I would wake, bodies intertwined.

Pacific Ocean sunsets.

Making love under the stars on the beach.

"When it comes to lost loves," I said lamely, "they say 'you can't go back.'"

"Maybe you and me can't," Farrelly said. "Rich people do anything they want."

I hung up with Farrelly, flashed back to White Dove. "Pack your camera and sunscreen, Pocahontas. I'll pick you up in twenty minutes."

"Shit," White Dove said as we drove down Pamela Watt Winston's street. "Can't see the house." The residence was situated off a winding, tree-lined residential road on a dead-man's curve and not visible from the street.

195

"Why does the client want to know so much about this broad anyway?" White Dove was tying her ink black, knee-length hair into a tight bun. A thirty-seven-year old Crystal Gayle look-alike, she kept her womanly form by running twenty-five miles a week, and doing pilates---whatever that was.

"You said she's married, right?" White Dove reached into a camera bag and snapped a telephoto lens onto her digital Nikon.

I shrugged just as a sixteen-wheeler whizzed round the curve and passed us. The turbulence rocked my rental car. "They used to date."

"Speaking of dates, been meaning to ask." White Dove checked the action on her camera before she continued. "Go on that match.com date the other night?"

"I cancelled." I slowed to make a U-turn. "Too busy."

"Doing what, drinking beer, watching the Yankee game?" White Dove slipped off layers of rattling jewelry-- Navajo turquoise bracelets, bejeweled Hopi necklaces--and placed them in her handbag. "Stop moping around like a wounded little boy and get over Wendy, for chrissake."

"I see your years of NYPD sensitivity training paid off."

"Look, she took advantage of you. Didn't she?"

"Yeah." I made the U-turn, hit the gas.

"You told me she wanted you to support her and her freakin' kids. Which you did for six years. That when you ran out of money she kicked you out."

"She didn't kick me out. I left."

White Dove sighed. "Whatever." She glanced toward a line of oak trees for what seemed like a long time. "What? You're not thinking of getting involved with her again?"

"No," I said.

Truth was, I'd jump at the chance.

I'd originally met the recently divorced, mother of two at a birthday party for the film director Stan Dragotti at a New York City restaurant, Bruno's on East 58th Street.

Wendy and I shared a sumptuous meal, a few drinks, a big-band dance, a 4:00 a.m. kiss---it was a kiss to build a dream on.

I began to visit Wendy at her home in San Diego, she visited me here in New York. It didn't take long for both of us to realize that we shared a unique chemistry, a molten psychological and physical attraction---I couldn't stay away from her, nor she from me.

Since she had two young daughters---a three- and a seven-year-old whom she doted upon---and worked as a part-time caterer for her philandering restaurant-owner ex-husband, and I was single, in business for myself--that is footloose and fancy free--I chose to become bi-coastal. Wendy and I rented a four-bedroom house together on a cul-de-sac in a gated Del Mar, California, community.

But as devoted as I was to Wendy and her girls, when I experienced financial difficulties---most of my clients had offices in the World Trade Center pre-9-11---and it became apparent that we could no longer afford our cul-de-sac home, Wendy turned on me. Although she refused to force her ex-husband Brad to pay thousands upon thousands in back alimony and child support---a state of affairs I never understood---she demanded that *I* take out loans, run up credit card debt, anything to maintain appearances, so as not to upset her children. I responded by suggesting that Wendy get a *full-time* job, and discovered that my beloved had an aversion to work. She found all available positions demeaning; she was pretentious and jealous of people with money, especially her girlfriends, some of whom married wealthy guys---guys she frequently compared me to, insinuating that I was less of a man because I'd gone broke. Yet in her last email she had the unmitigated gall to ask me for financial assistance---that was my Wendy.

I slowed the car at the base of a private home's manicured lawn. In upscale Oyster Bay, diligent residents would soon notice my vehicle and call police.

"You ready?" I said.

"Is a pig's ass pork?" White Dove said.

I hit the gas. Sped past Pamela's property, past an old colonial, then a split-level ranch and hit the brakes as I came abreast of a Cape Cod. White Dove opened the car door. Stepped out. Rolled onto the grass and scrambled for cover. I punched the accelerator and raced away.

White Dove moved quickly, stealthily, across several vast lawns. Looked and listened for signs of guard dogs. She crawled down and across a small ravine, through two front yards, then onto Pamela's property. Inching closer to the well-kept split-level house, she spotted a woman, Pamela Watt, in the yard sunning herself by a large, inviting pool. White Dove crawled to a vantage point behind a bush, and clicked away.

The call came on a Thursday night.

I was sitting home at the time, watching a *Law & Order* rerun. White Dove, along with several of our cop and firefighter buddies had called, asking if I'd meet them for beers; the guys were, as usual, on the prowl. But I came up with various excuses not to join them---beside not being in the mood, I still had to edit, organize and email the digital photos White Dove had taken of Pamela Watt Winston. And I'd never had much luck with the bar scene.

I muted Jack McCoy's aggressive cross-examination of a wily defendant, picked up the portable on the fourth ring. "Hello."

"Hi, Johnny, it's Wendy calling."

Wendy.

I pushed off the couch and began to pace. "Hi, Wendy."

"How are you?" Wendy said.

"I'm good." My stomach was churning. "And you?"

"I called for a reason, Johnny," Wendy said, getting right to it.

"All right," I said with a self-satisfied grin. Obviously, my last maneuver---not answering her email, ignoring her request for financial assistance---had worked.

She said, "I wanted to tell you that you were right about some things."

"Oh?" I wandered over to my living room window, looked down onto Second Avenue. Traffic was snarled. Horns honked. Drivers cursed. "Like what?"

"I didn't appreciate you," Wendy said. "You used to say that whenever we'd fight---that I didn't appreciate you, or our life. Well, you were right; I didn't."

I remembered those arguments: trying to convince Wendy that our life together was great, that she had beauty, brains, youth, and two beautiful healthy little girls. "Life," I used to say "doesn't get better than this." But Wendy was not capable of appreciating her gifts; she was obsessed, angst-ridden with her/our lack of financial independence, and how those circumstances affected her daughters.

"You really cared about me, Johnny---not like other men I meet," Wendy continued. "You were always there for me. I could always count on you. You were my Rock of Gibraltar."

I guess I should've felt validated by Wendy's long overdue revelation, maybe even I-told-you-so smug. But I didn't. "So, where does this leave us?"

Wendy took a long moment. "I don't know."

"You don't know?" I chuckled. "Whatever happened to the Wendy who's always so sure of herself?"

Silence.

"I have to go now, Johnny."

"No, don't. I was only kidding."

"I have to go get the girls. I'll be in touch," she said and hung up.

Baffled, I stood staring at the phone in my hand.

"Pamela has no felony convictions," I told the lawyer Farrelly on the phone the next day. I was sitting at the desk in my home office, perusing Pamela's file.

"She was a coke whore with a heavy booze problem a few years back," I said. "Locked up for DUI in 2001, again in 2004. Had her driver's license suspended for a year. Got some heavy credit card debts, and then there's the mortgage on the house."

Pamela and Robert Winston lived in the four-bedroom, three-bath, split-level ranch with Winston's parents and her two children by her former hockey player husband. Winston listed his occupation on his mortgage application as a personal trainer at a local health club, and reported an annual income of around eighty thousand a year.

"Sources tell me the husband's been dipping his wick in his client pool at the health club," I said. "They were separated. Pamela took him back."

Pamela, once a high-priced model with the Ford Model Agency in New York, listed her current occupation as a fit model for Ann Taylor on East 57th Street. She reported an annual income of nearly seventy-five thousand---a sobering decline from her heady $300-per-hour days. She commuted into the city five days a week and, following evening cocktails at a swank restaurant, Bice, at Madison and 54th Street, she caught the 7:03 train to Oyster Bay.

"She's still a beautiful woman," Farrelly said, referring to the digital photos I had emailed him. "Very beautiful."

"What's Browdy gonna do with all this info?"

Farrelly paused. "How'd you find out who the client is?"

"S'way I get the big bucks, Counselor." I could hear Farrelly puffing on a cigarette.

"If anything," Farrelly said, "he'll probably arrange to bump into her on the street, or a restaurant. You know, 'Fancy meeting you here. How've you been?' Yadda, yadda, yadda."

I pictured me bumping into Wendy. She'd be, as always, with her two girls, perhaps shopping for them at Nordstrom, chauffeuring them around Del Mar, or cheering them on at a soccer game. She could very well smile, say how good it was to see me--or not.

"Hope things work out for them," I said.

"Fax me your final invoice. I'll get a check cut by the end of the week and we're square. You did a great job, Stallone."

"Thanks," I said. "You need anything else on this coast, Counselor, be sure to call ."

"Count on it," Farrelly said.

A few months later I was sitting in Starbucks on Second Avenue, waiting for yet another Internet blind date that White Dove insisted I go on, analyzing for the umpteenth time the peculiar way Wendy ended our last conversation; agonizing over the fact that she was still not returning my calls, or even responding to my emails.

I had contacted a friend out in San Diego to see what I could find out. But the retired firefighter told me he hadn't laid eyes on Wendy or her children in a long time. Out of desperation I'd phoned her family.

"Wendy," her sister reluctantly told me, "was abusing Vicoden. She checked herself into a substance-abuse clinic. Refused to participate in their group therapy. Signed herself out. But she's all right now."

I phoned her father next. "She's depressed," he told me. *Depressed? Wendy?*

During our six years together, I'd never known Wendy to be depressed. On the contrary. Wendy was always "steady". Mood swings of any kind were virtually undetectable. I tried to recall what I knew about depression: only that depression is no different than the "blues"---and everyone gets blue once in a while. Right?

"I tried to get her to a doctor," her father said. "Even her ex-husband Brad tried. But she won't go. A shrink put her on some sort of medication. She seems to be doing O.K."

I told her father that I was willing to fly out to San Diego if he thought I could help.

"You know Wendy," her father said. "She's fussy, private. She won't appreciate you just showing up."

And so I let it go. Figured that Wendy would work out her issues and contact me when she was good and ready, although I still couldn't stop myself from over-analyzing our last conversation, trying to figure out what, if anything, I'd said wrong.

I sipped the last of my Starbuck's coffee, eyes on the door, on the lookout for my sixth, or was it my seventh, match.com date, doing my best to get on with my life, get over the now missing-in-action Wendy. But I wasn't having much luck getting over Wendy, or with Internet dates.

My very first cyber date had become belligerent after only one glass of wine, told me, twenty minutes into our date, that I was a son of a bitch--controlling, selfish, self-absorbed. She was apparently still very angry at her ex-husband.

My second Internet date turned out to have Tourette's syndrome, or something frighteningly similar. The third date was actually trolling for men interested in threesomes with she and her husband---he was bi-curious. My fourth date turned out to be a transsexual. The fifth spent our date speaking to her therapist on her cell phone. The sixth arrived drunk, or stoned---I couldn't tell which.

Starbuck's front door opened. A leggy knockout in a business suit stepped in and began scanning the place. She looked in my direction, smiled at me, and headed my way.

She didn't look anything like her match.com dating profile photograph, but then again most of the women I'd met on the Internet didn't look anything like their photos.

202

"Johnny Stallone?"

"That's me." I rose, all smiles and self-effacing charm.

She extended her hand and I reached to shake it.

"I'm serving process." She handed me a civil court summons.

"Have a nice day." She smiled, turned around abruptly, and strode out the door. My eyes and heart followed in her wake---I was flabbergasted. I sat back down, opened the folded blue summons.

Stallone & Lenahan Investigations was being sued for five million dollars, along with Browdy World Syndicate and Donald Browdy personally, by Pamela Watt Winston. The grounds for the civil suit was "stalking." A violent felony in New York State.

"Johnny Stallone?" A rather plump, fiftyish-something woman, wearing a wrap-around red dress that was too tight and too short was standing at my table smiling down at me---had to be my Internet date. I looked her over: she'd lied about her age---she was at least ten years older, her weight----twenty-five pounds heavier---and she reeked of cigarettes. I'd made it crystal clear in my online profile that I hated smoking.

I wanted to tell her, "No, I'm not Stallone," get up and walk out the door. But she had a copy of my online photo in her hand, and I didn't want to hurt her feelings.

"Yes, I'm Johnny." I rose to greet her. "Would you like something to drink?"

She smiled. "I'd love a latte."

I pulled a chair out for her, then walked over to the ordering line.

"Two tall lattes," I told the cashier. I checked the time; I could spend no more then twenty minutes with red dress----I had to speak to Browdy's lawyer Farrelly ASAP.

My cell phone rang.

"Stallone."

"Farrelly here."

203

"Hoped I'd be hearing from you. I just got served with the papers. What's the story?"

"Like I predicted, Browdy arranged a chance meeting with Pamela. He told me it went very well, that they were dating."

"You believe him?" I said.

"Why wouldn't I? But then I get this lawsuit."

I paid the cashier for the lattes. Stepped over to the pickup area and waited.

"You think Browdy stalked her?" I said.

"Off the record, he's obsessed, capable of anything."

"Great. Where's that leave us?"

"You'll need to retain your own counsel in New York. Mr. Browdy will cover all your legal fees and punitive damages, if any. But you'll still be vulnerable."

"In what way?

"Even if Pamela's attorneys do not prevail, they could file a complaint with the New York Department of State, seek to have your PI license revoked."

"I hadn't thought of that."

"Unless -"

"Talk to me, Counselor."

"You prove that Pamela set Browdy up."

"Level with me," I said. "That a possibility?"

"Browdy keeps telling me not to worry, swears the broad's playing him."

"What's that mean?"

"According to Browdy, Pamela wants it all."

"We screwed," White Dove said.

"That's the old American Indian fighting spirit."

"Look, fuck face, our client is a skell. A convicted felon. I told you that before we started. We facilitated his stalking of Pamela and we're getting our asses sued off for doing so. Case closed."

White Dove and I entered a building which housed *Vogue* magazine---on time for a meeting with a CI: confidential informant. We crossed a vast, gleaming marble floor, signed in with a couple of rather goofy-looking lobby security guards, then headed to the elevators.

"Tell me about our informant," I said.

"Eve McCourt. She was an executive at Ann Taylor. She was also boffing Pamela's husband. If I understood Eve correctly---we'd been drinking martinis---Pamela caused a major scene, went to Human Resources. Eve was forced to resign."

"How'd you find her?" I said.

"She trains at the health club where Pamela's husband works."

I noticed that the security guards were eyeballing White Dove, drooling like adolescents.

"Why she helping us?" I said. "Why she wanna get involved?"

White Dove grinned. "She likes me."

We stepped into an empty mirror-paneled elevator, pressed the button marked Vogue.

I looked at my reflection in the mirror, adjusted my knit tie, brushed some lint from my navy blue blazer. "What if Pamela did set Browdy up?" I said. "Led him on. Entrapped him."

"I don't buy it." White Dove checked her makeup, fiddled with a turquoise thing-a-ma-gig that was bobby-pinned to her hair. "I think Pamela straightened herself out. I mean, she's got a steady job. A husband. Kids. Hell, she lives with her freakin' in-laws."

"Doesn't matter. Coke whores might kick the habit, but they don't change."

"What's that, a grease-ball's philosophy: once a whore, always a whore?"

"Something like that," I said.

We entered a reception area: a rich, sparse, couched space adorned with fashion magazine covers, and walked through thick carpet toward a twenty-something female receptionist. We told her who we were there to see, that we were expected.

She made a call, hung up. "Eve," she said, "will be with you shortly. "

Moments later an impossibly attractive woman, dressed in a designer business suit, raised on four-inch heels, entered the waiting area and greeted us. First impression: Pamela's cheating husband had exceptional taste. And White Dove was correct: Eve McCourt had the hots for her---big time.

Eve led us down a corridor into her office. She took a seat behind a large neat desk, we sat on two leather chairs opposite her.

"Thanks for seeing us," I said, checking out the spectacular city view.

"Anything for White Dove," Eve smiled.

White Dove smiled.

I smiled.

"You're here about Pamela," Eve said.

I nodded.

"What do you want to know?"

"Is she happily married?" I said. "For starters."

"Depends how you define happy." Eve sat back, crossed a pair of dazzling legs---for White Dove's benefit, not mine.

"She and Robert, her husband," Eve said, "enjoy what might be referred to as an open marriage."

"I understand that you had an affair with Robert," I said. "That Pamela found out and caused you problems at Ann Taylor."

"Heavens no. My affair with Pamela caused the problem."

Yikes.

"I was a vice-president," Eve said. "Supervised the fashion division." She sighed deeply. "Company policy forbids becoming romantically involved with a subordinate. It's grounds for dismissal."

"But you did," I said.

"What Pamela wants, Pamela gets." Eve sat forward, elbows on her desk. "We were an 'item' for six months," she said. "When I ended the relationship, she threatened me."

I sat a little straighter; this sounded promising. "Threatened you how?"

"She told me she'd go to Human Resources, tell them about our affair. Claim that I forced her, that I sexually harassed her."

"Did she?"

"I told her I'd deny her allegations." Eve looked down at her hands. "That I'd retain an attorney and fight her."

We waited for her to continue.

"Pamela said she'd forget all about Human Resources," Eve looked at me. "If I paid her ten thousand dollars."

"She blackmailed you?" White Dove said.

"She tried," Eve said.

"So, you didn't pay her?" I said.

"No," Eve said. "I resigned."

"I don't get it," I said. "You told her you'd fight her."

"Yeah, well." Eve laughed a little. "Pamela taped our telephone conversations."

I looked at White Dove.

"What're you implying?" White Dove said.

"The bitch recorded me for six months." Eve looked directly at White Dove. "What the hell do you think I'm implying?"

The bar at Bice's, Pamela's East Side hangout, was beige and wood with brass sconces and indirect lighting. The place was relatively empty when we arrived around four, but those in attendance looked to be high-brow Euro-trash, fast and fashionable.

White Dove attempted to show Pamela's photo to a heavy-set male bartender. But he ignored her, walked to the far-side service area and busied himself.

"What's his problem?" White Dove said.

"He hates dirty injuns?" I said. Just then my cell phone rang. I checked the caller ID: a San Diego area code. "I've gotta take this," I said. "Hello?"

"Hi, Johnny. It's Wendy calling."

Finally.

"Wendy."

White Dove rolled her eyes, shook her head, made a disgusted face.

"Where you been?" I said, attempting to sound appropriately concerned, maybe a bit offended, careful not to let on that I knew about her problems. "I've called you three times, wrote five or six emails."

"I know. I'm sorry." Wendy giggled. "I've been busy with the girls."

"Well, you certainly sound like you're in a good mood," I said.

White Dove poked me, mimed that I was crazy, that I should hang up the phone.

"I've been reading Mother Theresa," Wendy said from out of nowhere.

"The Nobel Peace Prize winner?"

"She taught me about forgiveness."

"Really. There're people you need to forgive?"

"I've forgiven you." Wendy laughed.

"Oh?" I didn't know how to respond to that. "That's nice to hear."

"I've been thinking," Wendy said. "I want to see you again, Johnny."

"Really." My heart soared. "When?"

"I don't know. Soon. I miss you, Johnny. Miss what we had."

I wanted to tell Wendy that I hadn't changed the way I felt about her, that I still loved her, but not in front of White Dove---I couldn't take the abuse. "Hold on."

"I'll be right back," I said to White Dove.

She glared at me. "You idiot!"

I left the restaurant, walked out onto bustling east 54th Street, found peace and quiet in the doorway of the office building next door.

"Why don't you come to visit?" I said to Wendy. "I'll buy you a ticket. Get your ex-husband---what's his face, Brad---to baby-sit. I'll pick you up at the airport, we'll paint the town, just like old times. We'll have dinner at the place we first met. Bruno's."

I heard Wendy sniffling.

"You all right?" I said.

"I'm just so happy," Wendy said. "I was cruel to you in the end."

"That's the past. Let's concentrate on the future."

"Right," Wendy said without enthusiasm. "The future."

"So, you'll visit?" I said.

"Will you come and get me?" Wendy said.

"What're you talking about?" I said.

"Come and get me?"

"You mean you want me to fly out to San Diego and meet you, then we both fly back?"

"Yes, please?"

Desperation had filled Wendy's voice---an emotional plea. I didn't understand why the sudden mood swing, why she'd ask me to do something so ridiculous.

"C'mon, Wendy. I'll buy your ticket. You get on a plane. I'll be standing at the gate when you arrive at JFK."

"All right," Wendy said, her voice barely audible.

"I love you," I said.

"I love you too," she said. "Remember that."

"Call me tomorrow?" I said.

"Tomorrow," Wendy said and hung up.

I put my cell phone away, stepped out of the office building, and had to stop myself from jumping for joy, literally. I paced up and down East 54th Street, awash in the almost surreal reality that Wendy and I would soon be together again. I walked back into Bice.

White Dove was waiting for me.

"Don't tell me---you're gonna see Wendy again?"

"She coming to the city on business," I lied, avoiding White Dove's probing eyes. "We'll probably hook up for a drink."

"You should have your head examined," White Dove said. "That bitch fucks you over again, I don't wanna hear about it. You understand me?"

Bice's bartender stepped down to our end of the bar. "Can I get you anything?"

"We'll have two beers," White Dove said.

The bartender reached into an ice-filled sink, extracted two bottles of beer, twisted them open, poured them into glasses and placed them in front of us.

White Dove stuck Pamela's photo in the guy's face. "Ever see her in here?"

The bartender heaved a resigned sigh, glanced at the picture. "Nope. Never saw her before."

"I don't believe you," White Dove said.

"Gee," the bartender sneered. "I'm crushed."

I was about to whip out my wallet, bribe the guy with a $100 bill---the great memory enhancer---when I realized he looked familiar. "Hey," I said, taking a seat at the bar directly in front of him. "I know you."

"Great," the bartender said. "Now you can die a happy man."

"You got locked up, what was it, eight, ten years ago?"

"Hey." The bartender stopped what he was doing. Lowered his voice. "You a cop, or something?"

I saw no reason to tell him I was retired. "What was the charge?" I thought a moment. "Rape, wasn't it?"

"Look, I didn't do it. The bitch framed me."

"Do tell," I said.

Again White Dove stuck Pamela's photo in the guy's face.

The bartender took a closer look. "She used to come in here all the time, after work."

"Alone?" White Dove said.

"Last few times she was with a guy, a boyfriend by the way they acted."

"What he look like?" I said.

"Big guy. Didn't handle his booze well. You know, a loud mouth."

White Dove showed him a photo of Browdy.

"Yeah, that's him."

"Any idea where they'd go from here?" I said.

"I heard him make reservations once, up at that celebrity hangout up on east 88th Street, Elaine's."

"Hey," Duffy, Elaine's bartender said. "Where you two been hiding?"

"Here and there," I said as we walked into the lovingly seedy little bar and sat on stools. It was just after six and the place had only just opened. A couple of waiters were scurrying around, setting up tables.

Duffy shook my hand, then leaned across the bar and grabbed White Dove, gave her a hug. "C'mere, gorgeous."

"Get off me, you crazy donkey," White Dove teased as she broke the embrace.

"You wanna table," Duffy said, "or you going to eat the bar?"

I looked around; the restaurant was virtually empty. "Give us a couple of beers for now." I held up Pamela and Browdy's photos. "Ever see these two in here, Duf?"

Duffy placed two cold ones in front of us, then glanced at the pictures.

"Sure, that's Donald Browdy. Browdy World Syndicate. A bad drunk. Been coming here for years." He pointed at Pamela's photo. "She's a piece of work."

"How so?" White Dove said.

Duffy lowered his voice and spoke confidentially. "Last time they were in, they practically fucked at the table. Acted like a couple of assholes. Elaine was here. Told them to stop, threatened to toss them out."

Me and White Dove exchanged a glance.

"When was that?" I said.

"Two," Duffy said, "maybe three weeks ago."

I excused myself, stepped outside onto Second Avenue, took out my cell phone, speed-dialed the lawyer Farrelly.

"Farrelly, it's Stallone," I said, shouting to be heard above passing fire engine sirens. "Look, I've got some information that might shoot holes in Pamela's lawsuit--"

"Forget it," Farrelly said.

"What I said?" Sticking a finger in my free ear. "Say again."

"Forget it," Farrelly repeated just as the sirens faded. "I just spoke to her attorney. They're dropping the lawsuit, dropping the matter entirely."

I was speechless. My face must've gone slack.

"What is it?" White Dove said, suddenly beside me.

I hushed her. "They give a reason?"

"You won't believe this." Farrelly croaked a laugh. "Pamela and Browdy got quickie divorces from their respective spouses, and married last night in Las Vegas."

"Holy shit," I said.

"Exactly---looks like you were wrong, Stallone."

"Wrong?" I said. "Wrong about what?"

"When it comes to lost loves, sometimes you can go back."

My phone rang about a week later at 2:35 p.m.

I picked up the portable, checked my caller ID: a San Diego area code. I was smiling broadly when I answered, fully expecting to hear Wendy's voice.

Wendy and I had spoken several time during the last few days. Although she kept vacillating over if and when to come east---since 9/11 she claimed fear of flying---she finally committed. I purchased the e-ticket. Made dinner reservations at Bruno's. Secured two tickets to a Broadway play. In preparation for her arrival at JFK, I'd procured a bottle of high-priced champagne---her favorite---for the limo ride back to the city.

"Hello," I said.

"Tom, it's Brad."

Brad---Wendy's forever broke ex-husband. He was sobbing, I could barely understand what he was telling me.

"Wendy killed herself," Brad wailed.

"What?"

"She killed herself!"

I stiffened, went into panic mode. "What the hell're you talking about?"

"She rented a room at the airport Holiday Inn. Jumped out a tenth-floor window---how could she do it? How could she do that to our girls? What am I gonna tell the girls?" Brad blubbered things I couldn't understand and hung up the phone.

I stood frozen, listened to the dial tone.

My first reaction was disbelief. It had to be a joke. A sick fucking joke.

But I knew it wasn't.

I dropped the phone on the floor. Flopped down on my couch.

Killed herself? Jumped from a ten-story window? How could she? How could she do that to me, leave me like that? How could she do that to her daughters---she loved them more than life itself.

213

I placed my face in my hands---my head pounded, I felt sick to my stomach---and for the next half hour replayed our recent phone conversations. What had I missed? Wendy and her father had mentioned depression. Could it have something to do with depression?

I pushed off the couch, walked into the bathroom, and threw cold water on my face. I looked at my reflection in the mirror; my face was contorted with grief. I toweled off and cursed Wendy for the unthinkable pain she'd caused me. Cursed her for tearing my world apart. Thought about the irony of it all, the fact I'd been right. When it came to *my* lost love, I could never go back.

Date With an Angel

The pretty, young American woman arrived at Kiev, a Russian bar in Brooklyn's Brighton Beach, around 4 p.m., the start of happy hour.

Crime czar Vladimir Iwanczuk---a thorny, volatile, pressure-cooker of a man---was at his usual corner barstool which afforded him a sweeping view of the packed establishment. He had barely taken a sip of his ninth vodka when he saw her. She had been coming to Kiev every day for the past three weeks, a demure, refined woman of about thirty with an air of quiet dignity about her. She would sit at a secluded table in the corner, order a drink, avoid contact with the other patrons.

As always, she sat at her table, ordered a glass of white wine.

Iwanczuk tossed back his vodka, ordered his tenth, and, although he was no ladies' man, decided he would try to talk to the American, get her phone number, and pray that she was interested in an alcoholic, "well-preserved" sixty-year-old. Only consideration was that he hated abandoning his favorite barstool even for a few minutes. Knew that once he did, his two newly-employed, soft-hearted henchmen, brothers Alex and Victor, would not be capable of keeping the booze-ravaged, chain-smoking, phlegm-hacking regulars away.

Iwanczuk finger-combed his thick gray hair and made a mental note to fire the two brothers as soon as possible. He gave up his barstool, smoothed down his black, kid-skin leather jacket and made his way through the crowd---mostly retired or unemployed, down-on-their-luck Russian immigrants there to take advantage of Iwanczuk's endless generosity.

He arrived at the American's table.

Iwanczuk took a seat across from her.

"A woman as attractive as you," Iwanczuk said awkwardly, "should never be alone." He had a resonant, deep voice, and thick Russian accent.

She sipped her wine. Her hair was tied up in a tight librarian bun and she was conservatively dressed in a tailored business suit and sensible shoes. All at once Iwanczuk realized that she reminded him of his dearly departed wife.

"Do you mind that I join you?" he said.

"As I understand it, you own the neighborhood."

"This is true."

"Therefore you sit where you please."

Iwanczuk laughed. "This is also true." He sipped his vodka. "What is your name?"

"Ahren Mordashov. I'm called Angel."

"I am Vladimir Iwanczuk."

Angel did not respond.

"You have Russian name," Iwanczuk said.

"My parents were from Ukraine."

"Da? Where are they now?"

"Deceased."

Iwanczuk glanced at the free-loading, phlegm-hacker who had taken his barstool. Glared at his two inept henchmen---the brothers avoided eye contact. He thought about the fact that he might have known a family of Mordashovs---enemies of the Soviet Union---when he had been a Lieutenant Colonel in the KGB.

"Do I frighten you, Angel?" Iwanczuk was unsteady in the chair. "You look frightened. It is my ugly face?"

Angel smiled. "Your face is not ugly, it has character." She took a cigarette from a pack, but had difficulty lighting it.

"Your hands, they tremble." Iwanczuk took her matches. Lit her cigarette. She drew in a lung full of smoke, eyes fixed on the table.

"You have trouble, Angel?"

"Yes," Angel said. "I have trouble."

"What is trouble?"

Angel toyed with her wine glass. "It's not important."

"Please. Tell me trouble."

Angel looked at Iwanczuk as if trying to figure out his motives. "There's this man," she said. "He threatened to kill me."

Iwanczuk slugged back his vodka. "Tell me more."

Angel took a thoughtful moment before she spoke. "He's the superintendent of my building."

"What he wants?"

"Money he wants."

Angel told him the superintendent had banged on her door one evening, drunk. Told her she owed him a fixture fee for the apartment, for the air-conditioner, lights, wiring.

"I was stunned. I told him he was mistaken. Those were not the terms of my lease. He pushed his way into my apartment. Demanded I pay him $2,500 within two weeks or he'd cut me. Then he pulled a knife."

She paused, squirmed in her seat. "Creates an interesting dilemma for someone like me," she said through a delicate frown that touched Iwanczuk's heart---not much touched the Russian mobster's heart.

"What do you mean, like you?"

"I'm a hemophiliac," Angel said.

Iwanczuk turned the word over in his mind. "Ah, you are bleeder?"

"Yes, I'm a bleeder; rare for a female."

"My father was bleeder," Iwanczuk said. "As was his father before him."

"Hemophilia is hereditary."

"Da. But I am not bleeder."

"Your children could be."

"I have no children." Iwanczuk's finished his vodka. "When was last time man come?"

"Yesterday." She said that the superintendent had surprised her in the building's basement laundry room. Grabbed her and shoved her between two dryers. Pinned her against a wall. Pressed his knife to her throat.

"I was terrified. I told him the slightest wound to a hemophiliac was potentially fatal---he laughed at me."

Her voice cracked. She fought back tears.

"Is okay to cry." Iwanczuk used his calloused hand to pat her arm. "You are among friends."

Angel said she was convinced the super would cut her if she didn't pay him the money. That meant he could kill her.

"Talk to police? Landlord?"

She said the landlord lived in Vermont somewhere. The police talked to the super once. He denied everything, of course. Said they were lovers---which they were not, nor had they ever been. They said it was a domestic problem, her word against his. There was nothing they could do. That if she felt that threatened, she should move.

"If I don't have the money by tomorrow -."

Iwanczuk's eyes became slits. "What is superintendent's name?"

"Chuck Norris."

"Like karate movie actor?"

Angel nodded.

"Don't worry." Iwanczuk made a face that, in his world, passed for a smile. "I take care of trouble."

Later that evening, Iwanczuk, along with the brothers Alex and Victor, walked the ten blocks to Angel Mordashov's building. The superintendent who had threatened her was about to die.

Iwanczuk told his men to wait outside the entrance to the building. Alex and Victor took hunched positions by the curb, lit cigarettes and watched their boss walk up the

218

crumbling concrete steps and into the building---it was as they had been told. Iwanczuk conducted much of his business alone. No witnesses.

The Russian crime boss entered the building foyer, scanned the building directory, rang the superintendent's bell.

As a former KGB enforcer, Iwanczuk was accustomed to dealing with the criminal element. And not the way the feely-touchy American police did. In the Soviet Union you did not have the right to remain silent, you did not have the right to an attorney. In the Soviet Union you had two choices: cooperate with the KGB, or die.

And Iwanczuk had been involved in the deaths of countless men and women during his thirty-year career. Keeping an "enemy of the state" in the twilight between life and death by various means of physical torture, mind-altering drugs, and dismemberment, was not an exact science. And interrogation "incentives" did not always have the desired effects: innocent suspects sometimes died.

It was the blunders: the deaths of the guiltless shopkeepers, farmers, students and intellectuals, that haunted Iwanczuk---the horror in their faces, the screams for mercy, or pleas for a quick death. The stark reality that he would one day have to pay for his crimes against humanity in this life, or if there was a God, in the next, that kept Iwanczuk awake at night. Which was why he drank to staggering excess.

And why he'd become a benefactor to his countrymen.

True, Iwanczuk was a violent criminal who dealt in drugs, prostitution, money laundering, and contract murder. But when a law-abiding Russian came to him for assistance---a job, a loan to start a business, protection from thugs---Iwanczuk came to their aid. Although the mere mention of his name struck fear in the hearts of his enemies, he was both revered and loved by the average neighborhood immigrant.

To his surprise, Iwanczuk was buzzed through the flimsy security door. A tattered sign on a grimy wall informed him that the superintendent's apartment was in the basement.

The basement smelled of coal-oil and was lit by a single bare light bulb. Iwanczuk negotiated around old stoves, sinks, and other basement rubbish, and approached a door that had a red sign nailed to it: "SUPERINTENDENT". He noted the door was one of those wood-framed types, similar to the ones he'd kicked down a hundred times during his term in the KGB. Iwanczuk knocked. Inside he heard someone curse and a chair scrape across a bare wood floor. Two locks and a bolt later, a grizzly bear of a middle-aged man pulled the door open and stepped out into the basement.

"You are Chuck Norris?" Iwanczuk said.

"Da," Norris said.

Iwanczuk knew instantly that something was off; this was a Soviet using an alias---he must be a fugitive from the American police. Iwanczuk studied the man's Slavic face. He had never seen him before.

Norris spoke in Russian. "What is it you want?"

"I come on behalf of Ahren Mordashov," Iwanczuk said.

The punch caught Iwanczuk off guard. It knocked him off his feet and sent him crashing through a basement door into a garbage-strewn courtyard. As Iwanczuk struggled to free himself from a heap of over-stuffed plastic trash bags, Norris charged, moving in to finish him. But Iwanczuk struck unexpectedly with an uppercut to the groin. Norris screamed and collapsed hard to his knees. Iwanczuk freed himself from the plastic, whipped out an assassin's knife, yanked back Norris' head, and held the gleaming blade to his throat.

"That's enough," someone said in Russian.

Iwanczuk look toward the voice.

Angel Mordashov was pointing a gun at him.

Iwanczuk smelled coal-oil, heard distant voices.

He tried to wake but had difficulty. He felt pain. The deep throbbing ran from his neck to the top of his head. Now he remembered; someone had struck him from behind.

"He's coming around," a voice said.

Iwanczuk forced his eyes open. He was indoors, in Angel's building basement, seated on a heavy, iron chair. He tried to move, but his hands and legs were secured to the chair with duck tape. He saw blurred silhouettes, then two faces came into focus.

"Victor. Alex." Iwanczuk's two henchmen where standing there, staring at him. "What is meaning of this?"

The brothers did not respond.

Angel stepped into view.

Iwanczuk looked at her. "What is meaning, Angel?"

"I am the daughter of Anna and Doctor Aleksei Mordashov."

Iwanczuk's blood turned cold; now he remembered. He had indeed known a family of Mordashovs.

Alex spoke up. "We are sons of lawyer Vanik Grobowski."

"My brother was David Vnukovo," Chuck Norris said.

Angel walked over to Iwanczuk, stood by his side. "We were frightened children when your storm troopers came to our homes in the middle of the night."

"Beat our parents," Alex said. "Took them away."

"You tortured and killed innocent people," Norris said.

"Tonight you will stand trial for their murders," Victor said.

"Then you will die," Angel said.

Angel, Norris, Alex and Victor took seats behind a makeshift table---an old, chipped closet door laid atop two carpenter's horses.

Iwanczuk, seated in the center of the room in front of his captors, scanned the basement in search of an escape route. There was sunlight in the distance off to his left, the exit to the rear courtyard. He recalled that the stairwell he'd come down was behind him, around a corner. Iwanczuk struggled to test the integrity of his bonds. The duct tape was securely fastened. There would be no escape.

"Do you remember my parents?" Angel began.

"Da," Iwanczuk said solemnly. "I remember." His mind sunk back to the night he forced Angel's mother to submit to him, promising to spare her husband's life---a life he had already extinguished.

Norris stood. Opened a book, and began to read a long, mind-numbing roll call of Soviet citizens killed while in KGB custody during Iwanczuk's tenure. Norris read the list, paused after each name, and glared accusingly at the prisoner.

Next Angel took the floor, opened a folder, took out a piece of paper, and recited a list of formal charges that this "tribunal of the dead"---as she called it---was bringing against Iwanczuk.

"Murder," Angel said. "Rape. Torture. Conspiracy to commit murder. Gross violations of civil rights. Gross violations of human rights. Crimes against humanity." Angel folded the list of charges, placed them back in the folder. "How do you plead to the charges, Lieutenant Colonel Iwanczuk?"

Iwanczuk searched the faces of his captors.

He'd always known there was a chance this day might come. And he'd lain awake nights dreading it, imagining the different ways his life would come to an end: a shot to the heart, disembowelment, electrocution.

He was under no illusions, knew that no matter the outcome of this inquisition, more than any other human being on earth, he deserved to be punished. For he had been a government-trained and sponsored serial killer. A monster.

Iwanczuk thought about how to respond to the charges against him. He could deny that he was the same Iwanczuk who had been assigned to the KGB. After all, neither Angel nor Norris had seen him before. He could claim they simply had the wrong man. That could buy him valuable time. Or he could deny ever having been directly involved in the deaths. Claim that he himself was a victim: an uninformed, high-level bureaucrat who was as afraid as anyone else of questioning the supreme authority of the KGB. To do so would have meant death.

But as Iwanczuk's gaze settled on Angel's face---the face that reminded him of his deceased wife---he decided to do none of those things. For he was bone-tired from years of nightmares, worn out from drinking away his fears of reprisal, weary of living.

And he wanted to be with his beloved wife once again.

"I plead guilty," Iwanczuk said.

Norris jumped to his feet. "No denials? Excuses? Pleas for mercy?"

"Nyet." Iwanczuk shook his head. "I am guilty."

The captors exchanged astonished looks.

"It is trick," Victor said.

"It is no trick," Iwanczuk said.

Norris looked at the prisoner suspiciously. He reached under the table, took out a black bag, opened it.

"What is that?" Angel said.

Norris held a gardener's root cutter in his hand. He unhooked the safety, demonstrated the slicing action. "I start with his fingers."

"Nyet." Alex slammed his hand on the table. "His testicles. Start with his testicles."

"Da," Victor said.

"No," Angel said.

"What, nyet?" Norris said. "You want I cut his penis off?"

The brothers laughed.

Angel's eyes were wide. She spoke slowly, calmly. "The plan was to try him, convict him, then kill him."

"That was your plan," Norris said. He removed several more sharp instruments from the bag, laid them out on the table, arranged them in an order that apparently meant something to him.

Angel turned to Victor and Alex. "We can't allow this to happen."

"If you have no stomach for what must be done," Victor said to Angel. "Leave." He puffed his cigarette until the end was aglow. Then he walked over to Iwanczuk and forced the lit end into his ear, held it there.

Iwanczuk screamed.

"It is not a place for woman." Alex grabbed Angel by the arm, shoved her. "Get out. Now."

Victor dropped his cigarette, spun his brother around. "Don't you touch her. She is bleeder."

Alex shoved Victor. Victor shoved back.

"Stop," Angel screamed. She pulled her gun from her pocketbook and pointed it at both men. Motioned for them to get back behind the makeshift table.

"What is this?" Norris said. "You point gun at us?"

"You're not making us sadists like Iwanczuk," Angel said. "I won't allow it."

"You cannot stop us." Norris came around the table. Took a position between her and Iwanczuk. "So, you going to shoot us to defend *him*? The man who raped your mother, tortured and murdered your father?" Norris turned suddenly and struck Iwanczuk with a neck-cracking backhand.

Angel took a step back and fired at Norris' feet.

Norris leapt back.

Alex and Victor shrank away from her.

224

"Are you crazy?" Victor said.

"What are you doing?" asked Alex.

"What I came to do," Angel said. She turned her attention to Iwanczuk. "You have pled guilty to the charges against you."

"Da," Iwanczuk said. "I am guilty of it all."

"Your sentence is death," Angel said. "Do you have any last words?"

Iwanczuk took a moment. "Nyet."

"Shoot him," Victor said.

"Kill him," Alex said.

Angel hesitated. "You are not sorry for what you have done?"

Iwanczuk looked at her, knew he could not tell her the truth---that he was truly sorry for the pain and suffering he'd caused others. That if he had his life to live over again, he would have taken his wife and escaped from Russia, scaled the Berlin Wall, defected to the West, had a dozen fat children, opened a business, chased the American dream. But confessing now would only prolong his time on this earth, and therefore his agony.

Iwanczuk spit at Angel. "I apologize for nothing."

"What're you waiting for?" Alex said. "Shoot."

"She cannot shoot him," Norris said.

"Why?" Victor said.

"She knows truth."

"What truth?" Alex said. "What is truth?"

"Lieutenant Colonel Iwanczuk," Norris said, "is her father."

A collective hush.

Iwanczuk reared. He looked at Angel, realized that it was not his wife she reminded him of, but his mother---yes, he could see family resemblances; the proud face, big brown eyes.

"You are not child of love," Norris said bitterly. "You are a child of rape" He pointed a finger at the prisoner. "He is responsible."

Angel took a deep breath, trained her eyes on the man who had raped her mother, murdered her father. She placed the pistol to his temple, cocked the hammer.

"Nyet," Iwanczuk said.

Everyone looked at the prisoner.

Angel lowered the weapon. "You have last words?"

"Is not right for girl to kill father." Iwanczuk motioned to Norris. "You do it."

Norris regarded the former KGB enforcer. "He is right." Norris walked over to Angel. Reached for her gun.

And Angel handed it over to him.

"Go now," Iwanczuk said.

Angel took one last look at Iwanczuk, broke down, then hurried away. She climbed the basement stairs, ran through the building hallway, out the front door, down the concrete stairs.

There was a single gunshot.

DEAD EYE

by

R. Emmett Fitzsimmons
with
Thomas Fitzsimmons

"Show me a hero and I'll write you a tragedy."
F. Scott Fitzgerald

I hate guns. Always have. As a New York City cop, born to a family of cops, I know firsthand the pain and suffering guns can cause even in the "right" hands. Far as I'm concerned, the world would be a better place if we'd never even heard of Berretta, Browning, Colt, Glock, Smith & Wesson, Winchester.

Yet when I sensed someone rush up behind me on that nippy February morning, my survival instincts kicked in and I placed my hand on the cold steel grip of my S & W .38 special, ready to defend myself from ambush---it happens. Like most New York cops, I've never forgotten police officers Joseph Piagentini, Waverly Jones, Rocco Laurie and Gregory Foster, assassinated in two separate ambushes by members of the Black Liberation Army, way back in the 70s.

At the time I was standing on Williamsbridge Road, police call box phone in hand, receiving instructions from the 43 precinct desk lieutenant about where to pick up and drop off assorted reports. I glanced over my shoulder to see who was coming up behind me, and a woman wearing a dark blue work smock and light blue slacks stepped into view. She was short, thin, around 40-

years old with dyed black hair. Something about her heavy makeup and even facial features told me that she'd been a "looker" in her youth.

I relaxed my gun hand.

I hung up the phone, shivered from a sudden gust of stabbing winter wind, and turned to the woman fully prepared to hear yet another sob story about an inconsiderate neighbor, abusive husband, or complaint about an undeserved parking ticket.

"What can I do for you?"

I noticed that the woman's eyes were Frisbee wide, pupils dilated. She was obviously on drugs or suffering from some sort of shock. I checked her hands for weapons. She held no knife or gun.

"Three black guys just held up the supermarket," she said rapid fire.

"What supermarket?"

"Grand Union---they had guns."

I looked; Grand Union was diagonally across the street. "When?"

"A few minutes ago."

"Anyone hurt there?"

"No." Her eyes darted off to one side. "They went that way in a car." She pointed north on Williamsbridge Road with a trembling hand.

"What kind of car?"

"A dark car. Tan, I think."

"A Ford, Chevy, what?"

"I don't know."

As my eyes swept the area, I speculated that there could be more then one car and more than three perps. These days armed backups were common with stickup teams.

I opened the rear door of our police car. "Get in."

"What for?" she said, apprehensively.

"If we catch up, we need you to identify them."

228

Reluctantly the lady stepped into the back of the RMP. I slid onto the front passenger seat, filled my partner of the day (my regular partner was on another assignment), Kevin Moynihan, in on what was going on, and grabbed the radio.

"43 Peter to central, k."

"Go ahead, Peter."

"10-30, robbery at the Grand Union Supermarket, 1810 Williamsbridge Road. Less than five minutes old. We're looking for three armed male blacks, driving a dark, possibly tan car. No make or model. Last seen driving north on Williamsbridge Road. We have a female witness in the car."

"10-4," central said and then repeated our broadcast to all units city wide.

I opened my memo book, took out a pen, turned around and looked at the woman. Even though it was dead of winter, she was sweating profusely. She smelled faintly of perfume and cigarettes.

"What happened?" I said.

"Two of them walked in, went over to Anna's office."

"Anna?" I said, scribbling notes.

"Anna Herman, the bookkeeper." The woman looked off, remembering. "They told Anna to give her the money. She did and they ran out of the store."

"Then what?"

"I saw them getting into the car. There was another guy driving."

"Anything else you can remember?"

The woman thought a moment. "One of them had a shotgun."

Moynihan and I exchanged a glance; we were armed with .38s, six-shooters. Did we really want to take on three, or more, gunmen armed with at least one shotgun? I didn't.

And not just because we were outgunned.

I became a cop for all the right reasons: to put the bad guys behind bars, to save lives, make a difference in the world. My first few years I was one of the most "active" members of the 43 precinct; I made numerous felony arrests. Lost count of the number of cars I stopped in search of fugitives, weapons, or drugs. I stopped, frisked and harassed every punk in my sector at every opportunity, kicked ass whenever necessary. I showed up for work early, stayed late.

But after realizing that the criminal justice system is set up to glorify the rights of the accused, thereby rendering a cop's job, in many instances, all but futile, not to mention frustrating and demoralizing, I reevaluated my priorities.

As a result I no longer went looking for trouble. I did my job to the best of my ability, took what came, but never went out of my way to break balls---just the opposite. I worked hard at making friends. In lieu of arrests, I preferred to chase hookers, bookmakers, squeegee men, unlicensed peddlers, and floating crap or card games out of my sector. I rarely issued parking tickets. And, based on the disheartening fate of some of my fellow police officers, I was most cautious when dealing with the general public. Because even a reasonable error, questionable decision, or misspoken observation uttered under the most extreme circumstances could place a cop's future in jeopardy. If a citizen claimed that an innocent offhand comment I made offended them, for instance, and that person filed a complaint against me, the police department could very well penalize me if that decision was politically expedient. And then the citizen could sue me into the after life.

Moynihan pointed the car north on Williamsbridge Road and hit the gas. We would drive a short distance, estimate how far the perps could have gone in the time since the robbery, than make lefts and rights in an effort to sweep the area. I pulled my weapon, checked that it was loaded, thought about the fact that I'd never fired at a person before. I had serious doubts that I was even capable. I could never rationalize the taking a human life, of dealing with the physiological aftermath---there were always non-lethal alternatives.

I vividly remember the time I responded to a family dispute and was attacked by a schizophrenic parolee who was high on crystal meth. When I walked into that sweltering ghetto apartment, I discovered a young woman clutching an infant, cowering behind a torn couch, and the parolee stalking them---he held a butcher knife in his right hand.

"Police," I shouted, and ordered the physco to drop the knife. It was as if I'd startled him from a sordid dream. He looked at me and sort of blushed, embarrassed that I'd caught him. And then he charged me, knife slashing the air. Now, I had every legal right to shoot that crazy son-of-a-bitch, but the thought never occurred to me. Instead I sidestepped and punched his lights out.

In any case I wasn't worried that Moynihan and me would be tested that February morning. Common sense told me that the Grand Union robbers were long gone.

"Traffic's heavy," Moynihan commented. He slowed at each intersection so we could check the cross streets for the tan car. He looked left, I looked right.

Three blocks later the witness shrieked, "There they are." She was pointing straight ahead.

Sure enough, at the southeast corner of Williamsbridge Road and Pelham Parkway I saw a tan 1973 Plymouth that was attempting to negotiate around a clot of cars stopped at a red light.

"You sure that's them?" I said.

"That's them," the woman said. "I'm sure."

"What do you think?" Moynihan said.

I reached for the radio. "43 Peter to central, K."

The radio traffic was unusually heavy. Central did not respond..

"Central, 43 Peter is in pursuit of three armed male suspects, request immediate backup."

No response. The air waves were clogged.

"That light changes, they'll bolt," I said, feeling a sudden rush of adrenaline. I replaced the radio. "Let's take these mutts."

Moynihan tapped the gas, eased the RMP forward.

We stopped directly behind the tan car.

"Stay put," I told the witness.

Guns drawn, eyes alert for the robbers backup team, we stepped out of the RMP and approached the tan car from the rear. Moynihan was on the left driver's side, I was on the right. If all went well, we'd surprise the robbers, disarm them, have them out of the car and in handcuffs within seconds. We moved closer.

Although all of the car's windows were up, I clearly saw two men sitting in the front, one in the back.

"Out of the car!" I shouted at the passengers.

"Lemme see your hands!" Moynihan told the driver.

The robbers were talking to each other, probably arguing their next move.

Moynihan yanked the driver's door open. "Hands on the steering wheel!"

The driver did as ordered, placed his hands atop the steering wheel, in plain sight.

"Out of the fucking car, now!" I said and pulled the passenger door open.

Inside, a dark skinned, owl-eyed man pointed a .32 caliber handgun at my face---I knew I was a dead man. I held my breath, braced for the impact, thought about the fact that I was about to become the first cop killed in the line of duty that year. And then I thought about my mother---what was about to happen would break her heart.

The owl-eyed man fired his weapon.

#   #   #   #

A brilliant winter sun woke me early that morning. I fought my way through layers of sleep, rolled over, and realized that my wife had left early for her job as an office temp at Reader's Digest.

I forced one eye open, glanced at the nightstand clock, groaned, buried my face in a pillow dreading the thought of having to get up and work the 8 a.m. to 4 p.m. tour. The idea of leaving my idyllic Croton on the Hudson home with its pine-scented air and panoramic river views, driving down to the ghetto, donning the uniform, and breathing in the all-too-familiar stench of rotting garbage, made me want stay in bed forever.

And then there were the junkies, gang members, thugs, perverts, skells and low lives of every conceivable description that I'd have to deal with for the next eight hours.

I tossed the pillow aside, rocked from bed, dragged my shivering carcass across the cold parquet floor into the bathroom, turned the shower on and let it run to hot. I stepped to the mirror and considered my reflection. At six foot two, one hundred eighty pounds, I was in good shape, although the pressure of working in the South Bronx had slashed premature age lines in my face.

I stepped into the steaming hot shower, felt a stabbing pain in my lower back, and considered calling in sick---I couldn't get away with it. Even though the back pain was caused by a prior on-the-job injury, I was already on the department's chronic sick list; a negative if I ever hoped to be assigned to the detective division or achieve promotion.

I finished showering, shaved, dressed in warm clothes, stuck my off-duty, snub-nose .38 in my waistband and thought, once again, about how I'd make a living if I quite the NYPD. I had no idea.

I wrote a household expense check to my wife and left it on the kitchen counter---the irony of that familiar weekly routine underscored the tragic fact that, although we still loved each other, our marriage was in trouble.

We'd gotten married five years ago in a classic "hot-pants" haze. For the first few years we couldn't keep our hands off of one another. But when the physical attraction wore off, I realized that our relationship had evolved. My wife had become uncharacteristically introspective.

"I don't think I can take being married to a cop anymore," she told me one day. "I lay awake nights, not knowing if I'll ever see you again, alive."

And then the cultural differences between us became a major problem. I'm of Irish decent while she was born in Puerto Rico. Added to that was her growing religious fanaticism. The killer though was her shoplifting mania---a major embarrassment for a police officer. She'd been arrested for filching woman's clothing yet again only last week.

I slipped on a coat, grabbed my keys, headed to my trusty VW. As always, even in the dead of winter, the engine kicked right over. I palmed the stick shift, put the car in first gear, pulled from my parking spot, and told myself to relax and enjoy the 40-minute drive to the city. But a half-hour later, as I came off the Sprain Brook Parkway and merged onto the Bronx River Parkway, the flavor of the air changed. The sent of pine was utterly gone---the ghetto loomed ahead. The process of descending into its bowels triggered the usual taste of adrenalin that teased my nervous system and put tension in my back. I hunched against the steering wheel. My eyes became more vigilant.

Roll call that morning was as usual: organized bedlam. Between cat calls, fart noises, and airborne rubber bands, Sergeant Kennedy, a gray-haired, thirty-year veteran, called the fifty-man roll. Then he read several special orders which listed drug, and other high-incident locations, that were to receive "special attention" during that tour. He finished up by ordering my regular partner, Richard Passerino, to drive our RMP to the police garage for regularly scheduled maintenance. He assigned Kevin Moynihan, a Lou Costello (of Abbot and Costello fame) look-a-like, as my temporary partner.

"Fitzsimmons, Moynihan. Gonna give you two Micks a break today," Sergeant Kennedy said. "Take RMP 1221.You're working sector Peter." His crooked smile revealed small pointy teeth. "That means you owe me a beer."

"A" beer?---hell, I'd have bought him a whole case.

My normal sector, Eddy, was a teeming, explosive slum. Whereas sector Peter, on the opposite side of the 43, was a close-knit, predominantly Italian family neighborhood. And so I looked forward to a pleasant, uneventful day.

As Moynihan and I exited the station house, keys to our assigned RMP in hand, he talked hungrily about all the great Italian restaurants in sector Peter, and promised that lunch would be a gastronomical event. "I know a place," he grinned and patted his well-upholstered stomach.

Although we'd worked in the same precinct for years, Moynihan and I had never hung out. My take on him was that he was a loner who loved food and the racetrack. I was a social creature; a physical fitness enthusiast, I watched what I ate and hit the gym three

235

days a week. Bottom line: I didn't really know Moynihan. And he didn't know me.

Moynihan wanted to drive for the first four hours and I had no objection.

We drove to a local dinner and picked up a bacon and egg sandwich for him and dry toast for me; two coffees, a New York Times and a Daily News. We parked on a quiet, residential, tree-lined street, made small talk, ate and read. Afterwards, we visited a couple of the special attention locations that sergeant Kennedy had told us about; no drug dealers were out in the cold. All in all it was as I'd expected; a clear, quiet, winter morning.

An hour later, just as Moynihan had whittled our lunch choices down to three eateries---northern Italian, southern Italian and an Italian deli, we received a 10-1 (call the station house) transmission on the radio.

Moynihan steered the RMP to the nearest police call box on Williamsbridge Road, across the street from the Grand Union Supermarket. I bundled up, stepped out of the car, picked up the police call box phone, and called the station house.

#   #   #   #

I saw the muzzle flash. Heard the gunshot. Felt pressure in my right ear. Miraculously, the owl-eyed man missed.

What happened next happened quickly.

I stepped to the left and, shooting from the hip, fired four times. My first round tore into the gunman's neck.

I saw his left eye blown out of his head.

I heard Moynihan rapid-firing.

I saw the driver recoil in pain---he was hit.

"Shotgun coming at you!" Moynihan said.

Seeing the guy in the backseat swing a shotgun in my direction, I lunged from his line of fire, toward the back

236

of the car, and pumped two rounds into the rear window. Glass shattered. I took careful aim. Clicked on empty---I was out of ammo. I pulled my backup-gun, a DS22 Derringer Standard, aimed it at the perp and pulled the trigger. Misfire.

I tried again. Another misfire.

Shit.

The perp pointed the shotgun at me.

I saw Moynihan aim at the guy. Pull the trigger; click. Empty. I had no idea if he carried a backup gun.

I was on my own.

"Drop it, or you're a dead man!" I shouted, having no other choice but to bluff.

The perp froze. I could see his thoughts move across his face.

"You wanna die, asshole?" I said, pointing my useless derringer.

He rose the shotgun to his shoulder.

Aimed at my chest.

And for the second time in fifteen seconds I prepared to die.

"Drop it, now!" I screamed in utter desperation.

The perp hesitated, then lowered the shotgun.

I rushed him. Opened the car door. Grabbed the shotgun. Pulled the perp from the back seat by his hair. Flung him on the street like a bag of garbage.

Moynihan ordered the driver out of the car---he was leg shot---and shoved him to the ground alongside his accomplice.

Then I pulled the guy I'd shot from the front seat and threw him to the street. The stench of spent gunpowder was thick in the air.

Just then a heavy featured, local gangster I recognized from police mug shots appeared next to me, grinning ear to ear.

"Nice work," he said, then opened his coat to reveal a 9mm Beretta. "Wanna finish them mooks off with this?"

"Get the fuck outta here," I said.

"I'm gone," the gangster said and retreated into a store front.

I hurried to the RMP and grabbed the radio. "Central, this is 43 Peter. 10-13 Williamsbridge and Pelham Parkway. Shots fired. I need a bus forthwith. We have two perps wounded and three under arrest."

"3 Peter, any officer injury, K"?

"Negative, central."

Suddenly the hushed February morning filled with approaching sirens. Police cars, dome lights throbbing, came skidding onto the scene. The first to arrive blocked off the southeast side of Williamsbridge Road and Pelham Parkway: the crime scene. Others fought to control a growing horde of curious onlookers. Blue uniforms were everywhere.

That was when I noticed that the guy I'd shot had turned over onto his back and was choking on his own blood. As I rushed to roll him onto his side so he could breathe, a voice coming from the crowd of onlookers said, "Let the fuckin' nigger die."

Moynihan collected the prisoner's weapons and the bag containing the proceeds of the robbery, while I searched the prisoners---they carried no ID.

"You all right?" a distinguished-looking, Bronx borough homicide detective asked us. We assured him that we were fine. He suggested Moynihan and I head back to the station house, get a head start on the tons of paperwork that awaited us.

He said, "I'll take care of things here."

We sat in mostly reflective silence for the six minutes it took for us to drive back to the 43 precinct. I was trying to come to terms with my emotions: I had fired my weapon, critically wounded a man, and I expected to feel remorse, regret, maybe even guilt---I didn't. What I felt was pure anger, rage that the robbers had tried to kill us---fuck them.

"We ain't gonna get a chance to eat," Moynihan said, "once we're at the station house, what with all the interviews, paperwork."

I looked at him.

"Wanna pick up some ravioli with sausage and meatballs on the way?" He patted his stomach. "I know a place . . .."

The desk lieutenant was the first person to see us enter the station house, bag of aromatic Italian food in hand. He stood, applauded, and was joined by the TS operator, the 124 man, and about 30 cops who were in the sitting room, attending a training seminar of some sort. Cops I did not know started shaking our hands, slapping us on the back, telling us "good work." "You guys are heroes."

I didn't feel like a hero.

For the next six hours Moynihan and I were taken into separate rooms and questioned by various superior officers and investigators. I told the same story at least 20 times. A dozen eyewitness were questioned. The woman who'd alerted us to the robbery and witnessed the exchange of gunfire, Marie Sullo, backed our version of the incident 100%. As did two other witnesses, one of whom was the gangster.

Because of the size of the collar, five officers were assigned to help us process our prisoners and voucher the recovered Grand Union cash.

Afterward, Sergeant Kennedy took me to the side. He told me that he always knew I had guts, that he was proud of me, that I was his kind of cop. "I could see it in your eyes first time I met you." And then he said, "You all right, Fitzsimmons?" There was concern on his face. "I mean, really."

"I'm fine. Why?"

"Moynihan's a nervous wreck, getting worse by the minute. Shock's wearing off. He can't even eat---if you can believe that."

"Yeah," I said. "So?"

"You're acting like nothing happened---you were just in a shootout, for Christ's sake. Ain't nothing wrong with showing a little emotion; it's only human."

I shrugged. "I don't know what to tell you, Sarge."

A detective called Sergeant Kennedy over and whispered something in his ear. They both turned and looked appraisingly at me---my stomach sank. I knew something was wrong.

But what?

My mind raced. Could someone be making allegations that we opened fire on the suspects, execution style, without giving them a chance to surrender?

Sergeant Kennedy walked back over to me. "There's money's missing," he said.

I never saw that coming---the prisoners had robbed the Grand Union, and we caught them minutes later. How could money be missing? I stood there in stunned silence gaping at the sergeant.

"You guys recovered $1200. The store manager claims more was taken." Kennedy eyeballed me and let the information sink in. "You got something to tell me, Fitzsimmons?"

I shook my head, incredulous. "Whatever's in the bag is what we recovered."

The sergeant took a long moment before he sighed. "Have it your way."

He handed me a grand jury notice.

"Be at the grand jury tomorrow morning at 10."

Just then a man carrying a shoulder mounted video camera stepped in front of me. He switched on a bright light, and Gabe Pressman, a TV news reporter, stuck a microphone in my face.

I parked my VW, walked through light snow, and entered my apartment around 7:30 that evening. The phone was ringing as I walked in; it was my oldest sister, Maureen. She said my interview with Gabe Pressman was all over the TV news.

"You came off great," she said. "Very calm, professional. You OK?"

I assured her I was.

My two other sisters, Patricia and Carol, called in quick succession to check up on me. My identical twin brother, Tom, a cop in the 41st precinct "Fort Apache," phoned next.

"How's it hanging, Dead Eye?" Tom told me that, since one of my rounds had blown one of the perps eyes out, the cops were all calling me Dead Eye.

I didn't like the nickname one bit.

Tom and I went over the shooting in detail. He asked why I hadn't called for backup, the smart thing to do. I told him that I tried and couldn't get through. Then everything happened so quickly.

We talked about the missing money, and speculated as to who might have taken it. I recalled that, while Moynihan and I were dealing with the prisoners, the Plymouth's four doors were wide open.

"The cash was in a bag on the backseat," I said.

"Could someone have gotten to the bag of money without you guys seeing?"

I had to admit, it was possible.

My parents phoned last. My mother wept, happy I was alive.

My father, a hardened, retired 34-year NYPD veteran, didn't say much.

He never said much.

My wife came home about an hour later, carrying a bag of groceries.

"Hey, honey," she said.

I was sitting at the kitchen counter, staring into a glass of beer.

"What's wrong?" She placed the groceries on the counter.

I told her about the robbery and shootout.

"Holy Mary Mother of God." She put her arms around me, told me how much she loved me, said that she would always love me, and cried. We held each other for what seemed like a very long time.

Later, in bed, I couldn't stop thinking about that fact that Moynihan and I could very well become scapegoats for the thief who'd stolen the money. By seizing the initiative we had placed our futures in jeopardy. If the department could not account for the stolen cash, they could very well accuse us of grand larceny. Worst-case scenario: we could lose our jobs, go to jail.

I lay there with my sleeping wife's head resting on my chest, staring at the ceiling, listening to foghorns emanating from ships along the Hudson River.

A grand jury is comprised of 12 to 23 persons convened in private session to evaluate accusations against persons charged with crime and to determine whether the evidence warrants a bill of indictment.

Our Bronx grand jury appearance went as expected. An assistant district attorney led Moynihan and I into the grand jury room, one at a time, and asked us a series of leading questions. I'd appeared before a grand jury before, a humdrum experience where I'd actually witnessed jurors nodding off during my testimony.

That didn't happen this time. Every juror was awake, alert, and attentive. Within ten minutes, they handed down a "true bill." All three robbers, Robert Moody, John Taylor, and Gregory "Sonny" McFarland, were indicted for attempted murder, first-degree robbery, possession of firearms, resisting arrest, and held over for trial.

McFarland, the guy I'd shot, had an arrest record that dated back 30 years. He had spent time in prison and, at the time of the shooting, was on parole for another armed robbery.

Moynihan and I returned to the 43 precinct around 11:30. He was assigned a "winking" foot post---I believe he actually adjourned to a local Italian restaurant. I was driven to Jacobi Hospital to relieve a cop for lunch who was guarding a prisoner.

The cop I was relieving stood when he saw me enter the hospital's ICU.

"Hey, you shouldn't be here, Dead Eye."

"Don't call me that."

I looked in at the prisoner. He was the sole occupant in a private room. Tubes were stuck in his mouth, nose and arms. Electronic monitors were everywhere----Gregory "Sonny" McFarland was handcuffed to his bed. The cop was right. I shouldn't be there guarding the man I'd shot.

"What's his prognosis?" I said.

"The scumbag's in an irreversible coma," the cop said. "He's dead already."

Dead already---the words reverberated as the consequences of me firing my weapon struck me like a kick to the stomach; I'd actually killed a man. I felt my stomach knot, the blood leave my head, and my knees go weak. I stepped to the cop's desk and fell onto his chair.

"Hey, you all right, Dead Eye?" the cop said.

I looked at him. "Go eat. "

The cop grabbed his hat and headed to the hospital cafeteria.

I held my head in my hands and didn't think for a good fifteen minutes. Then I leaned back in the chair and looked at McFarland. I sat there, staring at the man who's life I had severed.

I told myself that McFarland deserved to die. He had tried to kill me. I had no choice. But those truths didn't make a dammed bit of difference. I felt like I'd done something immoral.

Another thought was bothering me. McFarland had fired at me at point-blank range. There's no way he should have missed. Was the ex-con a lousy shot? Was I just lucky? Or had McFarland missed on purpose? Maybe he would rather have died than go back to prison. He fired at me, knowing I'd shoot back---suicide by cop. It happens.

"You!" a voice said.

I looked up to see an owl-eyed, older woman standing there, glaring at me, hatred in her eyes. "I saw you on Gabe Pressman," she said. "Murderer!" The woman kept on screaming I was the white motherfuckin' racist who'd shot her son because he was black. I should be arrested and charged with murder. A nurse appeared and, with great difficulty, ushered McFarland's mother out of ICU.

An hour later, I was driven back to the 43 precinct. Sergeant Kennedy waved me over. "Whenever you're ready," he said. "Come see me and we'll write up your application for department recognition---you'll get an Honorable Mention. Maybe even the Combat Cross."

"I don't want any medals," I said.

"It's not up to you. Department recognition makes the captain look good, which makes the borough

244

commander look good which makes the commissioner look good---you get the picture. You and Moynihan are getting medals whether you like it or not."

"What's the story with the missing Grand Union money?" I said.

"The investigation's moving forward."

"They planning to charge us?" I said, half-kidding. "Do we need a lawyer?"

"Not yet," Kennedy said. "But don't be surprised if you're called down to IAD for questioning---then you'll need a lawyer."

I didn't like the sound of that.

I signed out at the regular time and drove home in a deep funk.

I unlocked my front door, walked into the apartment, and knew immediately that something was wrong. I looked around: a rectangular white spot was left where a picture once hung. A TV, lamp, and some other furniture were missing. At first I thought we'd been burglarized until I checked and saw that all my wife's personal belongs were gone. I looked for her suitcases.

Not there.

My wife had left me.

I checked my closet. My clothes were undisturbed. She'd left a couple of music albums on a high shelf, the ones she did not like. I walked into the kitchen. On the counter I saw one knife, one folk, one spoon, once cup, one saucer, one plate, one glass.

I found an unopened bottle of Irish whiskey in a cupboard, broke the seal, took the glass, sat at the kitchen counter, and poured a shot. I felt a sickening emptiness in the pit of my stomach; my world was coming apart.

Although my wife had given me no warning, had left me no "dear John" letter, I knew the reason she was gone. She didn't want to be married to a cop anymore.

Now, on top of being burdened with the guilt I felt over the McFarland shooting, and the possibility of being accused of stealing the missing Grand Union money, I found myself wondering where my wife had gone, if she was safe, was she with another man?

I downed the shot of whiskey. Threw the glass across the room, shattering it against a wall.

A few weeks later I was served with divorce papers.

Then the district attorney's office notified me that Robert Moody pled guilty to first-degree robbery and was sentenced to 7 to 14 years in state prison. John Taylor pled guilty to second degree robbery and received a 3 to 10-year sentence.

Gregory "Sonny" McFarland died soon after.

My life starting spinning out of my control.

Nights I sat all alone, haunted by McFarland's death. If I'd continued to call for assistance, waited for backup, I wouldn't have had to use deadly physical force. On top of this constant pressure was the still looming possibility that I could be charged with the theft of the Grand Union cash. I started suffering from insomnia. I showed up late for work. I started to drink on the job.

My steady partner of five years, Ritchie Passerino, covered for my tardiness and drinking as best he could. A Viet nam-era Navy veteran, he told me he thought I was suffering from post traumatic stress disorder and suggested I seek professional help.

I told to mind his fucking business.

By the time I was notified that Sergeant Kennedy was waiting to speak to me in the precinct muster room, I half-expected to be dragged off to a drunk tank, or placed in handcuffs and charged with grand larceny. Instead I walked into a room filled with my co-workers, where I was awarded an Honorable Mention medal for the shootout. The other cops applauded me enthusiastically. They saw me as a hero.

I saw myself as a failure.

Soon after, at a ceremony at Police Headquarters, the mayor awarded me and Moynihan the prestigious Combat Cross. The second highest departmental award is the Police Combat Cross. This form of recognition may be granted to members of the service who successfully and intelligently perform an act of extraordinary heroism while engaged in personal combat with an armed adversary under circumstances of imminent personal hazard to life.

The mayor handed me the medal, patted me on the back, shook my hand and told me I should be proud.

I didn't feel proud.

I showed up for work drunk the following day.

"If you hadn't won the Combat Cross," the precinct's commanding officer said, "I'd suspend your ass." He ordered me to take a vacation day and go home.

A few days later, Sergeant Kennedy informed me that Moynihan and I were no longer suspects in the theft of the Grand Union cash. "Someone in the store overestimated the amount of cash stolen," Kennedy said, sniffing my breath to see if I'd been drinking. "You guys are off the hook."

"A mistake?"

"A convenient one," Kennedy said. "They stood to collect the entire amount from the insurance company."

I went home that night thinking, at least I had one less thing to agonize over.

About a week later, during roll call, Sergeant Kennedy smelled beer on my breath and reported me to the captain. I was promptly relieved of my seat in a sector car and reassigned to a lowly one-man "fixer."

My new permanent post was the Jacobi Hospital emergency room. The message was clear---I was a burnout who was being buried in a place where I could do no harm.

Although the Jacobi Hospital post bored me, after a few months of working in the safe, relaxed environment, I found I was able to sleep at night. And I took comfort in the fact that I would never again be forced to use my firearm---I should have known that trouble would find me even there.

One evening, while I was trying in vain to convince a dazzling redheaded ER nurse to have dinner with me---she claimed she never dated cops---two Hispanic men barged into the ER carrying a third male who'd been shot. They carted the victim past me, placed him on an available gurney, and pleaded for a doctor.

"What happened?" I asked the three men.

The oldest of the three, a reed-thin junkie who I later learned was named Hector, said, "El es mi amigo. No menti dispararle. Fue un accidente. Es una arma vieja. Mojosa. No pense que pudiera disparar."

I speak a little Spanish. What I deciphered was: the victim was a friend of his. He was showing him a rusty old gun he'd found when it went off. It was an accident.

Groan.

Since the idiot had just admitted that he shot his friend, I would be forced to take police action---unless.

"Where's the gun?" I asked, hoping Hector would say it was anyplace other then in his possession. That way I could call a sector car, let them sort out the whole mess, and I could resume making time with the redhead.

Hector pointed to a black car in the hospital parking lot. "esta afuera. En mi Chevy."

Ay caramba. I asked two unarmed hospital cops to guard Hector and his pals while I went out to the Chevy to retrieve the gun.

I was in the back seat, rummaging around, muttering about the fact that I didn't want to make the God dammed collar, when, much to my surprise, Hector

248

opened the front passenger side door and reached under the seat.

What the hell? I stepped out of the car.

"You want to see my gun"? Hector said in perfect English. Then he pointed the rusty automatic at me and pulled the trigger---nothing happened. Hector quickly worked the slide, then pointed the weapon at me again. I snatched the gun from his hand. Cracked him on the head with the butt.

"Hey, Dead Eye." Two vaguely familiar 41 precinct plainclothes cops who'd obviously witnessed the incident alighted from an unmarked police car, guns drawn. "Why the hell didn't you shoot the prick?" the fatter of the two said.

"Yeah," his partner said. "The fucker deserved it." He picked up the gunman's weapon and inspected it. "This is an antique."

"You'll get another medal for this, Dead Eye," the fat cop said.

I didn't want another medal.

"How'd you like the collar?" I said.

The two cops exchanged glances: stupid question. Gun collars were much sought after and hard to come by. "You serious?" the fat cop said.

"As a heart attack," I said.

That went over real well at the station house.

"Hey, Fitzsimmons. Where the fuck do you get off, giving an 'attempted murder of a police officer' collar away," Sergeant Kennedy said. "And to cops from another command?"

It was the end of the tour, and I was in the middle of a long line of frenzied, raucous cops, anxious to sign out, and go home.

"What's the big deal?" I said, taking above the din. Since giving arrests away to other cops who wanted overtime and/or department recognition was routine, I didn't know what Kennedy's problem was. I reached over another cop's shoulder and scribbled my initials on the sign-out sheet.

"I didn't want the collar."

Kennedy stepped close to me, sniffed. "You been drinking?"

"No."

His expression said he didn't believe me. "They said you froze."

"Who?"

"The cops you gave the collar to. They said the scumbag pointed a gun at you and you just stood there, looking at him."

I shook my head. "I disarmed him, didn't I?"

"They said you took a stupid chance. Not shooting that skell when you had the opportunity jeopardized your life, maybe even theirs."

I noticed that several cops had stopped to listen.

"What, you gonna write me up for not shooting him?" I threw my hands up. "I don't believe I'm hearing this."

"Don't be a wise ass. What I'm saying is, had you arrested the asshole, you could've been awarded a second Combat Cross."

"I'm not interested in medals."

"Life ain't always about you." Kennedy shook his head, exasperated. "Look, Fitzsimmons, medals are good for the command, you know that."

"Fuck the command," I shot back, regretting the words the instant I said them.

All at once the room fell silent. All eyes were upon me.

"All right." Kennedy raised an unforgiving eyebrow. "I'll remember you said that."

A few days later, much to my surprise, the redheaded ER nurse, agreed to have lunch with me. During our meal break, we walked to a local Italian restaurant and ordered a three-course feast, including a bottle of red wine. As the meal went on I was increasingly puzzled by the fact that, although she seemed preoccupied, she was in no hurry to go back to work.

We lingered over coffee and cheese cake, stayed away longer then we should have. When we returned to the hospital, I saw a 43 precinct RMP parked at the entrance to the emergency room. Sergeant Kennedy was waiting for me.

Shit.

I stuffed my mouth with peppermint gum to mask the smell of wine and strolled into the hospital.

Kennedy was sitting in the emergency room waiting area, reading a newspaper. He saw me, checked his wrist watch, folded the newspaper and tossed it aside.

"A two-hour meal period, Fitzsimmons?" He looked at the nurse.

"Hello, Sergeant." The redhead smiled and winked at Kennedy.

At that moment I knew I'd been set up.

"Gimme your memo book," Kennedy said.

I handed it over and he made an entry.

"I'm writing you up for being off post," he said. "You got a bullshit excuse, you can tell it to the captain."

But I never got the chance.

Within a week I was transferred to the high-crime 44 precinct in the west Bronx. At the time the 44 was a dumping ground for cops who screw up, drunks, or those with disciplinary problems.

Tommy Ryan, a cop who once worked with my twin brother in "Fort Apache" was a member of the command. Ryan was under investigation for allegedly beating a prisoner, in his custody, to death.

I arrived at the 44 on a Tuesday afternoon, settled into my new locker, stood roll call with a crew of veteran cops, and was assigned to a foot post, patrol post 17, with a female. I didn't make an issue out of it, but I didn't like the idea of working with a female cop.

Sure, females were good at undercover assignments, traffic duty, and some other low-risk police work. But on the streets, if there was violence, most female cops were a liability---a fact police departments do not publicize. My apprehension about working with her led to the incident that finished me off for good.

We got a call: "Central to 44 Patrol Post 17, K."

"Tell them we're on meal," the female cop said. We were sitting in the rear of a bodega, on meal period. She was only halfway through a hearty plate of rice and beans. It was obvious from her physical dimensions that she'd never missed a meal.

I swallowed the last of my cuchifrito, and picked the portable radio. "44 Post 17."

"17, investigate a loud music complaint, 170th Street and Collage Avenue."

"Patrol Post 17, 10-4."

"What you do that for?" the female cop said.

"I'll take it." I handed her the portable radio. "You finish eating." I put my hat on, walked out of the bodega, and made a right.

Night had only just fallen, and the barrio was alive with pedestrian traffic. Drug lookouts were starting to slither onto the streets, hookers were peeking out of doorways. Thugs, pickpockets, three-card monte dealers and unlicensed peddlers were watching me from cars and tenement windows. They were checking out the new cop on the beat, no doubt wondering how much they could get away with.

As I approached Collage Avenue, I was reminded how much I hated patrolling the ghetto. There was no way to

252

avoid dealing with the crazies and the endless tide of criminals whose stock and trade is violence, cruelty, and mindless depravity. And then there are the destitute, the hopeless, and the multitude of neglected children who are the innocent victims of unrelenting poverty.

I could hear the offending music from half a city block away: a nerve-numbing fusion of rock and some sort of new wave electronica. I climbed the front stoop of a sludge tenement--- several scowling youth gang members dispersed---and pushed my way though a broken vestibule door.

The music grew louder as I climbed the poorly lit stairs. Empty crack bags popped beneath my feet. I was barraged with the stench of human excrement. Somewhere in the building a dog barked, a woman screamed at her children, a TV blared.

An elderly woman in a tent-size house dress---the complainant, I presumed---her face scrunched with anger and disgust, her hands covering her ears, was waiting for me on the fourth floor landing. She pointed to Apartment 4B.

I walked over, rang the bell, and then pounded on the door. Not surprisingly, the occupants could not hear me above the ear-rupturing music. I pounded again. Nothing. I tried the door. It was locked.

Last time I was in this situation I climbed to the top floor, went over the roof, down a fire escape and knocked on the occupant's window. I scared the hell out of the inhabitants, but at least I got their attention.

I told the elderly woman to wait in her apartment. Then I climbed two more flights and stepped out onto the roof.

Strangely, the music seemed even louder from up there. After a few moments my eyes adjusted to the darkness. I saw an old couch off to my right, littered with empty beer and soda cans. To my left was a stack of loose bricks that the neighborhood skells probably used to drop down on cops and firemen, sometimes with deadly accuracy.

I saw movement in the shadows ahead. I pulled my flashlight, thumbed it on, swung the beam toward the far end of the roof---I saw the guns pointing at me before I got a look at the men who were holding them.

I switched off the flashlight, lurched to the side, skidded over broken glass, found minimal cover behind a thin iron ventilation pipe, and drew my weapon. "Drop it!"

The men froze.

"Drop it, now," I said, but the men did not comply--- could they hear me above the loud music? "Put the guns down," I screamed. "Now!"

Still no reaction.

I glanced around: no escape. And I'd left the radio with the female cop. I cursed myself for being cocky and taking the assignment alone.

Movement. Were the two gunmen splitting up, setting up a crossfire?

I pointed my weapon.

Abruptly, the music stopped. The sudden silence was unsettling and affected my vision. I squinted, fighting to locate my targets in the darkness.

Noise to my left. I swung my weapon around, began the trigger squeeze---and heard whimpering.

I took a chance. Eased off the trigger, switched on my flashlight and pointed it toward the sound.

A black kid about 12 years old was hiding behind the couch. "Don't shoot, please," he cried.

"We're playing," I heard someone to my right say.

I swung my flashlight beam back toward the gunmen. Two pre-teens put there hands up to block the light from their terrified eyes.

"Don't shoot," the younger of the two said.

254

"Toss your guns over here," I said.

Two plastic guns clattered at my feet.

"We were playing cops and robbers," the older kid said.

"It's all right," I said as I stepped into the open. "I'm not gonna shoot."

I lowered my weapon.

And was sick to my stomach.

The door to the commanding officer of the 44th precinct was open. I knocked on the door frame, walked in, and placed my two guns, the off-duty and service revolver, on his desk.

"I've had it."

Deputy Inspector McKenna, a 30-year NYPD veteran, leaned back in his chair. "Was it something I did?"

"No," I assured him. "The problem is mine."

McKenna studied me for a few moments, directed me to a chair across from his desk, and then asked me to please tell him specifically what the problem was.

"Bottom line," he said.

"Bottom line?" There was no way I was about to tell him about my stupidity which led to the near tragic incident on the rooftop.

"I killed a man during an armed robbery a few years ago. It was a clean shooting. But I'm having trouble living with it. I don't want to be put in the position to use deadly physical force ever again."

McKenna said he was familiar with the incident.

"Running away won't help."

"I'm not running. But if I stay a cop, it could happen again."

McKenna shook his head. And for the next fifteen minutes he tried to talk me out of resigning.

He said that, as far as he was concerned, people who felt the way I did about violence, who had a conscience, made the best cops. He said the department couldn't afford to lose men like me. He suggested that I take an official six-month leave of absence; he would personally endorse it. Take a vacation. Go sit under a palm tree. Look at the ocean. Give it a rest for a while.

I told him I wasn't interested.

McKenna asked me a series of hard questions about what I planned to do with the rest of my life. He told me that "out there" in the real world, good jobs are hard to come by. "How're you planning to make a living?"

"Honestly, I have no idea." I stood. "Maybe I'll go into the bar business, or try Wall Street." I pushed my guns across the desk. "I only know I don't want to be a cop anymore."

McKenna threw up his hands. "Well, that's that." He rose from his desk and shook my hand. "Good luck, Fitzsimmons," he said. "You change your mind, or need to talk, I'm here."

"Thank you."

I walked out of the office, past the desk, out of the station house, and sucked in a deep breath. I was a free man: no more guns.

I felt as if a crushing blue stone had been lifted off my chest.

A Christmas Story

A banged-up Ford Taurus crept slowly along a snowy Queens, New York street, swerved into the oncoming lane around a line of double parked cars, and sloshed to a stop at a red light.

A group of bundled-up Korean teens, hands in their pockets, collars up against the cold harsh wind, passed through the Ford's headlights. A turning, oncoming garbage truck plowed up a shower of slush, forcing the Ford's driver, fugitive felon Adam "Tip Top" Neverson, to switch the windshield wipers to high.

"That be the place," Tip Top pointed a long, bony finger toward a row of shabby stores that were decorated, more or less, for the Christmas holidays.

Lee's Liquors was situated on the corner next to a rundown Korean restaurant with a scrawled "No Cat Meat" sign prominently displayed in its window.

The traffic light changed. Tip Top pulled to the curb. Shifted to park. Killed the engine. Snapped off his seatbelt. Smoothed the insistent wrinkles out of his polyester navy blue business suit.

"You sure 'bout this?" the hulking passenger, Booker T Webster said, eyeballing the row of stores, nipping at a pint of Old Sharpshooter gin. The fact that Booker T was one of the most inept criminals in New York—he'd been arrested for a dozen petty crimes and sent to prison twice for as many armed robberies—compelled him to question everyone's judgment, especially his own.

"Sure I'm sure, nigga," Tip Top said with absolute certainty.

"Why?" Booker T said. He adjusted the stained, two-dollar maroon tie that went perfectly with his slept-in, polyester gray business suit. "What's so special about this place?"

Tip Top fired up a fat joint, held a long drag. "Check the sign in the window."

"It say, 'No Cat Meat'."

"No, goddammit—Lee's Liquor Store on the corner. *That* sign."

"Oh." Booker T squinted. "No Credit Cards."

"Told you." Tip Top blew out the smoke and offered him the joint.

"No. Thanks—told me, what, dawg?"

From their vantage point, they could see inside the unremarkable establishment. Mr. Lee, a slight, elderly Korean man, was sitting behind an old cash register, a silly looking Santa Claus hat on his head, serving a long line of late-night customers.

"The man don't take no credit cards mean he deal in dough-ray-me." Tip Top cracked a window to let the marijuana smoke stream out. "Mr. Lee be hauling in the cash—take my word for it."

"Yeah, right." Booker T scowled, thinking that Tip Top's cadaverous appearance, green teeth, and obnoxious know-it-all attitude did not inspire confidence.

"Well," Tip Top said. "What do you think?"

"What I think—." Another swallow of gin. "One more felony conviction make me a three-time-loser." Booker T shook his head ruefully. "They will put my black ass away for the rest of my mutha fuckin' life."

Tip Top nodded, toked the joint. "That be true."

"Then again—." Booker T used thick fingers to open his cell phone, held it up and showed Tip Top a wallpaper photo of his wife and daughter, a beaming three year old. "She be my baby girl. My wife be my heart. And I ain't brought them shit for Christmas." He put the cell phone away.

"Look, nigga," Tip Top said. "We pull this off, you'll be able to move your family out of the ghetto. They'll be riding around in a chauffeur driven, Cadillac limousine."

"Yeah," Booker T snickered. "'Cause we gonna be the stars of our own reality show."

"What, you still don't believe me?" Tip Top pulled a newspaper clipping from his suit jacket pocket. "It say right here, *WANTED: Reality show ideas. Provide pro-spectus and audition tape.*"

"I know what it say."

"We pull this here robbery, grab the store's security camera tape—that be our audition tape. Then I write the pro-spectus for our show: 'Ghetto Robin Hoods.'"

"How you gonna write a pro—whatchamacallit?"

"You seen the awful shit on reality TV," Tip Top said. "How hard can it be?"

"You lucky you can write your own name."

"Why you always gotta be so mutha fuckin' negative."

Booker T took in a deep breath, let it out. "Awright. So, we rob this store, and we do what? Give the cash to a Baptist church?"

"Right. That what the real Robin Hood did. The mutha fucka stole from the rich and gave to the poor."

"Why?"

"How the fuck should I know."

"We gotta give all the cash?"

"Well, not all of it," Tip Top said. "We gotta keep some; you gotta buy your wife and baby girl Christmas gifts. I got my own operating expenses."

Booker T shook his head. "This sounds crazy, man."

"Look, that old gook runs that store all alone."

"I can see that," Booker T said.

"He ain't gonna offer no resistance." Tip Top reached into a brown paper bag, took out two Donald Trump Halloween masks, and handed one to Booker T.

"Why we gotta wear suits and Donald Trump masks?"

Tip Top sighed, exasperated at having to explain, yet
again "'Cause we gotta show the TV producer that we
got style—and the masks were free."

They slipped on their masks.

"Remember," Tip Top said. "We walk in like we be
regular customers. I stay at the front of the store, act like
I'm buying something, do the lookie loo. You go to the
register, collect the dead presidents."

"Why you always the lookout?"

"Why?" Tip Top said, taken aback. "What difference
does it make?"

"Shit goes down, you're the first one out the door."

"When I ever run out on you, huh? C'mon, tell me.
When?"

Booker T grinned. "You don't run 'cause you know
the consequences."

Tip Top had no response to that.

"Awright," Booker T said, relenting. "You do the
lookie loo, it make you happy."

"Awright." Tip Top perked up, rubbed his hands
together excitedly. "Now, once you get the cash, you in-
ca-pacitate the old gook; just a tap on the head so we can
get the security tape and get back to the car."

Booker T took a moment to consider the, uh,
intricacies of the plan; his brow furrowed.

"He's gotta have at least ten thousand in cash by
closing time," Tip Top persisted. "We give half to a
church, keep half; that's twenty-five hundred a piece.
That'll buy a whole shitload of Christmas gifts for your
family."

"Yeah," Booker T said, thinking that, for once, Tip Top
was making sense—and that's what concerned him.
"Too many people on the street," Booker T said.

"So? Makes it easy for us to blend in."

"It's a corner store," Booker T said. "Too many
windows. We be sitting ducks."

260

"We hand the guy a note. Keep the gats outta sight."
Tip Top took a dog-eared piece of paper out of his suit
jacket pocket and handed it to Booker T. The
handwritten note read:

**We r armed. Don't say notin. Give us all the
money or we pop a cap in your mutha fuckin ass.**

Booker T rubbed his cinderblock chin. "That be a long
note."

"Hey, I done this before," Tip Top said indignantly,
leaving out the fact that the last time he attempted to rob
a store with that very same note, the mean-as-a-snake
female proprietor had laughed in his face, beat the living
hell out of him, and left him bleeding on a Harlem street.

"What if the guy don't read English?"

"Don't be ridiculous," Tip Top said, his expression
giving away the fact he hadn't actually thought of that
possibility. "Hell, nigga, these days everybody reads
English."

"That a fact?"

"Fuckin' A."

"If you say so." Booker T focused on the store.

Tip Top looked at his wristwatch. "Five minutes they
close."

"Twenty five hundred apiece you say?" Booker T said.

"At least. Maybe more."

Booker T nodded, feeling troubled by the fact that he
was warming up to the idea. He gulped more gin, took a
long look around, scanned the area for cops or potential
witnesses. He spotted a drug lookout slouched in a
storefront doorway checking them out; he wouldn't be a
problem. An old woman walking a large dog loitered on
the opposite corner, her canine charge in full meditative
squat.

"Hey." Tip Top gestured to a man coming out of the
liquor store. "That be the last customer. Let's move
before the old gook locks up." Tip Top reached into a

261

brown bag, took out two plastic .38s, and handed one to Booker T.

"Fuck is this? Toy guns?"

"You got money for real gats?"

"No, but—"

"They be phony baloney guns," Tip Top said, "but they look real."

Mr. Lee, owner of Lee's liquors knew he was about to be robbed when he saw the two men wearing silly-looking Halloween masks enter his store. The shorter, skinnier of the two, dressed in an ill-fitting navy blue suit, perused a red wine display at the front of the store. His companion, a Sumo wrestler of a man in a rumpled gray suit, came lumbering down the aisle. He stopped at the register. Mr. Lee nodded nervously.

"What's that song?" Booker T said.

"Song?" Mr. Lee said.

"The Christmas music playin' on your sound system—I got it," Booker T said. "Silent Night." He handed Mr. Lee Tip Top's dog-eared handwritten note. "You gonna have a silent night you don't do what you're told."

Puzzled, Lee glanced at the note and forced a toothy smile. "What paper say?"

Booker T looked over his shoulder, shot Tip Top a death look. "Everybody reads English, huh? You dumbass mutha fucka." He turned back to Mr. Lee, pulled the phony baloney .38, and stuck it in Lee's face. "The note say gimme the money, mutha fucka."

Mr. Lee raised his hands. "No problem. Give money. No problem."

Booker T knocked the Santa Clause hat off Lee's head. "Now, mutha fucka!"

"Okay. Okay. Give money." Lee side stepped to the cash register, one eye on a dusty security mirror that allowed him a narrow view of the family-owned liquor store. He prayed that his son Kwan, who was in the basement storeroom reconciling their liquor inventory, did not choose this moment to emerge.

Lee's Liquors had been robbed three times this past year. During the last robbery, Mr. Lee had been pistol-whipped and hospitalized, his nephew executed—forced to his knees and shot in the back of the head. Kwan, American born, temperamental and quick tempered, had vowed revenge. Even though he was just short of legally blind, Kwan had managed to acquire a legal premises pistol license by greasing the palm of an NYPD-approved range instructor. Now there was a loaded .357 magnum under the register counter. Lee, a devout Buddhist, had never touched it.

"Hurry the fuck up, mutha fucka," Booker T said, brandishing the phony baloney gun, his massive, prison-conditioned frame threatening to burst from his suit jacket.

"Okay. Okay." Lee rang open the register, gathered all the cash, and stole a glimpse at another security mirror. The skinny man was still at the front of the store, his eyes on the street, bouncing from one foot to the other like a man in need of a bathroom break.

Lee stuffed the cash into a plastic bag and handed it to the gunman.

"What?" Booker T said, not happy with the weight and thickness of the bag. "You think I'm playin' which you, mutha fucka?" He leapt over the narrow counter, grabbed Lee by the shirt and bounced him off a wall.

Lee collapsed to the floor, bleeding from a gash on his forehead.

"Gimme everything." Booker T's toy gun was pressed to the back of Lee's head.

"Okay. Okay." Lee rolled to his knees and used his shirt sleeve to wipe the blood streaming into his eyes. He reached under the counter, saw the .357. But Lee did

263

not touch it. He lifted a small tin strong box, set it on the counter, flipped it open.

Booker T knocked Lee aside, stuffed whatever cash there was into the plastic bag. That was when Lee's son walked in, inventory register in his hand.

"Moreugesseumnida," Kwan said in Korean.

Booker T snapped around.

Through coke-bottle thick eyeglasses, Kwan saw the open cash register. Saw the empty strong box on the counter. Saw his father bleeding on the floor. Saw the huge man wearing a gray suit and a Donald Trump mask with a gun in his hand.

What happened next happened quickly.

Kwan dove for the .357.

Booker T threw a kick at Kwan. Missed.

Kwan got his hands on the gun. Fired.

The cash register detonated. Nickels, dimes and quarters exploded into the air. Kwan continued to fire.

Booker T bobbed and weaved. Liquor bottles, florescent lights, and security mirrors shattered, glass and booze spraying the store.

Kwan's next shot hit home.

Booker T yelped in pain. Grabbed the side of his head. Dropped the bag of cash. Dove back over the counter. Scrambled for cover.

Tip Top came rushing down the isle.

Kwan spotted him and fired two quick rounds.

Tip Top dove through a rack of wine. Bottles broke. He landed on top of jagged glass, slicing up his hands and knees.

Booker T crab-crawled across the floor, holding what was left of his ear. He pulled Tip Top from the debris of glass, bullets from Kwan's .357 whizzing over their heads.

"You get the security tape?" Tip Top said.

"Fuck the tape," Booker T said. "I'm outta here."

264

"I'm which you, nigga," Tip Top said.

"I'm telling you," police officer Nicky Costa said as we walked into the forty-first precinct station house around 3:30 p.m. on a Saturday, three days before Christmas. "Every girl I've ever dated had sex with me on the first date. Hell, I did most of 'em in the first hour. What, you think I'm bullshitting you?"

"No." I did a mental eye-roll as we made our way through the precinct. *Here we go again.* If Costa wasn't bullshitting about his expertise with women, he was spinning fantastic yarns about all the felony collars he'd made and gunfights he'd been in. Then there were the tall tales about his two master's degrees, how he paid for college by singing in a band (he'd never been to college, his singing voice was like a frog's croak)—it all depended on his audience, how much bullshit he could get away with.

"Wanna know my secret?" Costa said.

"No."

"I'm a sexual Tyrannosaurus."

My shoulders sagged with boredom.

"Face it, I'm a great lay." Costa graced me with his most winning smile. "I got a twelve-inch cock—that ain't an ankle holster I'm wearing." He chuckled at his own quip. "I can part my hair with my tongue. And I got a reputation. Women write my phone number in ladies rooms all over Manhattan. My phone never stops ringing."

"Really. How's your wife feel about that?"

We slipped off our coats, stopped in the sitting room, acknowledged the dozen or so early birds who had claimed their preferred roll call seats.

As was our habit, we perused the day's roll call, checked what sector teams were working, who was out sick, on vacation, or testifying in court. Then we read the latest special orders and incident reports that were tacked up on a bulletin board. As was expected during the holiday season, armed robberies were becoming epidemic.

It was time for us to change into uniform.

We climbed the stairs and entered the cold and cruddy fourth floor locker room.

"Hey, fuck face," a bald cop standing in front of an open locker said to Costa.

"*Mister* Fuck Face to you," Costa said.

"Oh, sorry. Mister Fuck Face—where's the twenty you owe me?"

"I gave it to your wife," Costa said.

Baldy faked a punch to Costa's midsection. Costa covered up, bobbed and weaved away.

"Hey, Costa," an older, Hispanic cop said as we walked by. "I waited at the bar for you for two fucking hours. "Where the fuck were you?"

"Up the fat ladies ass," Costa said, "looking out."

Costa continued to play grab ass with several other sector car teams as we negotiated the dimly lit tin-city that led, eventually, to our lockers.

We turned the corner, and I saw my former brother-in-law Charlie Pratt sitting on a chair. A St. Michael the Archangel pendant (the patron saint of police officers) dangled from a chain around his thick neck. His right elbow was resting on his left knee, fist under his lantern chin, holding a Rodin pose of moody reflection. There was a droop of bitterness at the corners of his mouth.

Not that *I* was happy about having to work—there was a Christmas party packed with single ladies that I was dying to attend. Both of us had, in fact, tried to get the tour off: I tried to bribe the roll call man with a bottle of top-shelf scotch, while Costa had offered a steak dinner. Together, we'd even debated calling in sick. But the approach of Christmas brought on a surge of street crime, especially in these harsh economic times—the understaffed NYPD was on full alert.

"Merry Christmas," Costa said to Pratt as we stepped to our lockers.

"Yeah," I said. "Merry Christmas, douche bag."

"Go fuck yourself."

I smiled. At least Pratt still loved me.

Pratt had been married for two boozy, drug-addled years to my estranged sister, disgraced former Police Officer Valarie Viselli, a beautiful, narcissistic sociopath. The fact that he survived the marriage with his life and sense of humor intact was nothing short of a miracle.

I dialed my combination lock, swung open my locker door, and took out a small gift-wrapped box. "Here, from me and Nicky," I grinned, offering it to Pratt.

Pratt heaved to his feet, looked at the gift as if it were an explosive device, then glared at us. "Now why'd you guys go do something like that for?"

"It ain't a Rolex, dick wad." Costa said. "Don't go getting all misty on us."

Pratt accepted the gift, tore off the wrapping, and opened the box. "Christ—it's a *Gucci* wallet," he gasped.

"A knockoff," I said. "Bought it down on Canal Street."

"Well, it's the thought that counts," Pratt said sagely.

I rolled my eyes; a gorilla with a heart. We proceeded to change into uniform.

Pratt stuffed his ID and cash into the new Gucci and tossed his old wallet aside. Then he reached into his locker, extracted, and handed us each a small box. It looked like a toddler whose baby food was laced with crystal meth had wrapped them.

"Merry Christmas." Pratt avoided eye contact and the corners of his mouth cracked. I think he almost smiled. "And a Happy—you know the rest."

We accepted the gifts and unwrapped them.

"An Omega!" Costa said.

"Yeah. The new James Bond wears an Omega—ain't you gonna put 'em on?"

We unstrapped our own watches, slipped on the *Omegas*. I knew that our wrists would turn green within a few hours. "Thanks, Charlie." I'd seen the crappy knockoff Omegas alongside the crappy knockoff Gucci wallets down on Canal Street. We'd paid fifteen dollars for the crappy Gucci. The Omegas were two for ten dollars. Pratt had skunked us.

"Know what this means," I said, "us exchanging gifts?"

"What?" Pratt said, his eyes narrowed in suspicion.

"That we're going steady." Costa blew Pratt a kiss.

It would be the only time Pratt smiled that tour.

"Costa! Viselli!" a voice called out.

"Yo," I said. "Over here."

The captain's clerical man, a skinny old cop with a red-veined drinker's face, came whistling around the bend. "Captain wants to see you guys; you, too, Pratt. Pronto."

"He's back from vacation already?" Costa said, hurrying to strap on his Sam Brown. He still carried an old .38 and wore the holster low for quick draw.

"What're you talking 'bout?" The clerical man stifled then swallowed a volcanic beer belch. "He was gone for a whole month."

"Not long enough if you ask me." I pinned on my shield.

"I hear ya," the skinny cop sighed.

The three of us entered Captain Ward's office, an institutional green space furnished with ancient, chipped tin furniture that looked like it belonged, well, in a police station. A dozen other cops were already there.

"Everyone's here, captain," the whistling assistant said.

The captain was sitting behind his tiny desk, arranging a miniature Christmas nativity scene, humming what sounded like "Grandma Got Run Over By A Reindeer". He sported a Florida tan and looked well rested. I was simply thrilled to see that he'd abandoned his assortment of ridiculous hair pieces (my personal favorite was the Elvis helmet) for hair plugs. Clumps of long thin hair protruded from each angry looking red blotch.

The captain placed the baby Jesus in front of the manger, smiled approvingly, then sat back and gave us the once-over. "As you all know, there's been a rash of robberies in the city during the last month."

The whistling assistant handed out a dozen mug shots and accompanying rap sheets of suspected stickup teams; a few were on the NYPD's Most Wanted list.

"First page—we named these two bozos The Trump Bandits," the captain said. "Booker T Webster and Adam 'Tip Top' Neverson, These mutts wear business suits and Donald Trump masks. Leave fingerprints all over the place. They hit a liquor store in Korea Town out in Queens. Got into the losing end of a gun fight with the owners and ran off empty handed—guaranteed they'll strike again, and soon."

I looked at the rap sheets and recognized the face of Booker T Webster—a male, black thirty-four years old, 6'6", 350 pounds. He'd been arrested for a dozen petty crimes, had served two stretches in state prison for armed robbery.

Costa and I had arrested Webster last year for beating the living shit out of a nitwit who'd snatched the purse of Webster's common law wife. The thief had knocked her and Webster's two-year-old daughter to the sidewalk. Unfortunately for the thief, Webster had stumbled onto the crime scene. What stuck in my mind most about the incident were the contrasts: like Webster, his wife was a fearsome-looking, heavyset thug who sported prison gang tattoos. Yet they were touchingly sweet, gentle, and loving toward each other and their baby—a regular Ozzie and Harriet. So impressed was I that, while Webster was under arrest, in our custody, I'd broken the rules and allowed his wife to visit him. Later, Webster thanked me for my kindness, and explained to me that he couldn't get a job; he was too damn stupid. That he robbed only to support his family.

I didn't know Webster's partner: Adam "Tip Top" Neverson was a male, black, thirty-nine years old, 6'1', 140 pounds. Although his early rap sheet was for mostly nonviolent crimes like larcenies, forgery, and fencing stolen property, he'd pulled one stretch in state prison for armed robbery, was discharged, then arrested shortly thereafter for burglary. He had made bail, missed his court date—he was now a wanted man, designated a fugitive felon.

It took another ten minutes for the captain to discuss the proclivities of each stickup team: One team impersonated cops, showed fake IDs. Another team, brutal and skilled at terrorizing their victims, always took a female hostage and released her once they'd made a safe escape. Yet another team dressed in New York Yankee apparel and was unfailingly polite.

"HQ is taking a lot of heat from the mayor's office," the captain said, "and the shit's running downhill." He sat back in his chair. "We gotta put an end to these robberies."

"You putting us on fixers?" Costa said.

"Stakeouts. Get back into civilian clothes."

"Oh, boy." Costa rubbed his hands together manically. "Fun and games."

The whistling assistant handed out sheets of paper with assignments.

"I want you to stake out those locations," the captain said. "A sergeant from Major Case has already checked out each site. You'll find diagrams of the stores, suggesting the best place to set up without endangering civilians."

I glanced at our assignment and the attached sergeant's diagram: Manny's Beer & Soda; a large distributor on Southern Boulevard and Hunts Point Avenue was owned and operated by one Manny Ramirez. Although I'd never been in the store I knew it to be a busy location. They'd have plenty of cash on hand just before Christmas.

"We'll need shotguns," I said, my eyes on the mug shots.

"Yeah," Costa agreed. "Most all of these mutts are three-time losers."

"They do show up," Pratt said, "they won't come quietly."

"I wouldn't get too worked up," the captain said. "Armed robbers are the undisputed, dumb-as-dirt bottom of the criminal food chain. Which is why they usually hit the same locations until they get caught. None of these particular skells have hit the forty-first precinct before. I doubt they will. But if you think you need shotguns, I'll authorize it."

We left the captain's office, changed into civilian clothes, and hit the street.

Pratt drove. We parked about a block away from our assignment on Southern Boulevard. Walking along the freezing ghetto streets, we heard the sound of Christmas music blaring in Spanish from a static-laced pawnshop speaker. We carried the NYPD issued Ithaca shotguns that the captain had authorized, and portable radios in black satchels.

Manny's Beer & Soda was a large, musty, crowded space with blinking Christmas lights dangling from the high ceilings. Piped-in holiday music drifted from hidden speakers. Holiday beer and soda displays packed the uneven concrete floor.

There appeared to be three harried young male employees, and one very attractive female, all of whom were serving a long line of impatient, assorted customers, anxious—from what I could overhear—to purchase supplies for holiday gatherings and parties.

"See her?" Costa said, drooling like a sex-crazed adolescent. The female employee stood at a shapely 5'5'. Her clothes were formfitting, tight; a big woman but sexy. The contrast between her dark skin and blue eyes was nothing short of astonishing.

"She's mine," Costa said. "Wanna bet?"

"Don't start that shit," Pratt barked. "This ain't a singles bar."

"Eat shit." Costa stepped over to the cash register.

"May I help you?" the woman said, her accent Jamaican, her smile brilliant.

"You may," Costa returned the smile, flipped out his shield and ID card. "The good-looking one is Officer Viselli. The old grouch is Pratt. You can call me Nicky."

"Cops." The smile on the woman's face collapsed.

"Let me ask you something," Costa glanced at the name tag over the woman's ample breast. "Lataesha, you ever play leapfrog naked?"

I cringed. Pratt shook his head, said something that sounded like "you asshole," under his breath, and huffed away. Lataesha looked startled.

"Pardon me?" Lataesha said.

"If you cook me dinner tonight, I'll cook you breakfast in the morning."

"What are you talking about?"

"Wanna go fifty-fifty on a rape charge?" Costa said.

272

"Are you crazy?" Lataesha glared.

"What, you don't like cops?" Costa said.

"No." Lataesha looked Costa in the eye. "I don't like you."

Costa's jaw dropped. His face turned bright red.

"The owner, Manny Ramirez around?" I interrupted, attempting to spare Lataesha from one of Costa's embarrassing, juvenile diatribes—saying that he didn't handle rejection well was a gross understatement.

Lataesha called out to Manny, turned her back to us, and strode away, Costa's eyes, heart, and pride trailing in her wake.

"I'm Manny Ramirez," an erect, distinguished middle-aged man said.

We identified ourselves.

"I'm glad you're here." Manny's handshake was firm, his smile sincere. I noted that his slightly accented English was flawless; he had the look and bearing of a maitre d'hotel.

"It's been two years since we were last robbed," Manny said. "A couple of drunk gang members. They vomited on themselves before they had even gotten out the door. But one can never be too cautious." He gestured for us to follow him to his office.

The office was directly behind the cash register; a small but neat enclosure with invoices, assorted paperwork and a tattered, ten-year-old automotive girly calendar tacked to the bare plywood walls. A sturdy looking floor safe was set alongside Manny's desk, on top of which was a control panel for an active security system. The large, rectangle window that overlooked the selling floor was actually a one-way mirror.

Since there was no place to sit, Costa and I stood around Manny's desk and discussed the Major Case Squad sergeant's observations and recommendations.

Pratt, furious at Costa's conduct toward Lataesha, chose to wait outside.

"First thing," I said, "is to talk to your employees," I said. "Make sure they know who we are. That they know to cooperate in the unlikely event that they do get robbed. And to duck if, God forbid, any shooting starts."

Manny called his employees into his office one at a time and introduced us. It was obvious they were suspicious of cops, but seemed happy to have armed protection—all but Lataesha who scowled and avoided eye contact with Costa. Who could blame her?

I thanked Manny as we left his office and joined up with Pratt. We then conducted our own risk assessment.

We noted the security system's half-dozen small bubble cameras that were affixed to the exposed ceiling beams. We found a rear exit and locked it. Ditto the skylight. Locked a crusty lavatory window that led to an alley and freedom—now there was only one way in and out.

"This is bad," Pratt said. "What do you think?"

"I don't like the setup," I said. "Too much customer traffic. Too many places for gunmen to duck and hide." I gestured at the forest-like stacks of beer and soda and a large ice maker. "We don't take them by surprise, things could go very wrong, very fast."

"We could stack those cases of beer over there." Costa pointed across the room. "Make ourselves a hunter's blind." He gestured back to the cash register. "One of us sets up behind the register, in the office. Maybe we'll be able to get them in a cross fire."

"Maybe," I said.

A battered Ford Taurus moved north on busy Southern Boulevard and slowed to a crawl as it came abreast of Manny's Beer & Soda Distributor.

"Why we slowing down?" Booker T Webster said, the left side of his head a mound of bandages, covering what was left of the ear that was shot off at Lee's Liquors.

"That be the place," Tip Top Neverson pointed.

A car honked behind them.

"Pull over," Booker T said.

Tip Top plunged through a small snow drift as he pulled the Ford to the curb in front of Manny's. He used a painful, bandaged hand to kill the Ford's engine and snap off his seatbelt. Picking up a half-smoked joint from the ashtray, he fired it up and took a hit. "Well?"

Booker T unscrewed a bottle of gin and took a gulp, wincing from the ear pain.

After the Lee's Liquors store shooting, the two criminals were forced to seek the aid of an unlicensed physician, not exactly a medical doctor. She was more a combination storefront gypsy fortune teller and self-taught veterinarian. Tip Top had to endure dozens of painful stitches to his right hand and both knees. Booker T's injuries were easier to deal with. Since part of his ear was blown clear off, all that was necessary was to arrest any infection and control the bleeding.

"What's it gonna be?" Tip Top said.

"Don't rush me, dawg," Booker T snapped.

Tip Top took another toke. "You still be angry about last night?"

"Naw." Booker T shook his head; much as he tried he couldn't blame Tip Top for last night's fiasco. After all, it was he who had dropped the bag full of cash and he who had neglected to grab the stores security camera video tape. Which was why when one of Tip Top's contacts told them that the busy Bronx beer distributorship took in $20,000 cash on a Saturday night, he'd agreed to check out the place, even though neither one of them were in shape to attempt another armed robbery—they were both dealing with intense pain, their minds numb from a mixture of gin, marijuana and stomach-churning, illicitly obtained, prescription painkillers. But Christmas was looming. Booker T was still flat broke. And he'd rather die than disappoint his wife and baby girl.

"We wait, Dawg,." Booker T said. "See what we see. Awright?"

"Awright," Tip Top said.

We built the hunter's blind as Costa had suggested, stacking beer and soda cases three deep and six wide with a missing case in the center about chest high as a gun port for shooting.

Pratt unpacked and loaded the three 14-inch Ithaca 12-gauge pump shotguns with two rifled slugs, and three .00 buckshots, and handed them out along with radios and wireless head sets.

"We get lucky tonight," Costa said. "I'd like to catch the collar."

"All right with me," I said.

"Yeah, sure," Pratt grouched and walked off towards the lavatory.

"Fuck's his problem?" Costa said, utterly incapable of understanding that his conduct toward the female employee Lataesha had been grossly inappropriate.

I shrugged. "You're his problem."

"Me? What I do?"

I wasn't about to waste my breath. "Where you wanna set up?"

Costa chose to stake out Manny's office where he'd enjoy a perfect view of the cash register and easy access to Lataesha—no surprise there, It was only a matter of time before Costa, a glutton for punishment, hit on her again, and she slapped him down again.

Pratt and I took positions behind our hunter's blind. Tested our radios and headsets. Got accustomed to the shooting angles and discussed several various robbery scenarios, the unspoken course of action being if gunmen did try to rob the place, and pulled weapons, we would shoot to kill, no questions asked—*this was not TV.*

"Look at that asshole," Pratt scowled, watching Costa loiter by the cash register, lascivious eyes fixed on Lataesha's derriere. "What's wrong with him?"

"You know Costa."

"That's the problem," Pratt said. "I don't like when police officers use their authority as leverage with women."

"You think that's what he's doing?"

"Don't play stupid with me, Viselli," Pratt snapped. "You're his partner. You know goddamn well what he's doing."

I felt my face flush, adrenaline hit my blood stream—I don't tolerate that tone of voice from anyone. *Ever.* But I bit my tongue, told myself Pratt was not only my former brother-in- law but, because he'd been genuinely good to my wacko sister, he was my friend. I took a deep breath, turned away. Took a position by the gun port. Spoke into my headset, told Costa to leave Lataesha the fuck alone and get into position.

"Blow me," Costa said over the radio. Then he stepped into Manny's office, closed the door, and took his position behind the one-way mirror.

Pratt sat on a stack of beer cases. Fiddled with his shotgun. "Look, Viselli. I didn't mean to—I mean, I'm not pissed at you, it's just that—"

"Forget it," I said, my eyes trained on the store's front door.

"No. I can't."

I turned to look at Pratt. He was rubbing the bridge of his nose like he had a migraine. There was a slight tremor to his right hand, his gun hand. "You all right?"

Pratt shook his head, frowned. "It's your sister."

Here we go again.

"She's been calling," Pratt said. "Writing emails. She wants to get back together."

Pratt and my sister had been partners for only a few days when they started having sex: on duty in the radio car, on the midnight-to-eight shift. Pratt fell in love. He didn't seem to mind that, before they'd met, she'd banged half of his co-workers along with a goodly number of bartenders and firefighters. He asked her to marry him.

"Don't do it," I told Pratt when I heard the news. At the time I'd been estranged from my sister for well over ten years and felt absolutely no affection or loyalty toward her.

"I love her," Pratt said.

"Yeah?" I told him a little about growing up with Valarie. The fact that in Catholic high school she was one of the Mean Girls. A boyfriend-stealing bully who tormented other girls, and, just for good measure, spread rumors that they were pregnant. "When we were kids, she was hateful, cruel. She got worse as she got older. Becoming a cop didn't change her; just the opposite."

As a reward for my candidness, Pratt stopped speaking to me. And married my sister.

In the years that followed Pratt chose to ignore Valarie's pathological lying, infidelities, and drug abuse. But then the FBI caught her on video tape, having sex and snorting coke with a drug dealer they were investigating, and she was forced to resign from the NYPD. Pratt had had enough; the marriage disintegrated.

And we became friends again.

278

"Last I heard, she was still up in Canada," I said, "with her sixth husband…or is he the seventh? Honestly, I've lost count."

"She says she misses me."

I snickered. "So the current husband must've run out of money."

"That she keeps thinking about all the good times we had."

"Ah, the good times—like the time she broke that whiskey bottle over your head? You got fourteen stitches. Or the time she hid her stash of cocaine in your precinct locker and you were almost fired? How about the time she emptied out your bank account, stole your car, and ran off with husband number five? Those the good times she's talking about?"

"I know how it sounds," Pratt said. "You think I'm crazy. But I love her."

"It's some sort of sexual obsession, Charlie, not love."

Pratt looked at me. "You'll excuse me if I don't take advice from a guy who's screwed up every relationship he's ever had."

I had nothing to say to that.

Just then a tall, skinny black guy, part of his face obscured by a pulled down watch cap, came though Manny's front door. He was wearing a baggy navy blue suit. "Charlie," I said. "Look."

Pratt came to the gun port, peered out. "That's Adam 'Tip Top' Neverson."

Neverson was trying to keep a low profile. He used a bandaged hand to shield the exposed part of his face from the ceiling security cameras as he walked among cases of beer.

"He's casing the place," Pratt said.

Lataesha approached Neverson; it looked like she was asking if he needed help. Neverson said something, showed her his bandaged right hand. Lataesha pointed him to the rear of the store toward the lavatory.

"Fuck she doing?" Pratt said. "He'll see us."

Neverson walked in our direction, his eyes sweeping the store.

"Shit." We crouched down and slipped out from behind the blind, ducked behind cases of Coke and Pepsi. Pratt crawled behind cases of tonic water, then dashed across open space, and bobbed down behind a large ice maker.

I whispered into my headset. "Costa?"

"I see him," Costa said. "He see you?"

"No. Not yet."

"Where'd he go?" Costa said.

I peeked around the soda cases. "He's by the bathroom, on his cell phone."

"Calling his partner, I'll bet," Costa said.

Neverson put his cell phone away. I plastered myself against cases of margarita mix as he walked past me to the front of the store and out the door.

"Get ready," I said into the headset.

The next customer stepped up to Manny's register, placed a case of beer on the counter, fished out his wallet. The store's phone rang. Lataesha answered it, found a pad and pen, and began writing down an order.

Booker T Webster, wearing a Donald Trump mask and gray business suit, the side of his head covered by dirty white bandages, lumbered into Manny's and made his way to the cash register. Neverson, now wearing his Trump mask, came in behind him.

I pointed my shotgun at the robbers, placed my finger on the trigger, but Manny and Lataesha were directly in the line of fire. "I don't have a shot," I whispered into the headset.

"Neither do I," Costa replied.

The two robbers pulled guns. Booker T shoved his gun in Manny's face. "Give me the money, mutha fucka." Then he pointed his gun at Lataesha. "You. Bitch. Hang up the fuckin' phone."

"Let `em do their thing," Pratt whispered. "I'll take `em on the way out."

"Put the phone down!" Booker T Webster repeated.

But Lataesha froze.

"He thinks she's calling 911," I said, panic in my voice. "He's gonna shoot her."

"Put the phone down!" Webster placed his gun to Lataesha's head. "Now!"

"Freeze!" I screamed from behind the blind. "Police."

Manny dropped down behind the counter.

Lataesha ducked.

Webster and Neverson spun, their guns pointing in my direction.

Charlie Pratt stepped out from behind the ice maker. "Merry Christmas, mother fuckers," he said, and pumped five rounds out of his shotgun.

A moment later, the only sound I could hear was the piped in Christmas music.

"Everyone stay down," I shouted as Pratt stalked across the floor and Costa rushed out of Manny's office. Together we approached the fallen gunmen, our weapons at the ready.

Adam Tip Top Nevilson's face was missing. His brains were splattered all over Manny's cash register and the one-way mirror.

Booker T Webster was bleeding from the chest but still alive. I bent down to check his wounds—he wouldn't be alive for long.

Webster looked into my face and recognized me. "I know you," he said.

Costa was on the radio calling for an ambulance.

"Be still," I said. "An ambulance is on the way."

"Plastic guns," Pratt said, incredulous, holding the realistic toy weapons. "They were carrying plastic guns."

"Tell my wife," Webster said to me, wincing through the pain, "that I love her. That I was trying to get some money to buy Christmas gifts for her and my baby girl."

"I will," I said. "I'll tell her."

Booker T Webster forced a smile, nodded a thank you, and died.

A furious face greeted Viselli, Costa, and Pratt when Booker T Webster's wife opened the door to her ghetto apartment at 8:05 Christmas morning.

"Fuck you want?" she said to the three white men who were carrying armfuls of gift-wrapped Christmas presents.

"Booker T asked us to drop these off the other day," Viselli said.

"Yeah," Pratt said. "The other day. Before—"

"Before the, er, accident," Costa interrupted.

Webster's wife regarded the three men with well-honed suspicion, realized that she recognized Viselli as a cop. She stepped aside.

The three men entered the cluttered apartment and saw a scrawny, sparsely decorated Christmas tree by a large window that hadn't been washed in years. They placed the pile of gifts underneath the tree.

They'd gotten the toys from the precinct's Toys for Tots Christmas drive. The knockoff Hermes scarf, Cartier wristwatch, and Chanel perfume they'd gotten on Canal Street.

"You there?" Webster's wife said. "When he died?"

The three cops exchanged glances. They could hear a kid's show, Scooby-Doo, playing on a TV in another room.

"We were there," Viselli finally said.

Booker T's wife knew what that meant. She nodded gravely and looked at a family photo that hung on a wall. "Did he suffer?"

"No," Viselli said. "He didn't suffer."

Webster's wife looked at the gifts that were piled under the Christmas tree and her eyes welled. "He was one dumbass mutha fucka," she said, "but I loved him." Then she turned her back as the three cops who killed her husband walked out the door.

Bodyguard

I knew at once that we were being followed—the metallic blue van, two cars back. But I was careful not to alarm the twenty-two-year-old D-list celebrity, Lindsay Andolini—of the Andolini waste disposal empire—who was sitting in the rear of the black SUV jabbering into her cell phone.

I kept checking the rearview mirrors. The van wove in and out of the pre-theater Ninth, Avenue traffic. I eased up on the accelerator. The blue van hung back. I hit the gas. The van sped up. I changed lanes. The van followed. Try as I might, I couldn't make out the numbers on the van's out-of-state license plate—the driver kept his high beams on.

I thought about pulling over, rushing the blue van, and accosting the driver, sticking a gun in the fucker's face—but that sort of conduct could cost me my bodyguard business, maybe even land me in jail.

Sirens. Ear-piercing horns.

A rush of fire engines, police cars, and ambulances came racing off of West 57th Street onto Ninth Avenue and roared south, forcing all vehicles to make way.

The blue van moved forward, angled left to allow the emergency vehicles to pass, and then stopped at a red light. The van was now one lane to the right and parallel to our SUV.

I did my best to penetrate through the van's illegally-dark tinted windows. Saw a man's silhouette. Got the impression of thick forearms. Long hair. A beard. I sensed that the van's driver was eyeballing me—this was not a member of the paparazzi.

I placed my hand on the butt of my .38.

But the light turned green and the blue van tore off. Raced one blocks south. Cut perilously across three lanes of traffic. Made a sudden right turn and disappeared onto West 55th Street.

I sat back, relaxed my gun hand.

"Everything, like, all right, Mr. Kruel?" Lindsay said from the back seat.

I turned around, watched as the beautiful young dingbat scooped a spoonful of cocaine from a small vile, placed it under her surgically enhanced nose, and snorted. It took every ounce of self-control that I could muster to stop me from calling her a stupid bitch, snatching the vile and pouring the coke out of the window. "Everything's fine, Lindsay," I said.

But everything was not fine.

And not just because my normally rabid intolerance of client drug use had relegated me to bodyguarding the very bottom of the celebrity food chain: has-been actors, over-the-hill athletes, and—worst of all—scheming politicians.

As an ex-New York City cop and former highflying, A-list celebrity bodyguard, I'd been hired to protect the very popular, but utterly talentless, reality star sitting in the back seat—Lindsay was dressed in an original Oscar de La Renta gown—on her way to the Ziegfeld Theatre for a movie première. The immediate problem being that I was alone and, therefore, understaffed, thanks to Lindsay's meddling neophyte PR agent, a clueless Hollywood phony and control freak who'd convinced Lindsay that she didn't need a security detail.

"The studio is supplying her security," the PR agent had said.

"No, they're not," I said. "They supply 'event' security, which guards the event's perimeter, the entrances, and exits. They do not guard the guests."

"But personal security makes her look like a diva!" the PR agent argued.

"She *is* a diva, you fucking moron," I said, thinking that assholes like the PR agent were just one of the many reasons that I longed to return to providing security to the A-list. "Her safety comes first."

"Look, the police already caught her stalker," the PR agent said. "Put him in prison. So who'd want to hurt her? Everyone loves her!"

"Tell me you're really not that stupid," I said. "They caught 'a' stalker. Besides, this is New York City, for Chrissakes. Crazies grow on trees."

"It's up to you," the PR agent said. "You're in charge of security."

"Meaning, I allow your 'Hail Mary' security approach, and nothing happens, you take the credit. Something goes wrong and I take the blame."

Rather than get into a pissing contest with the asshole PR agent, I had reluctantly decided to give in, forgo the requisite personal security detail, liaison with the event security company, and hope they were properly staffed for a worst case scenario.

Big mistake.

I checked the rearview mirrors for any more suspicious vehicles. Spotted two known paparazzi following in a Honda with NYP (press) license plates.

There was the indigent autograph hound known as "Radio Man" on a battered bicycle peddling furiously toward the première. Radio Man was such a fixture in the New York Film scene that George Clooney had invited him to be his guest at the 2007 Oscars—Clooney actually paid for the derelict's airfare, new clothes, a facial, hotel, and limo rides to the ceremony and after parties.

I swerved around a double-parked yellow cab, turned onto West 54th Street and saw the crowds that jammed the sidewalks from half a city block away. Several stretch limos were lined up in front of the Ziegfeld, waiting to drop off clients.

I pulled to the curb and stopped. I would wait until the other limos left before dropping Lindsay off, thereby garnering her more attention then normal from the press—she might be on the D-list but I intended to give her A-list service—I needed to do well on this job.

I eyeballed a group of gaping tourists who were staring into my back seat, trying to figure out which celebrity I was carrying. I reached into a satchel, pulled out and slipped on kidskin, lead-lined gloves. I could stop anyone with a single punch when wearing those gloves.

The other limos were pulling away from the Ziegfeld. I turned to Lindsay—the million dollar Harry Winston diamond necklace and matching earrings sparkled even in the SUV's dim light. "We ready?"

Lindsay smiled at me wonderfully. "Sure. What the fuck."

Show time.

I pulled out my cell phone, called Lindsay's asshole PR agent who was waiting for us at the front of the theatre. "We're here," I said curtly, hung up, and tapped the gas.

It was a mob scene. The exterior of the Ziegfeld Theatre was lit up with strobes and spotlights. Members of the legitimate local, national, and international press, their video cameras and microphones at the ready, were packed tightly behind metal police barricades that lined the entire length of the red carpet.

I spotted a former A-list client of mine, an Academy Award winning actor, entering the theater and felt pangs of regret. I'd lost that account by wrestling away his stash of coke, heroin, and oxycodine, and flushing it all down a toilet.

I pulled the SUV to the curb and sprang from the vehicle. I placed my hand on the rear passenger door handle and waited for the signal that Lindsay was ready to alight and make her entrance. I took that moment to scan the area.

There must have been a thousand frenzied pedestrians and fifty or so paparazzi packed behind metal police barricades on the south side of the street. A couple of tubby female police officers—of the five-foot, two-inch tall variety—stood guard by the barricades. If things got out of hand there was no way they could control the crowed.

I looked for the event security detail and saw only three or four men.

This was not good. I had to get Lindsay into the Ziegfeld as fast as possible.

I felt the vehicle door crack open so I peered inside. Lindsay graced me with a wink and a smile. But I didn't open her door. Instead I pulled out a handkerchief and handed it to her. "Your nose."

Lindsay checked herself in the SUV's overhead makeup mirror, saw the cocaine residue on her nostrils and upper lip, giggled, and wiped it off. "Okay?"

I gave her the thumbs-up, swung the door open, offered my hand, but positioned myself to momentarily obscure the cameras just in case Lindsay's dress rode up. Lindsay placed her hand in mine, then stepped ever so gracefully—even in six-inch heels—from the SUV.

There was an explosion of flashbulbs. A roar from the crowd. Lindsay stopped and waved. Waved to the red carpet press. Waved to the fans across the street. Worked them into a frenzy by blowing them kisses.

Lindsay's asshole PR agent found us, did an air-kiss routine then whispered something into her ear. Lindsay smiled and nodded. And then she did the unexpected, the unthinkable. She and the asshole PR agent walked away from me, away from the relative safety of the red carpet and theatre, across the street to sign autographs.

Fuck!

I abandoned the SUV, scrambled to position myself at Lindsay's side, did my best to control the situation while keeping a close eye on the pedestrians' hands. *Never mind their eyes or words. Watch their hands.*

"Lindsay!" Radio Man said and produced three 8-by-10 publicity shots of Lindsay for her to sign—rumor was that he sold them to a dealer who auctioned off autographed celebrity photos on the Internet.

Lindsay obliged then moved along the barricade, scribbling her autograph on everything and anything that the fans thrust at her.

"Take a picture with me?" a gushing twenty-something-year-old guy said, a small digital camera in his hands.

"I want a picture too," a teenage girl said.

"Me too," a tattooed biker type demanded. "I came all the way from fucking Baltimore!"

I didn't like the biker's tone. My eyes went to his hands: nothing but a digital camera.

"I'm, like, sorry," Lindsay said sweetly, signing autographs in quick succession. "I take a photo with you,"—sniffle—"I'll have to take one with, like, everybody. I'll never get into the première."

"Please, please, please," the teenage girl wheedled.

"All right," the asshole PR agent said. "One photo."

I wanted to strangle the guy. "That's not a good idea," I said.

"No one asked you," the PR agent said, "did they?" He took the girl's camera. Aimed it at the girl and Lindsay. "Smile," he said and snapped the photo.

That was when the crowd surged.

Metal police barricades fell.

The short, tubby female cops screamed that everyone should stop where they were—no one listened.

I grabbed Lindsay's hand. Pulled her away just as the throng poured over the fallen barricades.

I steered Lindsay toward the red carpet.

A couple of European paparazzi tried to block our path. I knocked them aside. Sent one careening into Lindsay's asshole PR agent, who fell and cracked his head on the pavement.

A half-dozen screeching soccer-mom types rushed Lindsay, begging for autographs. I plowed through them.

The tattooed biker from Baltimore came from behind. Grabbed Lindsay. Spun her around.

"Take a picture with me!" he said, hand gripping Lindsay's bare arm.

"I, like, can't...." Lindsay said, clearly alarmed.

"Let go of her," I said. "Now."

"Fuck you," the biker said.

I pulverized the guy, punching him in the face three times in quick succession. The biker crumpled to the ground, blood streaming from his nose and mouth. A pack of delirious groupies, screaming Lindsay's name, pitched forward, surrounding Lindsay and me, cutting us off from the red carpet and the theater.

Lindsay panicked, lurched to the right, away from the groupies; one of her high-heels broke and she stumbled—I grabbed her just in time. Picked her up. Cradled her in my arms—she couldn't have weighed more than a hundred pounds—and shouldered forward.

I carried Lindsay along the red carpet perimeter, bypassed the press, entered the theatre through the main entrance and placed her gently on the carpeted steps just inside.

"You all right?" I said.

"What the fuck?" Lindsay said catching her breath.

"Are you crazy?" The asshole PR agent was now standing alongside me, his hand pressed to an angry lump on his head. "You beat that man senseless for no reason."

"And you saw that when? While you were lying on your back?"

"I saw enough," the PR guy said.

"This is all your fault." I grabbed the asshole by his tuxedo lapels, slammed him against a wall. "If we had the necessary security detail none of this would have happened."

I let the PR guy go and turned to Lindsay. "This punk nearly got you trampled to death. Get rid of `im."

"I can't," Lindsay sniffled. "Daddy hired him."

"You don't fire *him*, the PR guy said, "I'll quit!"

Lindsay looked at the PR agent, then at me, and began to cry.

The PR guy pulled a handkerchief from his pocket and a little brown vile flew out, bounced off a wall, and fell to the floor.

I picked it up, examined the contents; it was cocaine.

"You know what?" I tossed the vile to Lindsay. "You two deserve each other."

"Thanks." Lindsay said and slipped the coke into her bra. "What . . ?"

"I quit," I said, turned and walked out of the Ziegfeld Theatre.

The Faggot

"Faggot!" a man shouted at a leggy blonde from a passing pickup truck.

"Cocksucker!" another man yelled from the pickup's passenger side.

The leggy blonde stopped and shot the truck's inhabitants the finger.

The pickup screeched to a halt.

Sean Gallogy witnessed the exchange as he and a recent acquaintance, Miss Moneypenny—he'd forgotten her real name—staggered out of the White Horse Tavern onto a sultry, nearly deserted Hudson Street in the West Village around two a.m. Gallogy had met the middle-aged, rather elegantly dressed businesswoman a few hours ago, charmed her away from a swarm of frisky off-duty firefighters, and spent a small fortune plying her with alcohol in an attempt to coax her to his friend's vacant apartment—Gallogy's intentions were less than honorable.

The doors to the pickup flew open, and three burly rednecks wearing brightly colored muscle shirts and sporting swastika tattoos piled out.

"We're gonna teach you a lesson, beaner," the largest of the trio, its apparent leader, said, raising a fifth of Jack Daniel's in his right hand.

The blonde stood her ground. "You're making a mistake."

The rednecks stopped in their tracks, exchanged quizzical looks.

"He's probably got a knife or a gun," a portly redneck said.

"I wouldn't put anything past a wetback faggot," the leader said.

"That it, greaser?" a freckled redneck said. "You carrying a gun?"

"I don't need a gun." The blonde kicked off her heels, pulled off the wig she had been wearing, tossed it aside, and stepped into a boxer's stance. "C'mon. One at a time."

The three rednecks broke into hysterical laughter.

"Look at this shit," Gallogy said to Moneypenny.

Moneypenny fingered the string of Mikimoto pearls that complemented her Dolce & Gabbana business suit. "Look at what?"

"Those three drunk assholes," Gallogy said.

Moneypenny belched a squall of bourbon, cigarettes, and burger grease as she squinted at the ruckus. "What're they doing?"

"Harassing that woman."

"That's a woman?"

It took a moment for Gallogy's beery eyes to focus; the leggy blonde woman was now an average-sized Hispanic man. Gallogy recalled an incident, not long ago, in which an Ecuadoran immigrant was beaten to death by three men with baseball bats yelling anti-gay and anti-Latino slurs. The assailants were captured, convicted, and sentenced to long prison terms.

"They're gay bashers," Gallogy said. He checked the pickup truck's license plate. "They're up here from Georgia."

His newest love didn't like the way the situation was developing. "Let's go, handsome," Monypenny said with some urgency. She took Gallogy by the hand and tried to pull him down the block, away from the disturbance.

Gallogy didn't budge. He looked south across Hudson Street. The Sixth precinct was located on Tenth Street just a few blocks away. He hoped that an RMP would come cruising north; someone had to save the guy in drag from the rednecks.

"Let's go," Moneypenny said with growing alarm. "I mean it. I don't want any trouble."

"Those assholes could kill that guy."

"What business of it is yours?"

Gallogy looked probingly at Moneypenny.

He usually told women when they first met that he was a defrocked priest, a reality TV show producer, or a Vegas lounge singer; all of those types conveyed a certain romance. In truth he was a New York City police sergeant—therein laid that night's problem.

Gallogy was recovering from a gunshot wound he'd sustained during a gunfight with an armed robber and had been out of work on sick report for over two months. If he were caught out of his residence drinking, in a street brawl, he would be fired from the NYPD. Guaranteed.

"All right," Moneypenny said nervously. "If you're trying to impress me, lover, you've succeeded. You're very brave." She placed a tanned, bejeweled hand to her bosom, batted her bloodshot baby blues and graced Gallogy with a pretty good Scarlett O'Hara. "I declare, Rhett, you are the bravest man I know." She cut the act, took Gallogy by the arm. "Now, are you going to take me back to your place and fuck me properly, or not?"

Gallogy's eyes had never left the rednecks.

They'd stopped laughing and returned to their pickup truck.

Gallogy thought for a moment that the confrontation was over. But the three didn't climb back into their vehicle and drive away. They pulled three baseball bats from the backseat.

The victim scooped up his shoes and wig and tried to hurry away.

But the rednecks spread out, cutting off his escape.

294

"We're gonna teach you a lesson, cocksucker."

There was no way Gallogy would allow what was about to happen, even if it meant losing his job. He removed Moneypenny's hand from his arm.

"Why don't you go back inside?" Gallogy took out his wallet, handed her a twenty. "Order a drink. Play the jukebox. I'll only be a moment."

She snatched the twenty. "Don't be too long, lover." Moneypenny walked unsteadily back into the White Horse Tavern, and was at once enveloped by the frisky firefighters—Gallogy never did like firefighters.

The leader let out a Rebel yell and swung his baseball bat.

The victim ducked.

The portly redneck charged and knocked the victim against a brick wall, then jabbed his bat into the guy's midsection, doubling him over.

The freckled redneck stepped up and cocked his bat as if testing out his home-run swing.

"Hold it," Gallogy said, training his .38 on the three. "Drop the bats or I'll drop you."

The three faces changed instantly from blood lust to fear. Slowly the rednecks lowered their bats, exchanged nervous, drunken giggles.

"You a queer-loving Jew," the leader said, "or you a faggot too?"

"One last time," Gallogy said. "Drop the bats."

"You ain't gonna shoot the three of us," the leader said.

"No?" Gallogy quickly closed the distance and slashed the leader across the face with the barrel of his gun, opening his face to the bone. The redneck collapsed to the pavement, spitting blood and broken teeth.

"Anyone else?" Gallogy brandished his weapon.

The two remaining rednecks dropped their bats.

The victim struggled to his feet.

"You okay?" Gallogy said.

"I will be." The victim took a moment to catch his breath, straighten his clothing

"Fucking, faggot," the portly redneck sniggered.

The victim took two steps forward and threw a left hook to portly's solar plexus. His breath roared out as he fell to the pavement and rolled into the fetal position.

Enraged, the freckled redneck charged.

The victim feinted left, grabbed Freckles by the shirt, spun him around, and threw him against a store's security gate. The gate acted like a trampoline, bouncing Freckles back into a flurry of brutal rib-cracking left and right body blows. Freckles was crying when he stumbled back into the store's doorway.

Gallogy had to admit he was impressed; the guy could throw a punch.

"C'mon, you Nazi pricks," the victim said, fists at the ready, daring anyone of his attackers to get up; there were no takers. The guy lowered his fists, stepped back into his high heels and pulled on his wig. As he checked his reflection in a storefront plate-glass window, Gallogy gave him the once-over.

He was wiry but muscular. Through some thick body makeup Gallogy could just make out the outline of a Special Forces tattoo on the guy's bicep—that explained the skills. If the tattoo was for real, the drunken rednecks were lucky to be alive.

The victim finished primping. "I'm Henrietta." He offered his hand.

The police sergeant shook. "Sean Gallogy," he said and noticed suddenly that lights had flicked on in several apartments on both sides of the street. Windows were open, and people were leaning out, looking down on the scene. "We'd better get moving," Gallogy said.

Someone moan.

The leader was struggling to his feet.

Henrietta kicked the guy once in the side, knocking the wind out of him.

Gallogy picked up the redneck's baseball bats and tossed them into the idling pickup truck. He turned off the engine. Removed the keys. Closed and locked the vehicle doors. Pitched the keys into an open sewer. "Let's go."

"I owe you." Henrietta was reapplying lipstick as they hurried away.

"Yeah? Well, maybe you can do me a favor?"

"Sure." Henrietta took out some breath mints, gave one to Gallogy, then popped one into his own mouth. "If I can."

"I was with this woman at a bar up the street. A group of firemen made a move on her. Maybe you could help me out, run some interference so I can get her back?"

"Firemen?" Henrietta said. "I simply *adore* firemen."

Considering what he had just witnessed, Henrietta's transformation from masculine to feminine was startling. Smiling, Gallogy offered his arm. "Shall we, Henrietta?"

Henrietta hooked Gallogy's arm. "Yes, kind sir."

Gallogy escorted Henrietta away from the crime scene, down Hudson Street, and into the White Horse Tavern—but Mrs. Moneypenny was nowhere in sight.

Gallogy cleaved through the crowd, searched both ends of the bar then checked the side room. Spotted Moneypenny at a table, sitting on a firefighter's lap, sucking face.

"Good God," Henrietta said over his shoulder. "Don't tell me that's her?"

"Yeah," Gallogy said glumly.

"What a slut," Henrietta said.

"That was the point." Gallogy turned back to the bar. "Want a drink?"

"Let's get out of here," Henrietta said.

"And go where?"

"A quiet little place. Around the corner."

Gallogy looked at Henrietta's silhouette, illuminated by the soft bar lights. There was a softness, even gentleness, in his face. He took a moment. Looked back toward Moneypenny—the firefighter had his hands under her blouse. His eyes swept the rest of the bar, looking for possibilities; there were none.

"I'm buying the drinks," Henrietta said.

"Sure," Gallogy said. "Why not?"

Henrietta took hold of Gallogy's arm, and he squired him though the bar, out the door, and down the deserted street.

Mad Dog Cole

"It's 'Mad Dog Cole'," said *New York Post* crime reporter Sean Egan over his cell phone to the *Post*'s city desk editor. Egan was out of bullet range, behind a large news truck, amid a surging wave of print and electronic media journalists. Directly around the corner was a group of flak-jacketed, armed-and-ready Emergency Service Unit (ESU) police officers.

"They got him trapped in an abandoned warehouse," Egan said. He took out an old Zippo, used it to fire up a Marlboro Red. "He robbed a Chase branch over on Twenty-Third Street. That detective, you know the one, the serial self-promoter, the one talks like a buffoon— Bo Welsh, yeah, that's his name. Welsh. Well, Welsh was waiting for Cole outside the bank." Egan jumped aside to allow a kamikaze bicyclist to pass. "How the hell should I know how Welsh knew? No. I don't believe in coincidences." Egan puffed his cigarette.

"Welsh chased Cole down Twenty-Second Street. Cole ran into the warehouse, barricaded himself in. Welsh backed off, called for reinforcements." Egan took another drag, blew out the smoke. "Where's Welsh now?" Egan looked around, spotted Welsh behind another network news van. He was surrounded by a news crew preparing him for a live TV interview; they were setting up a camera, checking the lighting and sound, and showing Welsh where to stand. A female makeup artist was applying makeup to Welsh's fat face.

"You can't make a silk purse out of a sow's ear, honey," Egan said under his breath, referring to the fact that Welsh possessed the look, cocky manner, and fractured vocabulary of an uneducated thug.

"I swear," Egan said to the editor, "that guy Welsh has never seen a camera he didn't like."

A police captain stepped from behind the safety of an ESU truck and spoke into a bullhorn. "Mike Cole. This is the police. Lay down your weapons and come out with your hands up."

"Something's going down," Egan said. "I'll call you back." Egan put away his cell phone, dumped his cigarette. He moseyed around the corner, through the police ranks, over toward the captain, and was yanked behind a van by a crusty old ESU sergeant.

"Egan," the sergeant said. "You wanna get shot?! Not that I give a shit. One less sleazy reporter is good for humanity."

Egan lit another cigarette, took a drag. "By my count, that makes seventy-three banks that Cole robbed. That beats Eddie Dodson's record of seventy-two—that's if you believe Detective Welsh's arithmetic."

"Who gives a shit," the sergeant said.

Egan shrugged. "Welsh's a media whore. Cole's a media darling. As of an hour ago, he's robbed more banks than anyone in history—that's according to Welsh."

"Yeah. So?"

"Don't it seem odd to you?" Egan said. "The rivalry."

"What rivalry?"

"Welsh and Cole," Egan said. "They're like a modern day version of Elliot Ness and Al Capone."

The sergeant sniggered. "Welsh is no Ness."

"And Cole's no Capone. I mean, sure, he's robbed a lot of banks, but he never hurt anyone. And he spends every dime he steals on his son's cancer treatments."

"Tell me something I don't know."

"What with all the violent thugs in the city," Egan said, "you'd think Welsh would focus his energies on one of them."

300

"What're you trying to say?"

"I don't know." Egan dropped his freshly lit cigarette, crushed it out with his foot. "It's just that Cole was a nobody until Welsh started calling him 'Mad Dog' and made him public enemy number one. Hell, weren't the two of them on the cover of *New York Magazine* recently? Thanks to Welsh, Cole's a bona fide celebrity."

The captain said into the bullhorn, "You're completely surrounded, Cole. Lay down your weapons; come out with your hands up."

Gunfire. The captain dove for cover.

Bullets strafed the brick walls above the police ranks.

The cops returned fire. There was a fusillade of shots. Warehouse windows shattered.

"Hold your fire," the captain yelled into the bullhorn. "I said, *hold your fire*."

Silence.

"Looks like Welsh didn't name him 'Mad Dog' for nothing," the sergeant said, waving the thick gun smoke away from his face. "Fucker's got a death wish."

"I doubt that's the plan," Egan said.

"Plan?" the sergeant said. "What the hell're you talking about?"

Egan heard a commotion. Looked and saw that Welsh had finished with his TV interview. He had slipped off his suit jacket and was pulling on a bulletproof vest. One production assistant helped Welsh fasten the Velcro straps on the vest while another played valet and held Welsh's jacket. The makeup artist touched up Welsh's makeup.

"A cop wearing makeup." The sergeant shook his head. "I admit I cringe every time that prima donna opens his big mouth, but Welsh's a hardworking cop. You gotta hand him that."

"Here we go," Egan said.

301

Welsh swaggered across the street, toward the warehouse, stopped when he saw Egan, and nodded— Welsh always had time for a member of the mainstream press. "How ya doin', Egan?"

"Ready for your close up?" Egan said.

"I wuz born ready." Welsh adjusted his suit jacket, straightened his tie, pulled his Glock, and racked a round into the chamber. "It's time I brought Cole out," he said, as if all the other cops were there as his supporting players.

"Where you think you're going, Detective?" the sergeant said.

"To get Cole," Welsh said.

"Negative. ESU has it now."

"I been chasing fuckin' Cole for two fuckin' years," Welsh said, an edge to his voice. "Hell, I chased the skumpbag here. It's my fuckin' case."

"Yeah, sure," the sergeant said. "You can interview him after we bring him out, or ID the body. Either way, stay the fuck out of our way."

Welsh started to protest then stopped. Unlike TV cops, Welsh knew better than to give lip to a uniformed sergeant, that's if he wanted to remain a detective.

Welsh stormed off pouting. He strode across the street, stopped in a store doorway. He glared back at the sergeant, paced in angry circles then pulled out his cell phone.

"Who do you think he's calling?" Egan said.

"Fuck should I know?" the sergeant responded irritably.

"I'll bet he's calling Cole."

"Cole?" The sergeant looked toward Welsh then back at Egan. "You know, I don't like Welsh, but I like you even less. Get the fuck away from me, Egan. Go on. Get outta here before I hit you in the head with something. Go on. I'm not kidding."

302

Egan grinned at the old sergeant. "I'm going." He stuck a cigarette in his mouth, lit it, and sauntered across the street. He stopped when he got within a few feet of Welsh, then faded into the throng of news people and rubbernecking pedestrians—he cocked an ear. Watched. Waited.

Egan finished his smoke, reached for another, and realized he was out. He crushed the empty pack, tossed it in a nearby trash can then tried in vain to bum a smoke off of someone, anyone—it pissed him off that almost no one smoked anymore.

Egan thought about dashing to the corner store and buying a pack, but he knew that, if what he thought was about to happen was happening, it would only be a matter of minutes before someone came looking for Welsh.

"Captain wants to see you," the old ESU sergeant said to Welsh not five minutes later.

"Yeah?" Welsh smirked. "Why's that?"

"Cole's willing to give himself up, but only to you."

Egan stepped out of the crowd, came up behind the sergeant.

"Hear that, Egan?" Welsh said.

"I heard," Egan said.

"Well ain't that somethink," Welsh said with a smug grin. "C'mon, Egan—and the rest of youse guys from the press. Youse're gonna wanna see this." Chest out, Welsh strutted across the street to the ESU truck, a dozen reporters in tow.

"Yes, chief," the captain said into the cell phone. Welsh's here now. You'll know as soon as I do." The captain closed his cell phone.

"You wanna see me, captain?" Welsh said.

"Fuck is going on here?"

"Excuse me?"

"What's with you and Cole?"

303

"I been chasin' the skumpbag for years," Welsh said. "Him and me have a, a whatchamacallit; a kinda rapport. Ya know?"

"No, I don't know." The captain noticed Welsh's makeup and made a disgusted face. "I don't like grandstanding, Welsh."

For once Welsh kept his mouth shut.

"You'll go in," the captain said. "You bring Cole out—no fucking around."

"Understood," Welsh said.

"Cole wants you unarmed," the captain said.

Welsh hesitated one lone theatrical moment. "Fine with me."

The captain regarded Welsh. "You sure you wanna go through with this?"

"*Try to stop him*," Egan mumbled and the sergeant shot him a look.

"I'm sure," Welsh said. He surrendered his Glock to the captain, then his backup .38 then took off his suit jacket and handed it to one of the cops.

"Things go wrong, try to get him close to a window," the captain said. "A sniper will take him out. Otherwise, you got ten minutes."

"Ten minutes?" Welsh said. "What if it takes longer, I mean, I might hafta talk the fuckin' mutt down. Who knows how nuttso he is."

The captain shook his head. "If you're not out in ten minutes, I'm sending in backup."

Welsh heaved a sigh. "All right. Ten minutes."

"You ready?"

"Let's do it." Welsh took a deep breath, walked toward the warehouse entrance. Several flak-jacketed cops patted him on the back, wished him good luck.

And then Welsh entered the warehouse alone.

Ten minutes later, Egan heard a roar from the crowd and saw an explosion of flash bulbs. Shouts of "roll tape!" were followed by reporters and camera crews rushing to get close to Mad Dog Cole and Bo Welsh.

Cole's hands were cuffed behind his back. Welsh had him by the arm. The ESU troops held the media back as Welsh guided Cole to a waiting police car and placed him in the backseat. Welsh got in beside him. The driver switched on the lights and sirens and pulled away from the scene.

Egan was waiting for Welsh three hours later when Welsh walked into the Bullpen Pub, a cop hangout on First Avenue and East 88th Street. The old-time bartender, Paul "Squeaks" McGuire, placed a cold bottle of Budweiser in front of Welsh as he bellied up to the bar.

"Christ, you're all over the news," Squeaks said, indicating the dozen large flat-screen TVs that were fixed to the walls around the bar. Squeaks shook Welsh's hand. "Good job."

"Yeah. Thanks." Welsh took a long drink from his bottle, turned to shake hands with a few active and retired cops who were regulars, when he noticed Egan sitting at the far end of the bar.

Egan lifted his scotch on the rocks and toasted Welsh.

"Be right back," Welsh said to the guys at the bar then took his beer and sat alongside Egan. "What brings you here, Egan?"

"Was hoping to run into Mike Sheehan or Big Frank McDarby."

"Yeah? Why's that?"

Egan sipped his drink. "I'm writing a novel."

"No shit?"

"I need a collaborator. Someone who can fill me in on the inside workings of a top detective's mind, how a cop really thinks and feels—you wouldn't be interested. Would you?"

"Depends. I get credit?"

"Sure," Egan said. "Below the title will read 'by Ed Egan and Bo Welsh'."

"How about 'by Bo Welsh and Ed Egan'?"

"Sure," Egan chuckled. "Why not?"

"What's the book about?"

"How about we sit at a table," Egan said, "and I'll sketch it for you."

Egan ordered two more drinks then he and Welsh got up to sit at a corner table.

"Here's the premise," Egan said after they'd settled in. "We have a hard-working, middle class guy; we'll make him a construction worker. He's got a wife and small son. He and his wife have the usual marital problems, not enough money being the main one. But all in all, they're a happily married couple—then their kid gets leukemia.

"Within a couple of months both the guy and his wife get laid off. They lose their medical coverage, have no way to pay for their son's treatments. What with the economy neither one can land a decent job. She takes a job at McDonald's. Waits tables. He pumps gas days. Tends bar at night. But the money's not enough. The couple's forced to borrow what little they can from their families. Friends at their old jobs take up collections, throw fund raisers for them. The Catholic Church gets involved. But no matter how hard the couple tries, they can't come up with enough cash to pay for their son's intensive chemo and radiation treatments.

"When things seem like they can't get any worse, the guy's wife says she can't take anymore. She has a nervous breakdown, deserts the guy and their son. Takes off for parts unknown. Without her measly paychecks, the guy falls behind on their rent. Gets evicted.

"So the guy's devastated. His wife's gone. He's watching his son die before his eyes, and there's nothing he can do about it. He tries going on public assistance, but qualifying is a long, drawn-out process that his son won't survive—the kid desperately needs a bone marrow transplant. The guy goes into a deep depression; starts drinking heavily. He probably considers suicide. But he snaps out of it, gets sober. And then he gets angry. Rather than allow his son to die he begins go rob banks."

"Hey," Welsh said, "that's Cole's story."

"That's where I got the idea," Egan said. "But don't forget, we're writing fiction."

"I get it," Welsh said.

"Anyway," Egan says, "so this guy—let's call him Cole for the sake of discussion—becomes a master of disguise and robs about thirty banks. Now enters our protagonist, the cop who's gonna bring Cole down."

"Beautiful. I love it," Welsh said. "Keep talking."

"Well, this cop's very ambitious. He's not satisfied being just another cop. He wants to be known as the best cop in New York. He wants fame, notoriety, and the financial rewards that go with it."

"A man after my own heart," Welsh said.

"Exactly. So, this cop—"

"Let's call him Welsh," Welsh said. "For the sake of discussion."

"Why not?" Egan said. "So Welsh's unit, Major Case, is working day and night investigating all of these bank robberies. Welsh comes to the conclusion that they're all being committed by one man. But no one agrees with him. So Welsh starts working on his own time, trying to prove his theory. What initially tips him off to Cole is two parking tickets that were issued to Cole's car in the vicinity of two bank robberies. Welsh checks the plate number on the two tickets, finds out where Cole lives. He starts following Cole when he's off duty. Watches him pump gas. Tend bar. Watches him visit his son

307

every day at Sloan-Kettering. What cinches it for Welsh is when he investigates Cole's finances: his credit's a mess. After being evicted from his residence, and having virtually no credit, Cole's found a way to rent another apartment, buy a used car, and pay for his son's medical expenses. Welsh decides that Cole's either a drug dealer, or he's the elusive bank robber."

"So far this is all true," Welsh said. "Thought you were writin' fiction."

"What I'm telling you is only an outline, more or less," Egan said. "We'll change things as we go, take liberties with the facts. For instance: maybe we introduce a leading lady—Cole and the cop could both be in love with her."

"A love triangle?" Welsh said. "Fuckin' beautiful."

"And what if we make Cole's character a handsome black guy. And the cop, what if we make him bisexual, a guy struggling with his sexuality. Maybe he's attracted to the lady and Cole?"

"That's a terrible fuckin' idea."

"I'm just tossing shit against a wall," Egan said. "See what sticks. I mean, the last thing we wanna do is wind up paying Cole a piece of our action."

"So Cole don't have to be a nigger?" Welsh said. "The cop don't have to be a queer?"

"No. Of course not," Egan said. "If you want we'll make the cop a ruggedly handsome romantic lead…you know, a Sean Connery type."

"Like me."

Egan did a double take. "Yeah. Like you. Okay. Where was I—oh, yeah. After following Cole for a couple of months, the cop—"

"Welsh," Welsh said.

"Right. Welsh gets lucky. He tails Cole to a bank, watches him get out of his car wearing a disguise, sees him go into the bank and actually rob it. Welsh's

308

ecstatic. He can't wait to show up all the other boneheaded detectives in his unit who scoffed at his theory. He follows Cole, is about to pull him over and arrest him, when it suddenly dawns on him that Cole's not your average bank robber. The guy is working two menial jobs, robbing banks and spending every cent he earns, legal and otherwise, on his son's medical expenses—in this economy, the public might see Cole as a hero. Which gives Welsh an idea...

Mike Cole nearly had a heart attack when he saw the man sitting at his kitchen table, in the darkness, pointing a gun. Cole leapt back from the open refrigerator, backpedaled, and fell over his son's toy fire engine.

"Easy, Cole," the man said. "I ain't here ta hurt you."

Cole struggled to his feet, did his best to recover some semblance of dignity. "Who the fuck're you?" trying for tough but falling short.

"Bo Welsh."

"That supposed to mean something to me?"

"Detective Bo Welsh." Welsh produced his badge. "Siddown."

Cole's mind raced. Did this cop know who he was? Was he here to arrest him? Would he ever see his son again? Cole glanced out to the street. Didn't see any flashing lights or police cars. If this cop were here to arrest him, he'd most certainly bring backup. Cole sat down at the kitchen table across from Welsh.

"What's this about?" Cole said.

Welsh slipped his gun into his shoulder holster. "I gotta proposition for ya."

"A proposition?" Cole smirked. "You couldn't just call me up like a normal person? You gotta break into my apartment in the middle of the night, stick a gun in my face? My wife and kid are sleeping in the back bedrooms."

Welsh smiled. "Your son's a patient at Sloan-Kettering. Your wife left you."

"How the fuck you know that?"

"I know."

Cole sat back. "Well? Let's hear it."

"You got any beer?"

"What?"

"You heard me—beer. You got any beer?"

Cole got to his feet, opened the refrigerator, took out two bottles of beer, handed one to Welsh, and sat back down.

Welsh twisted off the bottle cap. Took a long pull, made a disgusted face. "Yuck. What, this have lime in it?"

"What in the fuck do you want?"

Welsh put the beer down. "I'm here to do you a big favor—I'm your, whatchamacallit, your white fuckin' knight."

"Do tell."

"You're a bank robber—now don't bother to deny it," Welsh said. "You've got style—the way you disguise yourself. The fact you've never hurt anyone."

"I don't know what you're talking about."

"But most importantly, you ain't stealin' for greed or because you're a lazy wackadoodle skumpbag. You're stealin' to pay for your son's medical expenses. Which is admirable. And is why I chose you."

"Chose me. For what?"

Welsh sipped some beer. "Know what makes people great?"

"This is a riddle?"

"Rivalries," Welsh said. "Think Ali versus Frazier. Red Sox versus Yankees. Lakers versus Celtics. The FBI versus the Mafia. Get the picture?"

Cole shrugged. "No."

"Remember Frank Lucas? Richie Roberts?"

310

"Who?"

"Frank Lucas, only one of the most powerful black gangsters that ever lived in Harlem— public enemy number one. Richie Roberts was his adversary, the cop that made Lucas famous. They made a movie about them, American Gangster?"

"Oh, right."

"Denzel Washington played Lucas in the film. Russell Crowe played the cop—we do this right, they'll make a film about us."

"Us?" Cole leaned forward. "Do what right?"

"Create, implement, orchestrate a rivalry—and not just any rivalry. We'll be the talk of the town. We'll be on Entertainment Tonight. Page Six. TV shows will follow our exploits."

"Man, I don't know what the fuck you're talking about."

Welsh broke into a wide grin. "You're a crook, you dumb fuck. I'm a cop. I'm gonna make you the next Frank Lucas. The next public enemy number one."

"Say again?" Cole gaped at the cop.

"Public. Enemy. Number. One."

"You are?" Cole sniggered. "And what? I'm supposed to thank you?"

Welsh got up, walked over to the kitchen window, gazed down to the street. "Look, I can arrest you right now and you'll do a hundred years in a federal prison. But then your son will die of leukemia. But if I don't arrest you, allow you to go on robbing banks, several things happen." Welsh sat back down, looked directly at Cole. "First and foremost, you'll be able to keep taking care of your son."

Cole leaned forward. "Yeah?"

"I'll run interference for you when I can," Welsh continued. "Maybe help you pick the safest banks to rob." Welsh sat back, crossed his legs. "Of course I'll *have to help you find a safe house, a hideaway that only you and me will know about."*

"What's in it for you?"

Welsh grinned. "With my help, it's only a matter of time before you set the record for most banks robbed. Once you get close to the record, that's when we go public: I ID you, plaster your face everywhere, get your featured on America's Most Wanted. *I'll talk to every reporter in every newspaper and TV show. Every cop in the country will be looking for you. The whole world will be watching, waiting for you to be captured or break the bank robbery record. And when you do, that's when I move in and arrest 'Mad Dog Cole'."*

"Mad Dog Cole?" Cole said.

"Yeah. I came up with it the other day. Catchy, right?"

"Ya think?" Cole knew he had to get away from this crazy cop. But he was too big to take in a fair fight. And he'd shoot him if he attempted to run. Cole decided to use his beer bottle to hit the cop over the head if he got a chance, and then make a run for it.

"Hell, your arrest'll be a media event," Welsh said. "The news coverage will be unprecedented. The trial will be bigger then O.J. Simpson's. And I'll go to bat for you at trial. Admit that economic circumstance and the lack of affordable health insurance left you no choice. That you were the victim, a poor working slob who did what he had to do to save his son's life. By the time I get done, the media will be calling you an American hero. The poster boy for all that's wrong with out-of-reach medical insurance in this country."

Cole picked up his beer bottle, took a swig, then lowered it below the table, out of the cop's sight, and gripped it like a club. Soon as the cop gave him the chance, he'd flip the table over, hit him on the head.

"You'll go to jail, of course," Welsh said. "But here's the kicker. I'll get rich and famous making you famous. We'll be the next Frank Lucas and Richie Roberts. There'll be book deals. Movie deals. Now you can't profit legally from those proceeds, but I'll set up a private trust. And I promise you, on my word of honor, that your son's medical expenses will be paid for."

Cole froze. "Repeat that?"

"I said I'll pay for your son's medical expenses."

Cole put his beer bottle back on the table. Took a deep breath, blew it out. "Hypothetically speaking, let's say I'm who you think I am. How do I know you'll keep your word?"

"You won't." Welsh sipped more beer. "But you have no choice."

"Meaning, you arrest me now—"

"And your son dies."

"Or I do what you ask—"Cole said.

"And your son lives."

"So Cole goes for the plan," Egan said. "He sets the record for the most banks robbed. Welsh arrests him; a spectacular media-fueled event just like your arrest today. There'll be a long, televised trial. Like you, our protagonist will spend days on the witness stand. Weeks, maybe even months in the newspapers and on TV. He'll be one of the most famous cops that ever lived, a household name. Another Wyatt Earp. A Pat Garrett. He gets filthy rich off the notoriety and fame—you with me so far?"

Welsh sat back in his chair. He looked like he'd swallowed a hairbrush.

"Well?" Egan said. "What do you think so far?"

"It's thin."

"Anorexic," Egan said.

"The premise is ri-fuckin'-diculous," Welsh said. "No one's gonna believe a New York City detective would

313

enter into a criminal conspiracy with a notorious bank robber."

"Oh, they'll believe it all right," Egan said.

"Yeah?" Welsh squinted at the reporter. "You think so, huh?"

"They'll believe it because it's true," Egan said. "Isn't it?"

Welsh looked down at his beer. "You wearing a wire, Egan?"

"No." Egan stood, took off his suit jacket, stepped around to Welsh's side of the table and spun around.

Welsh executed a thorough, practiced pat-down.

"Well?" Egan said as he sat back down.

"You're not writing a book," Welsh said, "are you?"

Egan shook his head. "No."

"A story for the *Post*?" Welsh said.

Egan took a moment. "Not exactly."

"What then?"

"I don't know." Egan finished his drink. "There's no way I can prove my theory. Long as you keep paying for Cole's son's medical bills, he won't flip."

Welsh thought about that then grinned self importantly. "Now what?"

"Even though I think you're a self-serving narcissist and belong in jail, in the end you're saving a little boy's life. There's no way I'd interfere with that."

"You're saving your own life too."

"Come again?"

"If you ever print that story, I'll put a bullet in your fuckin' head, dump your body over in New Jersey, blam it on the mob."

Egan looked at the detective, forced a laugh. "You're kidding."

Welsh got angrily to his feet, picked up his beer. "I kid you not."

314

Egan watched Welsh stop at the bar and ask for his check.

"He's on the way out," Egan said into the microphone that was hidden under the table.

Welsh paid his bill, left a tip, and headed for the door.

The first thing Welsh saw when he stepped outside was the crusty, old ESU sergeant glaring at him, shaking his head in apparent disgust. Then he noticed the ESU captain, standing alongside a police car, flanked by two Internal Affairs lieutenants. Suddenly a line of news vans and cars scratched to a stop. A crush of reporters and photographers piled out.

"You wanted fame," Egan said from behind him. "You've got it."

"You set me up," Welsh hissed, "you fuckin' skumpbag"

Egan lit a Marlboro Red. Watched as Bo Welsh was placed under arrest, read his rights, handcuffed, and placed into the back of a police car.

The Demon Child

"Shush!" Joe "The Runt" Saldavari said. "Hear that?" Runt stopped and listened to a chorus of baying hounds; a chill ran up his spine. He blessed himself, said a silent prayer. Used his tiny hands to block the glare from a rapidly rising, eerily bright Harvest moon. "Not good."

"Now vhat?" Max Schultz was the size of a mountain gorilla, but his voice was that of a small child. "Vhat in hell is freaking you out this time, Runt, the fact it is Halloween?"

The two men were sequestered in a plush Central Park thicket behind a stone wall, their eyes trained on a Manhattan mansion, a spooky looking fortress that housed a closet satanist: Doctor Harold Watkins III, the richest, most successful abortion doctor in America.

"How many times I gotta tell you, Max: don't call me Runt!"

"Hokey dokey." Max giggled like a girl. "Runt. Runt. Runt. Runt. Runt. Runt…."

For the hundredth time since meeting Max, Runt thought about pulling his Glock 9mm automatic and blowing the big jerk's brains out. But he needed Max's strength and shooting skills if they hoped to execute The Church of the Buzzer Chosen's plan: invade the Watkins residence, circumvent the formidable security system, overpower any resistance, abduct ten-year-old Harold Watkins IV, and hold him until Watkins III closed his one-hundred-plus abortion clinics.

"One of these days, Max—" Runt relaxed his gun hand.

They'd been rivals when they'd first met in the nation's bible belt while performing in The Church of the Buzzer Chosen's Christian Ministry Circus. Runt was a member of The Dwarfs For Jesus, an acrobat troop. Max the Avenging Angel, an ex-convict who'd done time for burglary and manslaughter, was the ministry's strongman and sharpshooter. Both happened to be in love with the same woman: Tatiana, a tattooed Hungarian missionary. She dumped them both and ran off with an up-and-coming, smooth-talking TV evangelist.

"Well," Max said. "Vhat is problem?"

Runt hesitated—he believed wholeheartedly in Heaven and Hell, God and the Devil, the supernatural. And he believed the rumors that Doctor Watkins was a Hitleresque demon sent from hell, a practitioner of black magic. That he harvested the unborn fetuses that he acquired during abortions and used their genetic material for satanic rituals like casting spells and nourishing a growing army of the undead.

"A full moon. Baying hounds. They're bad omens," Runt said.

"Bah! Vhat you afraid of?" Max was incredulous. "Ve vatch parents leave. Child is home alone with babysitter. Vhat can hurt you?"

"That's just it. I don't know. But I got a bad feeling, a *really* bad feeling."

"Bah! You vatch too many horror movies, little man."

Max pulled a folded .22 caliber sniper rifle from a backpack and snapped it open. He checked the scope and then twisted on a silencer—the plan was for him to shoot out the mansion's security lights then shoot the exterior alarm system-phone circuit box thereby preventing the system, if tripped, from calling 911. They would then break into the mansion from a rear basement window without fear of the police.

"Wish the dammed dogs would stop howling." Runt looked to the sky; the full moon was dodging behind thick, fast-moving clouds. A violent thunderstorm had been forecast. "They give me the creeps."

"Not dogs." Max cocked an ear. "Wolves."

"Wolves?" Runt's skin crawled. "Wolves in Central Park?"

"Da." Max gestured with the rifle. "Zoo that way."

"Oh. Right. The zoo." Runt relaxed a bit, chuckled at his own foolishness. He looked toward the Central Park Zoo. "I didn't think they had wolves in the park zoo. Wolves creep me out more than howling dogs."

"Everything creep you out." Max loaded the weapon, checked the action.

Runt stood nearby, wringing his hands and pacing in tight circles. "You're sure you wanna do this tonight?" Runt said; the howling seemed to be getting closer. "I mean, we can come back when there's no moon."

"Ve have job to do, little man," Max said. "Ve must stop the murder of the unborn. Every day counts."

"You're right," Runt reluctantly agreed. Even if horrific deaths awaited them, they had to at least try to stop Dr. Watkins' assembly-line abortion clinics. Runt reached into the pocket of his jacket, took out two pair of plastic surgical gloves, and handed a pair to Max.

"Put those on."

Max squinted down at the four-foot-tall dwarf.

"Sorry," Runt said. "*Please* put those on."

"Da." Max snapped on the gloves.

Runt pulled on his own gloves, then reached into the backpack and extracted an architect's blueprint of the Watkins house that they'd gotten off the Internet. Based on the blueprint and a full week of surveillance, they were pretty sure that the child's room was located on the second floor at the rear of the house. "You need to review this?"

"No," Max said.

Runt replaced the blueprint then checked to see that they'd remembered to bring lock picks, rope, masking tape, plastic restraints, two ski masks, and a black body bag with holes for breathing—that's where they planned to place the Watkins child.

Max glanced across the street. "Look."

Runt peered over the stone wall.

A man wearing a white shirt and tie had walked out of the Watkins mansion. He was standing by the curb, smoking a cigarette; a big guy, formidable. There was a .45 automatic on his hip. He smoked leisurely, glanced up and down Fifth Avenue. The streets were still and quiet, desolate at that time of night.

A little known downside to living on the fashionable avenues of Fifth, Madison, and Park was that there was no commerce of any kind. No restaurants, bars, drug stores, or groceries. The nearest signs of life were a ten minute walk over to Third Avenue.

The man dropped his cigarette and took a last lingering look around. Stretched. Yawned. Turned to walk back to the mansion.

Without saying a word, Max stood, stepped into a shooter's stance, aimed, and fired.

The man's head snapped back. He went rigid. Fell face forward into the mansion's foyer.

"What the fuck!" Runt said.

"Is easy way in," Max said and quickly broke down the weapon.

Runt looked north on Fifth Avenue, then south.

There were few cars and no people.

"Ve must hurry." Max shoved the rifle into the backpack, strapped it on.

Runt blessed himself then kissed the crucifix that was dangling from a chain around his neck. The two men pulled on the ski masks. Max bent down to allow Runt to climb onto his back into a piggyback position. If and when the police checked the many NYPD street and private building security cameras along Fifth Avenue, all they would see would be a lone monster of a masked man with a large backpack on his back.

Max vaulted over the wall, dashed across Fifth Avenue, and into the mansion.

Runt dropped off Max's back and helped drag the dead man into the vestibule.

Runt flipped the dead guy over, removed his .45, shoved it in his own waistband. He searched the guy's pockets, found his wallet, removed the cash, and peremptorily tossed the wallet aside.

"Don't forget jewelry," Max said. "Must look like robbery."

Runt pulled off the guy's watch and ring then stopped. "Hey. Look." He lifted the guy's hand; on the back "666" was written.

Max squinted and pointed his flashlight beam. "So? Is tattoo."

"No." Runt shook his head emphatically. "It's 666; three sixes. The sign of the devil."

Max looked closer. "Is flower."

"It's three sixes, I'm telling you."

"Bah!" Max switched off his flashlight, closed and locked the front door.

Runt heard movement to his left. Then noise to his right. He heard a floorboard creak upstairs, followed by a gust of wind—or was it the sound of someone breathing?

Runt pulled his Glock and the dead guy's .45 and, a gun in each hand, quickly scanned the residence.

The first floor interior was decorated like a 1950s TV version of a haunted house. There were large, dark furnishings, old dusty paintings, something out of the Addams Family.

"You seeing what I'm seeing?" Runt said.

"Da." Max had to swat thick cobwebs away so he could check out a couple of sadistic paintings and sculptures; there was a giant bat's head mounted on the wall like a prize deer.

"I didn't know bats grew that big," Runt said.

Max laughed heartily. "Is Halloween joke, no?"

"I wanna go." Runt inched back out of the foyer toward the front door. "C'mon, Max. Let's get out of here while we still can. I'm not kidding."

"Shut mouth." Max grabbed Runt by the collar and yanked him inside. "Stop nonsense."

"I can't help it, Max. I'm scared."

"I give you something to fear." Max stuck a finger in Runt's face. "You run away, I find you, squash you like bug." Max seized Runt by the shoulders, shoved him forward. "What can hurt you with two guns?"

They moved into the interior of the house. Past a rusting suit of body armor, past a vast collection of human skulls that were lined up on a wall of book shelves, until they came upon a foreboding, sweeping staircase.

They climbed the stairs.

According to the blueprint the master bedroom was the first room on their right. They opened the door. Max pointed the flashlight; the room looked as if it had been ransacked. There were piles of cash and expensive jewelry laying out in the open—that didn't make sense.

"The guy you shot," Runt said, "had to be a burglar."

"A burglar, in shirt and tie, smoking cigarette on sidewalk? No. He was babysitter."

"Yeah? But who'd leave all this shit out in the open?"

"Someone who has no fear of thieves," Max said.

They entered the master bedroom, stuffed their pockets and the backpack with the cash and jewelry.

"Hey." Runt stuck his nose in the air. "What's that smell?"

Max tested the air. "That is smell of decaying flesh; something dead here."

"Oh, Christ." Runt scurried behind Max. "I don't like this, Max. Something's not right. You gotta trust me on this—let's go."

Max walked out of the master bedroom, pointed the flashlight beam at the far end of a long corridor. He walked down the hall, past several empty bedrooms, testing the air. His eyes came to rest on a half-open door with an abandoned tricycle by the entrance. "Smell come from that room."

"That's the kid's room," Runt whispered. "I ain't going in there, Max."

Max moved down the hall.

"Max, no—"

Max kept walking. He reached the kid's room, pushed the tricycle aside, eased the door open with his foot. He stepped inside and disappeared into the darkness.

"Max?"

The child's door slammed shut with a boom. A lock tripped. There was a flash of lightning that sent a sheet of light throughout the house. A loud and rumbling clap of thunder followed. Outside the wolves howled, long and loud.

"Max?" More howls, terrifying and closer—they sounded like they were in the house.

An unearthly scream.

"Max!?" Runt bolted for the stairs, started down, stopped when he saw that the man Max had killed was not where they'd left him; someone had moved the body. A low guttural growl came from out of the first floor darkness.

"Who's there?" Whoever it was started to move.

Runt could hear the footfalls. A snarl. Heavy breathing. Someone or something was waiting for him in the darkness.

322

Nearly frozen with fear, Runt brought both guns to bear and strained his eyes. He could just barely make out a hulking shape—eyes glowed eerily, its breath was visible. What the fuck was it? A large dog?

"Hi, doggie," Runt said softly. "That's a good doggie."

A wolf-like creature stepped out of the darkness, eyes blazing, mouth dripping with blood—had to be the dead guy's blood. The creature roared and started for Runt who turned and darted back up the stairs, into the master bedroom; he closed and locked the door behind him.

The creature crashed into the door, which rattled from the force. Runt pointed both guns at the door and fired, emptied both clips as fast as he could pull the trigger.

Silence.

Runt dropped the empty guns. Started looking for an escape route; there was no way he was going back through that bedroom door.

He dashed to a window, saw a large tree with sweeping branches outside—yes, if he could get a good running start and hit the old cast-iron radiator, then the window sill at full speed he could propel himself into that tree.

He looked down to the street. Fuck. The mansion was encircled with a spiked, wrought-iron fence. If he miscalculated and missed the tree, he would be impaled on the fence.

A chorus of terrifying, ungodly howls filled the air. Runt's skin crawled. He hurried to shove chairs, lamps, and other furniture aside to clear an unobstructed path.

He checked his calculation, started at the door, paced the length of the room to the window; yes. A professionally trained acrobat like himself could do it. He picked up a chair, threw it at the window, and shattered the glass.

A snarl from the other side of the bedroom door. Sudden ferocious, repeated pounding. The door began to splinter with each subsequent impact. Paint fell from the walls and ceiling. The creature would be through the door in a matter of moments.

Runt made a beeline to his starting position, set his feet, got into a crouching position, and was about to make a run for it when he heard an unearthly shriek. The snarling and pounding stopped and the door lock clicked. Someone had unlocked it from the other side.

Runt peed his pants.

Slowly the door swung open.

"Max!" Runt said. "God, am I glad to see you—"

Max did not respond. He stepped aside, zombie-like, and a ten-year-old boy walked past him and into the bedroom—the air stopped moving.

Runt forced himself to breathe and make eye contact with the Watkins boy; his eyes glowed as red as a demon's. He radiated an evil as tangible as that smell of decaying flesh.

Runt screamed in terror, made a run for it, dashed across the room, stepped on the radiator, then the window sill, and took flight. Leapt outward toward the street, arms flailing as he reached for the tree branches.

The police car arrived at seven a.m. the following morning.

"This way," a building superintendent said and led two officers to the head of the alley which separated his high-rise apartment building from the mansion next door. The superintendent pointed down the alley to the base of a wrought-iron face. "Over there."

The cops walked about fifty feet. The fence and ground beneath it were wet with blood.

"Christ," a male cop said.

"That's a lot of blood," the female cop said.

324

The two cops searched the immediate area, walked slowly up and down the alley, looked behind and under dumpsters, and through a dozen assorted bags of recyclables.

"That's window glass," the male cop said. He bent down to pick up a piece then checked out the apartment building and mansion's windows that faced the alley. "But I don't see any broken windows."

"And where's the body?" the female cop said.

"Yeah," the male cop said. "Hey, check that out."

Halfway up a large oak tree, a branch appeared to have snapped.

"I'll bet some kids climbed up that tree," the male cop said, "and the branch broke."

"Climbed up it," the female cops said, incredulous. "Why?"

"Peeping Toms. They'd have a great view into the apartment building windows."

"Or that mansion," the female cop pointed to the Watkins residence.

The male cop glanced at the mansion, then scanned the apartment building's first few floors. Saw an attractive female in a bra, slipping a blouse on. "My money's on the apartment building."

"So the branch broke and one of them was impaled on the fence?" The female cop grimaced. "Christ, that must've been horrible."

"His friends must've lifted him off the fence, taken him to a hospital."

"So we knock on doors?" the female cop said. "Check for witnesses?"

"Negative." He shook his head. "I'll call it in. Let the lazy assed detectives do the grunt work. We'll check the hospitals."

325

As the two cops moved back up the alley to their patrol car, the female cop sensed something. She looked toward the mansion, saw a curtain move, and felt a chill.

Someone, or something, was watching them from the mansion's second-floor window.

www.ingramcontent.com/pod-product-compliance
Lightning Source LLC
Chambersburg PA
CBHW060836280326
41934CB00007B/799